How the West Lost the Peace

How the West Lost the Peace

The Great Transformation Since the Cold War

PHILIPP THER

Translated by Jessica Spengler

polity

Substantial parts of this book were published in German as *Das andere Ende der Geschichte. Über die große Transformation* © Suhrkamp Verlag Berlin 2019. All rights reserved by and controlled through Suhrkamp Verlag Berlin.

This English edition © Polity Press, 2023

Publisher's note: Chapter 7 and the Afterword are new for the English edition. The material in Chapter 6 and the Preface has also been revised and updated.

The translation of this book was supported by a grant from the Goethe-Institut.

Polity Press
65 Bridge Street
Cambridge CB2 1UR, UK

Polity Press
111 River Street
Hoboken, NJ 07030, USA

All rights reserved. Except for the quotation of short passages for the purpose of criticism and review, no part of this publication may be reproduced, stored in a retrieval system or transmitted, in any form or by any means, electronic, mechanical, photocopying, recording or otherwise, without the prior permission of the publisher.

ISBN-13: 978-1-5095-5059-3
ISBN-13: 978-1-5095-5060-9 (pb)

A catalogue record for this book is available from the British Library.

Library of Congress Control Number: 2022946158

Typeset in 11 on 14pt Warnock Pro
by Cheshire Typesetting Ltd, Cuddington, Cheshire
Printed and bound in the UK by TJ International Limited

The publisher has used its best endeavours to ensure that the URLs for external websites referred to in this book are correct and active at the time of going to press. However, the publisher has no responsibility for the websites and can make no guarantee that a site will remain live or that the content is or will remain appropriate.

Every effort has been made to trace all copyright holders, but if any have been overlooked the publisher will be pleased to include any necessary credits in any subsequent reprint or edition.

For further information on Polity, visit our website:
politybooks.com

Contents

Preface: The Great Transformation after 1989   vi

1 From Neoliberalism to Antiliberalism: The Enduring Relevance of Karl Polanyi   1
2 Lost Social and Political Equilibrium: The USA after the Cold War   36
3 The Price of Unity: Germany's Shock Therapy in International Comparison   68
4 *La Crisi*: Italy's Decline as a Portent for Europe   88
5 The West, Turkey and Russia: A History of Estrangement   121
6 Eastern Europe as a Pioneer: Polanyi's Pendulum Swings to the Right   158
7 Systemic Competition during the Covid-19 Pandemic   183
Afterword: A Bad End: The War against Ukraine   222

Postscript and Acknowledgements   235
Notes   237
Index   268

Preface: The Great Transformation after 1989

The West appeared to be history's sole victor in 1989. The feeling of triumph was especially pronounced in the USA, the main power during the Cold War. Nowhere was this better expressed than in Francis Fukuyama's famous essay on 'the end of history'. In the summer of 1989 – before the fall of the Berlin Wall, and long before the collapse of the Soviet Union – Fukuyama predicted the lasting hegemony of liberal democracy and an absolutely free market economy.[1]

The title of my book refers to a different end to history. With Russia's invasion of Ukraine, the age of transformation as it was envisioned after 1989 is well and truly over. The new order after the end of state socialism was based on the premise that states and societies – including those that emerged from the former Soviet Union in 1991, and from the former Yugoslavia after four years of war – could develop freely within their recognized borders. Following the liberal and neoliberal thinking of the time, it was believed that fortune would favour the industrious. Russian dictator Vladimir Putin, however, adheres to a different doctrine: might makes right. Ukraine therefore deserves the full support of the West and the entire world – otherwise Russia's pursuit of a multipolar world order with a Russian sphere of influence in Eastern Europe will instead lead to maximum global disorder.

That said, it would be wrong for the ostensibly united West to point fingers only at Russia. The Covid-19 pandemic was a major rupture which weakened the political dogmas of the post-1989 world even before the war in Ukraine. Interventionism suddenly made a comeback, replacing the concept of a 'lean state' which largely withdraws from the economy and many other public duties. Western governments locked down their economies and societies for months on end to contain the virus and prevent mass deaths. They also pumped billions into pharmaceutical companies to support vaccine development, and they subsequently organized nationwide vaccination campaigns. Despite these efforts, humanity will have to live with the novel coronavirus and its variants in the long run – there is no going back to the time before 2020. The one–two punch of the pandemic and the biggest war in Europe since 1945 have brought an end to the era for which historians have not yet found a name. It makes no sense to put a second 'post-' in front of post-war, the term used by Tony Judt to describe the long period from 1945 to 1989.[2] 'Post-Cold War' would also be a strange construction considering the current talk in Europe and Asia of a new Cold War now under way. I therefore propose the *age of transformation*.

Transformation can be understood and defined in two ways. After the end of state socialism, Western 'transitologists' essentially followed Fukuyama's ideas, though his political opinions were naturally not shared by all social scientists. Economists like Jeffrey Sachs and David Lipton spoke in 1990 of a 'double transition' with respect to Poland, which was considered a reform pioneer. They held the view that democratization and the creation of a market economy were closely linked. It was clear from the outset that there was a tension between these two processes, and this inspired a number of interesting research projects and publications. But the most important paradigm in the study of systemic political change was the 'consolidation' of democracies, not the weakening and dissolution of them as witnessed in the lost decade after the global financial crisis. Social scientists tended to take a fairly critical view of the economic reforms and privatization of the 1990s. These critics included David Stark, who introduced the broader concept of 'transformation' here.[3] But for all their critique of the details, scholars primarily considered the changes to be a top-down process after 1989, which is why the concept of reform played such a major role.[4]

It is also possible to view the transformation as a social process, however, which raises the question of what it does to people and vice versa. This perspective is exemplified by the book *The Great Transformation*, the magnum opus of the historical sociologist Karl Polanyi, which is the subject of my first essay. Three aspects of this work make it valuable to critically examining the transformation as it was envisioned after 1989: Polanyi looks at social upheavals which can (but do not necessarily) trigger economic changes, he explores political counter-reactions (which he describes as a 'double movement') and though he mostly focuses on England, his perspective is ultimately global. This can help us escape the territorial confines of Eastern Europe where the transitologists got bogged down (aside from their occasional forays to Latin America, which I talk about in the first chapter of this book). The post-1989 transformation produced winners and losers not only in post-communist Europe – where 'transformation losers' became a stereotype – but also in the West: in the Rust Belt of the USA, the former industrial regions of central and northern England and many other places. In the West, however, such people were referred to not as 'transformation losers' but as 'globalization losers'. The post-communist transformation and globalization were closely connected and shared an ideology, namely, neoliberalism – which Polanyi would probably have continued to refer to as global 'laissez-faire capitalism'.

Preface: The Great Transformation after 1989   ix

I want to stress here that I use the term 'neoliberalism' analytically, not polemically. Quinn Slobodian recently published an excellent analysis of neoliberal thinking,[5] but intellectual historians to date have paid scant attention to the social consequences of this top-down economic and societal transformation. I foreground this perspective in my essays and address another relevant issue as well: the unintended repercussions of the reforms and the fundamental question of whether the economic policy goals at the heart of neoliberalism were actually achieved.

Polanyi's long time frame is important as well. The global hegemony of neoliberalism (see chapter 1) obviously did not arise overnight or only after the Berlin Wall fell. It goes back to the 1980s and the governments of Ronald Reagan and Margaret Thatcher. Countries on the periphery of the global economy, like Chile and later Poland, also played a significant role. And globalization, which would come to be constitutive of post-communist economic development and the contours and social consequences of the reforms, was older still and had accelerated since the 1970s.

There are commonalities, however, between Polanyi's arguments and the post-1989 concept of transformation. Both interpretations deal with a profound and accelerated rupture which simultaneously and synchronously affected political systems, economies and societies.[6] This short working definition of transformation can, in principle, also be applied to other periods following deep historical caesuras, such as the time after the French Revolution or the collapse of Europe's continental empires in 1918. The end of an *ancien regime* has always created space for a more far-reaching transformation.

However, as Polanyi takes pains to point out, transformations can also generate counter-tendencies. For example, ever since Vladimir Putin's second term in office, the former KGB officer has sought to bring about an 'anti-1989' counter-revolution through repression at home, military interventions in the 'near abroad' and now the war in Ukraine.

Some of the revolutionaries of 1989, Václav Havel first and foremost, felt that time sped up in the years that followed – not physically, obviously, but in people's perception and as a political tool. Covid-19, a kind of bookend to the age of transformation, brought about a massive deceleration. Many overworked fellow academics were initially relieved when their travels came to a halt in March 2020. At the time, they had no inkling of how long the lockdowns and other restrictions would last. Of course, developments stretching over more than three decades are never linear, so this book will also look at the many internal ruptures in the period between 1989 and 2020. Three major turning points are worth mentioning straight away: the transition to radical neoliberalism around the turn of the millennium, which provoked the first populist counter-reactions, the global financial crisis of 2008–9 and the political *annus horribilis* of 2016.

This book probes the question of how the West could emerge victorious from the Cold War but then lose its global hegemony and, above all, its internal peace in an accelerating cascade of crises. The term 'crisis' is generally used to stress the urgency or drama of a particular problem – see the various financial crises since the mid-1980s (as mentioned, sometimes we will have to go back to the period before 1989, and in general it is important not to place too much weight on individual dates), the 'refugee crisis' of 2015–16 and the much-discussed crisis of liberal democracy. I use 'crisis' differently here. Crisis discourse always emerges when a political system reaches the limits of its creative possibilities, when it can only react to changes instead of shaping them. But this interpretation of crisis is an expression of helplessness which is rarely productive.

From a historian's perspective, crises are heuristically valuable because they bring to light structural problems and deficits that have developed over a long period of time. The global financial crisis revealed the contradictions inherent in globalized financial capitalism and provided an opportunity to critically interrogate the neoliberal order that had been dominant to that point.[7] The surprising majority support for Brexit and the election of Donald Trump laid bare the deficits of (neo) liberal democracy. The Covid-19 pandemic can be interpreted as a crisis of globalization and its associated dependencies, one which aggravated existing tensions between world powers, social classes and generations. The social and economic blow of the pandemic was cushioned by the formerly maligned interventionist state, but trust in liberal democracy has eroded further. This is the continuation of an unsettling trend that began with the 'great' transformation starting in the 1980s. The emergence and global spread of new viral diseases also throws our ruthless exploitation of nature into sharp relief. We know that all these problems exist, but they crystallize and become more obvious in times of crisis than in supposedly 'good times'.

At this point, a notoriously sceptical Central European might ask: when have times ever been good? The 1990s generally have a good reputation because economic growth picked up again, particularly in the USA, while inflation and unemployment sank, as did government debt, eventually. After their planned economies collapsed, the first post-communist countries made it over the hump in 1992 (with Poland leading the way), while China began its unprecedented economic ascent, and progress was made in the fight against poverty in Asia and Latin America.

The main thrust of this book is at odds with the optimism of that time, however. Even during the supposedly 'golden 1990s' (which were not especially glittering in Germany or Italy), economic policy took a wrong turn. This is certainly true if we look at the economy in a wider context and ask which social groups benefited from this growth, how sustainable it was and what environmental price was paid for it.

Polanyi v. Fukuyama

When I read the essay by the then-unknown Francis Fukuyama as a young student in 1989, I was struck not so much by his predictions as by his polemic against 'the Left'. Fukuyama celebrated the West's imminent Cold War victory as a triumph of both foreign and domestic policy, placing left-wingers in 'Cambridge, Massachusetts' on a par with the last remaining communists in Managua and Pyongyang.[8] The neoconservative Fukuyama apparently felt that Western social democracy had landed alongside communism on the trash heap of history. Fukuyama's essay is an important historical source inasmuch as the term 'liberal' became an insult in the USA soon after it was published.

Polanyi was a later discovery for me. I had read his work as a student at some point in the early 1990s, but I was not particularly interested in the history of England's industrialization in the nineteenth century, which makes up the bulk of his book. I was reacquainted with him during a book tour in the USA in 2016, when I revisited the legendary Strand Book Store in New York. There was a copy of *The Great Transformation* on the shelf, one of the many paperback editions published in the 1960s and 1970s. When you find too many untouched copies of a book on the second-hand shelves of the Strand, you know that the work has not been well received. But when you find a worn book with underlined passages to boot, you can be sure that it has been studied carefully.

Polanyi was not an especially original discovery on my part, as he has always had a lively following amongst political scientists, particularly those researching 'varieties of capitalism'. I knew of him from social scientific works, but most other historians are unfamiliar with the Austro-Hungarian historical sociologist, even though his magnum opus can be read as a social history of England. *The Great Transformation* was also an attempt to write a global history *avant la lettre* of the long nineteenth century. The concept of global laissez-faire capitalism is relevant even now. Friedrich Hayek and other pioneers of neoliberal thinking never directly referenced Polanyi, but the democratic socialism he espoused was, in their view, the greatest enemy on the home front in the Cold War.

As I read Polanyi on my journey to Princeton and Philadelphia, his writing fit with the industrial ruins flanking the train tracks through the Northeast Corridor. His book depicts British agriculture and the rural population as victims of the global division of labour in the nineteenth century. Is there a parallel here to the fate of industry in the USA and northern England since the 1980s? Historical analogies are tricky, as I realized a few days later at the annual congress for Eastern European studies, where the newly elected Donald Trump was compared to all manner of authoritarian rulers and dictators from the 1920s and 1930s. As a contemporary historian, I thought first and foremost of Silvio Berlusconi (more on this in the fourth essay). Under Berlusconi – the longest-serving Italian prime minister after 1945 – Italy involuntarily became a testing ground for right-wing populism and what was, in many respects, a neoliberal economic and social policy. Polanyi avoided historical analogies for good reason; as a sociologist, he was more interested in abstract models and timeless statements.

Reading his book helped me understand why, even in times of growing prosperity, social tensions can fester and erupt in the form of political counter-reactions. Regardless of whether or not you embrace the term neoliberalism, there is no question that capitalism was 'disembedded' after 1989 (to pick up on Polanyi's concept of 'embedded capitalism'). Another Polanyian term that plays a key role in my book is 'double movement', meaning the political counter-reactions that can be triggered by the social effects of unfettered global capitalism.

The majority support for Brexit in the UK and Donald Trump's election in the USA in 2016 are interpreted here as a counter-movement to neoliberalism and liberal democracy. Italy's failed constitutional referendum at the end of the same year also came down to growing distrust of reforms crafted by party officials in the capital and imposed from above. Was 2016 therefore an *annus horribilis* for Western democracies, a counterpoint to the supposed *annus mirabilis* of 1989? The victories of Donald Trump and Boris Johnson put a great strain on both major Western alliances, the North Atlantic Treaty Organization (NATO) and the European Union (EU). Only very recently, as a result of the Russian war against Ukraine, did 'the West' re-emerge as a political unit, though it remains to be seen how long that unity will last.

The drawback to the notion of the *annus horribilis* is that those of us living through the era cannot really know when or whether neoliberalism has come to an end. Cornerstones of the ideology – such as trust in functioning markets, rational market participants, deregulation, liberalization and foreign direct investments – had already been fractured and delegitimized by the global financial crisis. The political fallout only became apparent eight years later, after most Western countries had seemingly overcome the crisis. The classic analytical problem facing historians is that economic, political, social and cultural changes are seldom synchronous and congruent. A rare modern exception to this was the transformation of the post-communist states and societies, where almost everything changed in one fell swoop after the end of state socialism. The year 2016 was not the same kind of concentrated historical moment, though it did bring about a deep political rupture. But political history alone does not explain either Brexit or the election of Donald Trump. I am therefore not convinced by the popular theory that Trumpism is a product of the increasingly polarized and dysfunctional American political system.[9] To get to the deeper roots of the decline of liberal democracy, we have to look beyond Washington and examine the social and economic changes since the 1980s which plunged some parts of the USA into conditions comparable to those of the early post-communist world.

I want to add a personal observation here, one which is more than just an anecdote (I will return later to the question of how historians can employ 'personal sociology'). On the tenth anniversary of 1989, an older colleague of mine from Germany took me to the big annual convention of the Association for Slavic, East European, and Eurasian Studies for the first time.[10] It was held in St Louis, Missouri, and as we ambled through the city with a few Eastern European and Russian colleagues to get lunch, we came across huge shopping centres with ancient linoleum flooring and display cases holding just one or two kinds of deli meats and cheese, nothing more. The empty, dying shops made it feel as though we had been transported back to the era of late-stage state socialism, and we joked about the post-Soviet city in America's heartland.

What was the political fallout of this social and economic decline? I deal with this question in my first essay, provocatively titled 'From Neoliberalism to Antiliberalism'. In the past, like many political scientists, I used the term 'illiberal', but I have since discarded it because it is one of the chimeras brought into existence by Viktor Orbán. An illiberal democracy is an oxymoron – something Hungary's prime minister apparently figured out for himself, since he later abandoned the term and claimed to follow a policy of 'Christian democracy'.

When it comes to the *annus horribilis* and every other historical rupture, we have to look at the chronology of events from a somewhat broader perspective. Poland's Law and Justice party (Prawo i Sprawiedliwość, or PiS) first won the presidential and parliamentary elections in 2015. Poland's recent history bears similarities to Hungary's, where the global financial crisis and collapse of the 'Eastern European bubble' paved the way for Orbán to ascend to power in 2010 and then win a supermajority of parliamentary seats in 2014, giving him the authority to change the constitution. Eastern Europe is not the focus of this book (as it was in its predecessor, *Europe since 1989*), but it is important to look closely at the region, as I do in the sixth essay here, if we want to understand what can happen when right-wing populists and nationalists win a second election.

Orbán's victory was overdetermined after the global financial crisis, since the post-communist social democrats who preceded him had been engulfed by corruption scandals and offered no remedy for the looming collapse of Hungary's national currency and economy. Another decisive turning point came with Orbán's re-election in 2014, when he achieved a two-thirds parliamentary majority despite losing votes, thus cementing his power indefinitely. Hungary is ultimately just a small country with barely 10 million inhabitants which accounts for a good 1 per cent of the entire gross domestic product (GDP) of the EU, but it is on the brink of changing from a democracy once considered 'consolidated' into an authoritarian regime. It is a regime inasmuch as the separation of powers now exists only on paper in Hungary, and the country's freedom of the press has been massively restricted (luckily the USA never reached this stage under Trump, and there are still critical media outlets in Poland). The fundamental question now facing the EU is whether it can endure as a mixed system in which liberal democracies exist alongside antiliberal regimes.

The political pendulum in Eastern Europe and democracy's Anglo-Saxon motherlands swung far to the right in 2015–16, not to the left as Polanyi would have hoped and expected. But reading Polanyi can help us better understand the reasons for this rebellion against the neoliberal economic order and liberal democracy. We know that an aversion to large-scale labour migration from the EU played a major role in Brexit, though Polanyi's book is less helpful in this regard, as he generally does not address the role of migration in global laissez-faire capitalism, even though he himself had to emigrate twice in the course of his life.

There are also limits to Polanyi's insight when it comes to analysing nationalism and racism. I say this at the outset mainly to emphasize that my aim is not to construct yet another cathedral to a great political thinker. This can sometimes happen when the authors of books on political theory or intellectual history identify too closely with their subjects (just think of the cathedrals built over the years to Hannah Arendt, Michel Foucault and Walter Benjamin). There is no need for an iconography of Polanyi, and such a thing would have been strange to a man of his modest nature anyway.

Historical research into neoliberalism (to which this book aims to contribute) has generally revolved more around its intellectual history and ideology than concrete practices and economic policies. The research is even patchier when it comes to social issues, though it is important not to turn neoliberalism into a bogeyman. Not every negative social development of the past thirty years can be traced back to governance effects or 'high politics', since every ideology has limited social reach. Multicausal explanations for historical events are always more convincing than monocausal ones, and sometimes coincidences and a confluence of different developments play a decisive role.

The fourth essay in this book, which deals with Italy, shows that a fundamental distinction can be made between *neoliberalism by conviction* and *situational neoliberalism* in which certain principles and measures are implemented primarily because they seem to be the most reasonable option in a certain context. One good example of this is the privatization of state industries, which can take place either out of ideological conviction (as a way of curtailing the state's role in the economy) or simply to make money in the short term and plug holes in the state budget.

These differences become most apparent when we compare the economic policies of various countries. Unfortunately, it is beyond the scope of this book to provide a systematic international comparison based on precise data which analyses the approaches of different historical actors. In light of this, I can only make spot comparisons and accept that there will be gaps in my coverage. For example, there is no essay specifically about the UK here, even though from the 1980s the country led the way in liberalization, deregulation, privatization, the reduction of state influence on the economy, and global financial capitalism. These five areas of activity formed the core of neoliberal policy, and they serve here as a definition of neoliberalism. We will, however, encounter the UK under Thatcher and Chile under Pinochet several times in the other essays. Chile makes an appearance because it was a pioneering neoliberal reformer in the 1980s, just as Poland was in the following decade. The USA, Germany and Italy are dealt with in more detail in the book, as are Russia and Turkey. I chose these countries based on the premise that social historians should only write academic books about nations whose culture they are familiar with and whose language they can speak, or at least read.[11] Google Translate and 'English only' will not get you very far if you want to understand the world, much less write a history of it.

As a polyglot, Polanyi was particularly well placed to think globally. He owed this to his roots in the assimilated Jewish bourgeoisie of Habsburg Hungary and his life as an emigrant who had been forced to start fresh in several different countries. Compared to Polanyi, Fukuyama had a comfortable existence. He grew up during the golden years of American capitalism, which may explain why he felt that the free market economy was the superlative model and believed that it was tied to liberal democracy. Three decades later, we know that capitalism can function well without democracy, or with no more than a democratic façade. This is obviously not a new insight, so the more interesting question is why Fukuyama's so eloquently expressed expectation came about in the first place after 1989.

The West's unabashed feeling of superiority after the victory in the Cold War affected relations with states and societies that had long looked to the West for orientation. This is the subject of the fifth essay, which reflects on why Russia and Turkey have so brusquely turned their backs on the EU and USA since the start of the twenty-first century. Domestic policy is the main driving force here, but not everything can be blamed on the 'bad guys' Putin and Erdoğan. The behavioural parallels between the two countries and the deepening crisis in their relations with the EU, and Germany in particular, should be reason enough for us to turn the lens on ourselves and ask what has gone wrong in the West. This self-critique and brief discussion of NATO's eastern enlargement are absolutely not meant to relativize Russia's attack on Ukraine, however. There is no justification for the way Putin wants to re-write the end of history – with the creation of a new Russian empire.

Essentials and social consequences of neoliberalism

From a socio-historical perspective, the neoliberal order had two main negative consequences. The first was only partially intentional and can be summed up in a single sentence: wealthy individuals, social classes, big cities and countries prospered, while poorer regions, communities and vulnerable social groups fell even farther behind, especially in developed industrial nations. This is often portrayed as a case of growing social inequality, something Branko Milanović has studied internationally for many years.[12] But the regional divergence is just as pronounced and significant, especially in terms of politics. Opportunities for individual development increasingly come down to where you are born and raised – in an economically dynamic area, or in a small, stagnating town which might be in a rural or deindustrialized region to boot. But even in booming metropolises, your opportunities will differ depending on whether you reside in a 'good' or 'bad' part of the city. Social diversity is obviously an important issue, but it is rarely debated as such.

The second key problem with the neoliberal order was the way in which it mobilized the population for the labour market – namely, through the threat (and, all too often, the experience) of poverty and social decline, particularly for members of the lower middle class and anyone dismissed as a welfare freeloader. The dimensions and consequences of this social decline varied depending on the country and local context, meaning that it could lead to either relative or absolute poverty. The social reforms in the Global South and post-communist Europe demonstrated neoliberalism's reliance on state control and simultaneously resulted in existential hardship. The same applies to the USA, where the emphasis on food stamps in the 1990s had disastrous effects on the future prospects and health of poor Black Americans as well as whites. Poverty in the deindustrialized Rust Belt and many big cities took on positively Eastern European dimensions, as reflected in life expectancy rates. The welfare state remained somewhat more intact in the UK because even the Iron Lady dared not break up the National Health Service (NHS). But the former industrial centres of central and northern England face the same lack of prospects as the small and medium-sized cities of the Rust Belt.

More than fifty years ago, the British social historian E.P. Thompson noted that a social group's material living conditions do not automatically translate into a shared consciousness or political agenda. The neoliberal rhetoric of 'unavoidable' economic and social reforms initially led to political demobilization, which stood in contrast to the utilitarian mobilization of the population for the labour market. The effects of this demobilization can be seen in the declining voter turnout rates found in every democracy where the social gap between rich and poor yawned especially wide – a problem which has been further exacerbated by Covid-19.

The political vacuum has been filled largely by right-wing populists and nationalists in the past decade. This theory is not entirely new; Adam Tooze, for example, has written a groundbreaking book stressing the role of the global financial crisis in Brexit and the election of Donald Trump.[13] Growing social and regional inequality had toxic political effects in continental Europe as well, particularly in the post-communist East. The stock markets bounced back from the financial crisis remarkably quickly, at least compared with the Great Depression of the 1930s. But many homeowners with mortgage debt, including approximately nine million Americans, lost their property and their wealth, and the EU subsequently had to face the 2011 euro crisis, which was disastrous for Southern Europe.

The socio-political delegitimization of liberal democracy began long before this, however. From the mid-1990s, and even earlier in the USA and UK, the transformation of the labour market and accompanying social reforms changed the everyday life and future prospects of the lower and middle classes alike. This is yet another argument for viewing the post-1989 transformation as an experience which shaped both East and West as well as the newly industrialized countries duly referred to as 'emerging markets' from the 1990s onwards.

The Law and Justice party (PiS) in Poland, the Republicans under Trump and the now-irrelevant United Kingdom Independence Party (UKIP) in England received most support in the isolated and impoverished regions we might call 'the rest of the West', in a reversal of the triumphalist title of Niall Ferguson's book.[14] It is therefore neither a coincidence nor a mere consequence of the global financial crisis that Poland, the UK and the USA all lurched to the right in 2015–16.

There were other causes and contributing factors, of course, which are beyond the scope of this book to discuss – not least the electoral system. Majority voting systems fostered political polarization and the rise of right-wing populists. Contingency also played a role, as it so often does in history. Trump might not have won in 2016 had he faced a more persuasive opponent, and Brexit happened in part because the influence of the Eurosceptics was woefully underestimated and voter turnout was low. In Poland, PiS achieved an absolute majority in the Sejm in 2015 only because several other parties (especially on the fractured left) failed to meet the percentage threshold for winning parliamentary seats.

But pondering counterfactual scenarios rarely accomplishes much because there is no getting around the actual course of history. The fact remains that social divisions preceded the political polarization. This is particularly true in the USA, where the usual indicators for income and wealth inequality have increasingly come to resemble those of Latin America ever since Reagan was president. This trend intensified under Bill Clinton due in part to his social reforms and the aversion to 'big government'.

I should say in advance that I cite data and statistics sparingly in this book, partially because they do not fit easily into the format of an essay, and partially because it is important not to rely solely on a quantitative perspective in social history. That said, these essays are very much based on statistics and hard data which I have collected for more than a decade. This particularly applies to the chapter on Germany's transformation, for which I collated the regional GDP of the 'five new German states' in order to compare the former East Germany with the neighbouring Czech Republic. It is also impossible to analyse recent Italian history without a detailed knowledge of sovereign debt, which involves dealing with very large numbers. Indicators such as youth unemployment and income upon entering the labour market are also crucial to understanding Italy's decline since the mid-1990s.

The USA and UK tended to pity the newly unified Germany back in the 1990s. Germany was considered the 'sick man of the euro',[15] ranking amongst the bottom three EU states in terms of economic growth from 1995 to the turn of the millennium, and again from 2002 to 2005. In the essay on Germany, I probe the reasons for this 'unity crisis', which I experienced first hand while visiting numerous provincial towns in the former East Germany for my dissertation. At the end of the 1990s, the entire Federal Republic of Germany seemed to be caught in a vicious cycle of rising unemployment, sovereign debt and taxes and weak economic growth.

There is also a deeper meaning to the term 'unity crisis'. It refers here not to the former East Germany, which was reflexively blamed for all manner of problems in the 1990s, but rather to the mistakes and unintentional side effects of the unification of the two German states. Most literature about the post-communist transformation mentions that Poland underwent 'shock therapy', claiming in the same breath that this was the basis for the country's subsequent prosperity.[16] As my comparative analysis shows, the former East Germany also experienced shock therapy in many respects, though it was hardly a success story. In the case of Poland, too, this is a one-sided and monocausal theory. The most important prerequisite for the economic upswing starting in 1992 was the availability of highly qualified, low-paid workers.

This high level of education did not just suddenly materialize in 1989, of course. In the era of state socialism, access to education and skilled jobs had been an opportunity for individual advancement for many people. The growth in human capital (which is not strictly a neoliberal concept, as it requires a strong state that invests in resources for its citizens in the long term) cannot be attributed to reform policies of any flavour. Even during the post-communist transformation, what mattered was whether and how a new government invested in education. All in all, we can say that universities benefited, but schools and vocational training institutions did not.

When I speak and write about past historical mistakes, I am often asked whether there were any alternatives at the time. The course of history implicitly speaks against this, which is why historians of all stripes (not just Marxists) tend to take the view that things happened the way they had to. It is hard to counter the power of the factual. This is especially true for the period after 1989, when reforms were all too often presented as having 'no alternative'. But at many recent historical turning points there were, in fact, opportunities to take a different economic course, and these alternatives were debated. It is important to remember this to avoid any ex-post confirmation of the paradigm of inevitability.

Margaret Thatcher's famous claim that 'there is no alternative', which became a mantra in post-communist Europe just as it did in the West, proved to be politically toxic over the years. It was also responsible in part for the much-discussed 'crisis of democracy'. To get to the root of this crisis, however, we have to start earlier than the *annus horribilis* of 2016 or the global financial crisis (Colin Crouch did this back in 2004 in his book on post-democracy, and Cas Mudde also published important theories at about the same time).[17] In the mid-1990s, a growing number of moderate leftists and social democratic politicians began to adopt Thatcher's slogan, and they faced repercussions at the ballot box and a general loss of legitimacy for doing so. The evolution of the moderate Left is a thread running through all the essays here, but to answer the question of how right-wing populists come to power, we really have to look at the stance taken by centre-right conservatives.

This book is obviously not the first to deal with the crisis of the Left and liberal democracy and the rise of right-wing populism. American and European bookshops have been flooded with the subject since 2016, as have professional journals, popular magazines and social media. Maybe this wealth of publications is actually a kind of academic populism. The very term contains a demarcation, as demonstrated by the fact that I have never met anyone in academia who has openly claimed to be an adherent of Trump or Orbán. However, pointing fingers at right-wing populists does not get us very far, especially not in a political sense.

Political scientists often use the term right-wing populism to describe a *form* of politics; I address this in more detail in my essays on the USA and Italy. But as a historian who has intensively researched modern nationalism, I am acutely aware of the ideological *content* of this populism – namely, an ethnic, exclusive and xenophobic right-wing nationalism. And if a historian is allowed to prognosticate, I would say that this will remain a major and dangerous challenge in the years and decades to come.

This book closes with an essay on the Covid-19 pandemic. In the first wave of the pandemic, countries with relatively intact social safety nets and well-developed health care systems fared better than the USA. The number of victims was relatively high overall in the UK, too, especially amongst the lower classes. This highlights the long-term consequences of neoliberal politics and short-term effects of populist right-wing governance. Donald Trump and Boris Johnson (to say nothing of Jair Bolsonaro in Brazil) were clearly out of their depth during the pandemic. During the first wave, Germany in particular was considered an international role model – though, like the EU member states in Eastern Europe, it had the benefit of having seen how hard the pandemic hit Italy and Spain, so it could react accordingly.

The tables turned during the second and third waves, especially when it came to vaccination campaigns. The UK and USA moved faster and more effectively, mainly because they were more willing to take risks and they mobilized every available resource to develop vaccines, which they then approved more quickly. Germany and the EU took a more cautious approach to vaccine approval, negotiating with the pharmaceutical industry about liability in the event of damages and ensuring data protection before finally organizing their vaccination campaigns.[18] This resulted in a delay of two to three months which cost many lives and necessitated further long lockdowns in the spring of 2021.

I interpret the differing approaches to Covid-19 as an example of the systemic competition waged between the USA and China right from the start of the pandemic in the spring of 2020. Political competition could be found in Europe, too, with Boris Johnson, Viktor Orbán and Serbian president Aleksandar Vučić all claiming that sovereign nation-states resolved the health crisis more effectively than the sluggish, supranational EU. The rates of infection and excess mortality in their three respective countries speak against this theory (as does the slow pace of vaccinations in Switzerland). But from the start of 2021, it was the vaccination campaigns that received the most attention – and in this regard, the three countries were, in fact, faster than their neighbouring states and the EU.

Much is at stake here for the European Union, which must prevail in this competition to avoid losing even more support and legitimacy. It is still too early to write a history of the pandemic – no one knows how the disease and the measures employed to fight it will be viewed in a few years' time, or how effective the Chinese and Russian vaccines that have been used in Serbia and Hungary will prove to be. What is certain is that Donald Trump will not be the only right-wing populist to lose office on account of the pandemic; Czech prime minister Andrej Babiš was also punished at the polls for his poor management of the health crisis. But frustration and anger about the pandemic's economic and social consequences could just as easily turn voters against liberal politicians (in France, for instance). We know it is not possible to 'learn' from history in the literal sense. At most, we can try to avoid making the same mistakes over again. This is yet another argument for learning more about the accumulating crises of the three decades after 1989 and their economic and political fallout.

Preface: The Great Transformation after 1989 xxvii

The format of this book

At first glance, essays might not seem like the best format for examining the problems of our time, seeing as they are more discursive and subjective, and less oriented on facts and figures, than traditional articles in scholarly journals. But the benefit of focusing on propositions and personal opinions is that it forces the author to be transparent about their own standpoint, something which is taken for granted in cultural and social anthropology. The personal remarks and experiences included in these essays are therefore certainly not anecdotal or random.

One of my sources of inspiration was the 'personal sociology' of Didier Eribon, Steffen Mau and other social scientists who have returned to the sites of their childhood as a starting point for analysing the social, economic and political transformation of the past thirty years. Contemporary historians are always revisiting the recent past anyway, some of which we probably lived through ourselves. As a result, personal experiences often influence our research and interpretations, though this influence is rarely made explicit and thus put to good use.

Reading essays can be exciting, too. As a student, I was fascinated by Isaiah Berlin, Albert Hirschman and Leszek Kołakowski, and by *Kultura*, the Polish exile magazine. When he was a young newspaper editor, Karl Polanyi wrote countless essayistic articles which are still worth reading a century later. Tony Judt was a famously gifted essayist who wrote 'Reappraisals' and 'Memory Chalet' shortly before his premature death. Mary Beard also reaches a wide audience with her essays, and like Ingrid Rowland and Hannah Arendt before her, she helps balance out the preponderance of male authors in this genre. Tony Judt, with whom I share many political views, took a very personal approach to his work. I myself do not think too much emphasis should be placed on personal experiences (which have often just been a product of biographical coincidence in my case), so I only mention them in this book when they prompt new questions or open up new perspectives.

Most famous essayists have been leftists or liberals, and I feel comfortable in their company. Many went on the defensive after 1989, and while this was understandable, it probably also contributed to the hard-right swing of Polanyi's pendulum in recent years. We can slow the pendulum by carefully analysing the reasons for this recurrent 'double movement'. Perhaps doing so will give us a chance to swing it in the other direction, opening up new opportunities for a progressive politics and society.

1

From Neoliberalism to Antiliberalism
The Enduring Relevance of Karl Polanyi

'Presentism' has become something of a trend in professional historiography. Switzerland has an online magazine called *Geschichte der Gegenwart* (History of the Present); a German contemporary historian brought out 'A Brief History of the Present' with a well-known publisher in 2017; and textbook publishers try to make past eras more appealing to their young audience by drawing connections to the present day.[1] In the USA, too, the best way to promote a book is to say that it covers a timely topic.

Referencing current academic debates is also more important than ever. Mentioning prominent colleagues is a good way to score points on social media because it increases the likelihood that they will recommend your own work on Twitter or Facebook in return. Presentism and discursivity attract a lot of public attention, but there are limits to what they can achieve. After all, even the most diligent students and political activists only have so much time for reading. Academics today live in an economy of overwhelming supply, where the growing abundance of information and texts bumps up against naturally limited capacity and demand. In other words, more and more information is being sent out into the world, but more and more cannot be received and read. This daily competition for our attention makes it easy to lose sight of more distant periods and older publications and sources. This is a great loss, especially for history as an academic discipline.

I always encourage my students to read older works – and not just history books. You can learn a tremendous amount, particularly about the late nineteenth and twentieth centuries, from the social scientists who were writing at the time. Their studies are historical sources, but many also contain theories and models that help explain the problems of their time as well as our own. The epistemological value lies not in looking to history for answers to new questions and interpreting these findings in a presentistic way based on current needs, but rather in taking past approaches, theories and explanatory models and laying them like a matrix over the present.

The works of the historical sociologist Karl Polanyi are social scientific classics that are always worth revisiting.[2] Polanyi's magnum opus, *The Great Transformation*, was published towards the end of the Second World War and reached a wide audience in the following thirty years. During Polanyi's lifetime (he died in 1964 in the USA), even the bastions of the liberal market economy – the USA and UK – thought that 'laissez-faire capitalism' was outmoded. This attitude stemmed from their all-too-fresh memories of the stock market crash of 1929, the Great Depression in the 1930s and the rise of fascism.

As a result, even economists who embraced the concept of neoliberalism in the 1950s called for heavier regulation of the markets and legislation against cartels and monopolies.[3] Most of society was in favour of taming the free market and creating an 'embedded' capitalism, as Polanyi vividly put it. Polanyi fell out of fashion in the 1980s. No new editions of his book were published, and even the translations dried up.[4] You were most likely to find his work in a library or second-hand bookshop, a sure sign that it had been relegated to history.

But then the crises of capitalism began to pile up at the end of the 1990s. The Asian financial crisis, which ultimately dragged down Russia and the rouble in 1998, was followed by the dot-com crisis. Polanyi was suddenly relevant again, and he experienced a renaissance. Beacon Press in Boston, which first published *The Great Transformation* in paperback, brought out a new edition in 2001 with a foreword by Joseph Stiglitz, an unwavering critic of neoliberalism and the Chicago Boys under Milton Friedman. Stiglitz received the Nobel Prize in Economics not long after, further boosting the popularity of *The Great Transformation*.

There were other, longer-term reasons for the renewed interest in Polanyi. It was clear by the turn of the millennium that only certain social classes, industries, countries and regions had profited from the 'great transformation' after 1989. Post-communist Europe oscillated between optimistic awakening (Poland, the Czech Republic, Hungary) and depression (Russia and other post-Soviet states). Political reformers in the East could fall back on an obvious excuse, however: the misery was the fault of the communists, state socialism, mismanagement prior to 1989, *Homo sovieticus*.

This Manichean view of history also fed into the post-transformation promise of modernization as it was envisioned after 1989. Once countries had made it through the long drought, or the vale of tears, or some other essentially Biblical trial, they were expected to achieve a state of developed capitalism and become as wealthy as the West.

But in the age of neoliberalism, this promise was on shaky ground from the start. Unlike their counterparts in the East, political elites in the USA and Germany did not have the option of badmouthing earlier economic and social developments or the social democratic welfare state. Moreover, it was not clear where the development of these countries was supposed to lead. The West, and especially the USA, had already reached the modern capitalist stage. Aside from increasing consumption or improving the efficiency of the system, there was no place to go from there.

This lack of direction made globalization a hot topic which sparked considerable opposition and resistance right from the start. How did it benefit factory workers, or even microelectronics experts, for cars to be made in Mexico and mobile phones in China? At best, consumers enjoyed cheaper prices for more and more imported goods, though they all too often had to go into debt to afford them. Old industrial regions had started to decline back in the 1970s, and now yet another generation was growing up in a state of late-capitalist or post-communist tristesse.

Globalization thus offered a second promise of modernization, one that was both economic and normative.[5] Thanks to the global division of labour, workers in Guadalajara in Mexico or Shenzhen in China were expected to earn more. Outsourced industrial production jobs in these regions were supposed to lead to the creation of a thriving middle class, which would then step up in support of democracy. This optimistic vision of the future seemed to be borne out in Chile, where voters in the 1988 referendum refused to grant Pinochet another term in office. Wages in China, Mexico and the Global South were also expected to rise, thus easing competition for workers in the USA and Western Europe. The most pioneering modern industrialized states would continue to lead the development of new technologies, doing away with grimy old factory jobs and instead offering clean jobs in the service economy and high-tech sector. Globalization thus promised to modernize the whole world, but its universality made it difficult to grasp. The middle class in the West started to hear that life would not be as comfortable as before, and that you had to be flexible, efficient and willing to learn if you wanted to withstand the harsher winds of the free market economy.

Despite their different promises of modernization, the post-socialist transformation in the East and late-capitalist transformation in the West shared a framework: neoliberal globalization. This triggered rapid and profound economic and social changes across every sector. Harking back to Polanyi, we should note that these changes did not happen automatically; they were deliberately imposed from above by the respective political and economic elites.

Even if you agreed with the neoliberal progressive thinking of the 1990s, it was clear and deliberate from the start that the transformation would take a different course depending on your country, region, social class, occupation and individual resources. As mentioned earlier, not many people were reading Polanyi at the time, though it would have been worth their while to do so. He described how England's industrialization and global free trade impacted different population groups, and he turned an almost anthropological gaze on the social consequences of the 'great transformation'. Together with his insights into the workings of global financial capitalism and his knack for coining new terms, this was the deeper reason Polanyi was rediscovered around the turn of the millennium.

His book was like a matrix for this new era, which is actually quite astonishing considering the vast distance between the present day and the environments that had shaped him and his work. Polanyi was born in what was then Austria-Hungary and studied law and economics in Budapest, where he came into contact with a circle of radical students at the university.[6] Marxism was still a matter of faith at the time, not so much an academic method for analysing contemporary or historical problems, as it is today.

When Hungary began to hound communists and Jews after the conservative counter-revolution, Polanyi settled in Vienna, where he made a living as the editor of a business magazine. He emigrated again in 1934, this time to England, then worked as a visiting professor in the USA during the war and subsequently taught at Columbia University in New York. Looking at his oeuvre, it seems most accurate to classify him as a historical sociologist, though he was active in various disciplines. His interdisciplinarity proved a hindrance to his academic career, however, and he never became a tenured professor. But his academic position says very little about the quality of his works, in which he presented himself as a well-rounded intellectual.

In terms of his world view and methodology, Polanyi was a revisionist Marxist.[7] As such, he focused on analysing the economic upheavals he believed were responsible for the outbreak of the First World War, the Great Depression and fascism. In contrast to the classic Marxist interpretation of history – and unlike some liberals and neoconservatives who peddled short-sighted theories around 1989 – Polanyi was not a determinist. There was no telos of history for him, either in the form of a world proletarian revolution or one of its preliminary stages, namely, the bourgeois society of industrial modernity.

One of the main themes in his magnum opus is the dialectic between the principle of the free market and society's need for protection. According to Polanyi, nineteenth-century laissez-faire capitalism and globalization had plunged millions into hardship, by which he did not necessarily mean hunger and material deprivation, but rather the collapse of social communities and their value systems. After 1989, this also seemed to apply to most small and medium-sized towns in industrial northern England and the American Rust Belt, as well as many industrial regions in post-communist Europe.

Polanyi argued that the labour movement and unions arose as a counter-reaction to the globalized free market. This counter-reaction had an influence on governments, which became increasingly interventionist and protectionist in the late nineteenth century in response to growing economic competition. Polanyi was less able to explain nationalism and the outbreak of the First World War, however. He attributed the latter to 'the dissolution of the system of world economy which had been in progress since 1900' and the collapse of the balance-of-power system.[8] Polanyi's contemporary Joseph Schumpeter has shown that international corporations tried to prevent the global conflagration – not out of pacifism, obviously, but because they were worried about their business.

In Polanyi's account, the war's winners and losers returned to their free-trade regime in the interwar period, and to the gold standard in the international monetary system. But then came the Great Depression and final collapse of the liberal global economic system in the 1930s. Polanyi considered fascism to be the result of the 'market system' and the irresolvable conflicts between capitalism and democracy. If this interpretation sounds familiar, it is because similar ones have been put forward by other Marxists, including those of the Soviet school.

Polanyi explicitly rejected the materialism of orthodox Marxists, however. The main problem, in his view, was the uprooting and destruction of social communities, and the feeling many people had of no longer being up to the demands of the economy. It was this anthropological dimension, the focus on basic human needs, which helped make Polanyi's magnum opus a classic.

Another Polanyian concept also gained widespread traction, namely, the 'double movement' between the principle of the self-regulating free market and the need for 'social protection'. But what does 'movement' mean in this case? Who is actually moving? Polanyi does not have a satisfying answer to this question because, as a sociologist, he primarily thought in terms of structures and dealt only marginally with historical actors. He goes into most detail at the end of his book when discussing the early socialist ideas of Robert Owen. They probably fascinated Polanyi in part because they fit with his interwar life in Vienna, where the social democrats had tried to establish a form of bourgeois socialism from the middle of society outwards by means of consumer, production and building cooperatives. But the earlier sections of Polanyi's book revolve largely around counter-reactions from above and the growing protectionism amongst nation-states.

Unlike Polanyi the sociologist, a historian would probably try to construct a chronology of these counter-movements. This would be a very ambitious undertaking, however, even if you focused only on a single area, such as cooperatives and unions. I therefore tend to interpret Polanyi's double movement more abstractly, as a swing of the political pendulum. As soon as Polanyi's pendulum is nudged in the direction of social protection, it can swing in one of two ways: left towards democratic socialism, or right towards fascism.[9]

We do not know the extent to which Polanyi's work was read by political elites in Western industrialized countries after the Second World War, but he was certainly not read as often or intensively as Keynes. Regardless of how Polanyi was received, pendulums everywhere swung in the direction of the welfare state and heavier economic regulation after the war. Even the USA and UK, the leading global economic powers who had benefited most from the free exchange of goods and capital up to that point, established complex and costly social welfare systems. This stemmed from the tradition of the New Deal in the USA and the overwhelming victory of the Labour Party in Britain in 1945.[10]

In West Germany and the founding states of the European Communities (EC), systemic competition between East and West played an important role as well. These countries adopted an 'embedded capitalism' model in order to counter Eastern Bloc propaganda about exploitative capitalism and keep the communist electoral victories in countries like France and Italy in check. This model was typified not least by the EC itself, an economic community which also tried, little by little, to ensure minimum standards of social welfare.

The embedded capitalism advocated by Polanyi was flanked on a global level in the post-war period by the Bretton Woods system, which regulated international exchange rates and capital flows using the US dollar as its anchor currency. In combination with the low exchange rate of the German mark and other Western European currencies, Bretton Woods facilitated the German 'economic miracle' and the *Trente Glorieuses* throughout the EC. By contrast, the post-communist states had to build up their market economies after 1989 with far fewer protections.

The Bretton Woods system collapsed in 1973 when it became impossible to maintain the high dollar rate in the face of American budget and current account deficits and rising inflation. The holes in the state coffers, along with the oil crisis that followed soon after, halted the expansion of social welfare systems and led to the first regression. On top of this, doubts were growing about Keynesian economics and the state's ability to exert control, and companies were becoming increasingly critical of rising tax burdens.

The global hegemony of neoliberalism

When low growth and high inflation led to stagflation, the hour of the neoliberal economist had finally come. As mentioned, neoliberalism was originally an affirmative term, so it can be used analytically here. The centre of neoliberal thought was the Chicago School of Economics which formed around the Austrian economist Friedrich Hayek and Milton Friedman, who was thirteen years younger. In the 1960s and 1970s, the Chicago School's theories spread throughout the USA and around the world, growing more radical in the process – with momentous consequences. Friedman in particular was fundamentally critical of the state and leaned towards the principle of laissez-faire. In 1980, the eloquent professor became an important economic policy advisor to Ronald Reagan, a position which enabled him to put his ideas into practice. The European counterpart to Reaganomics was Thatcherism, though it was only after Thatcher's second electoral victory that the Iron Lady adopted a policy of radical market liberalism and deliberately sought conflict with the trade unions.

Chile played an important role for emerging nations, and for Eastern Europe after 1989. General Augusto Pinochet implemented a two-phase process of comprehensive market privatization, liberalization and deregulation.[11] Economists from the Chicago School were instrumental in this, though Friedman apparently had enough political sense and decency to distance himself from the dictator. It is a matter of debate whether the boom in Chile, which lasted until the Asia crisis in 1998, can be traced back to this neoliberal shock therapy or to the subsequent economic policies of the Christian and social democrats. After the change of government in Chile in 1990, these parties strove to improve the purchasing power of all classes and achieve a 'social equilibrium'.[12] We know about this thanks to the files of the World Bank, which was initially sympathetic to this mixed economic course before it also went down a neoliberal route from the mid-1990s.

'Social equilibrium' was a phrase coined by Alejandro Foxley, Chile's first post-dictatorial finance minister. It was somewhat provocative, since international debates at the time were all about 'economic equilibrium'. But Foxley, who was influenced by Catholic social teaching, was thinking on a larger scale and in social dimensions. His arguments were additionally based on a classic Keynesian insight (further developed by Paul Samuelson and other proponents of the neoclassical synthesis) which held that strengthening the purchasing power of the masses would drive the economy forward. As it happened, Chile did see high rates of growth until the end of the 1990s.

The international community, however, attributed this growth primarily to the radical reforms of the 1980s. Foxley was unable and unwilling to undo these reforms because it would have meant re-nationalizing public companies that had been privatized. International belief in Chile's apparent neoliberal success story was further stoked when Pinochet had to step down as president in 1989 after losing the referendum. This created the illusion that neoliberal reforms had led to democratization.

Polanyi's pendulum thus swung back in the direction of laissez-faire capitalism in the 1980s. This was associated with a sharp rise in the global flow of commodities and capital, a development Polanyi had identified in his study of the nineteenth century. With the collapse of state socialism and disintegration of Yugoslavia (which had been a prominent proponent of a 'third way'), neoliberalism achieved a worldwide hegemony in economic policy from 1989 to 1991.

The key document from this turning point in world history was the Washington Consensus, agreed upon in the year the Berlin Wall fell by representatives of the International Monetary Fund (IMF), the World Bank, debtor countries, US Congress and high-ranking economic experts. While the consensus was originally intended for the Latin American countries plagued by high foreign debt and inflation, it evolved into a kind of blueprint for the economic reforms in post-communist Europe and other parts of the world. The top priority was macroeconomic stabilization (which, in practice, always meant strict austerity policies), followed by the holy trinity of liberalization, deregulation and privatization. Foreign direct investment, and thus global financial capitalism, also made an appearance.

Is it accurate to call this consensus 'neoliberal'? The economist John Williamson, who wrote the paper in which the term 'Washington Consensus' was coined, objected to this label after the turn of the millennium because he found it pejorative and he did not want to be lumped in with the Chicago Boys.[13] But key elements of the Washington Consensus were in alignment with the new economic thinking and diverged from the 'neoclassical synthesis'. This was particularly true of privatization, which reached a whole new level from the end of the 1990s, as well as the unbounded liberalization of foreign trade and the deregulation of national and global financial markets.

Post-communist Poland was the first European country to follow the recommendations of the Washington Consensus. In the autumn of 1989, the democratic government that had been in power in Poland since June of that year adopted a package of reforms that would soon come to be named after its originator, finance minister Leszek Balcerowicz. Like the Washington Consensus, the Balcerowicz Plan aimed at wide-ranging privatization and liberalization. Even though it was clear that the reforms would lead to massive social spending cuts and caps on wages, the majority of the left wing of Solidarność and prominent proponents of Catholic social teaching approved of them. Like its Washington predecessor, this 'Warsaw Consensus', as it were, was formulated as a 10-point decalogue.[14]

Germany's 'shock therapy' followed in the summer of 1990 (see the third essay in this book), and even the initially hesitant Czechoslovakia jumped on the neoliberal bandwagon under finance minister Václav Klaus. Klaus, an ardent supporter of Margaret Thatcher, invented what was known as voucher privatization, the aim of which was to create a 'nation of shareholders', as had previously happened in the UK (the privatization of British Telecom being a prime example).

International and domestic experts applied this model to the Russian Federation, but the future oligarchs there snapped up the vouchers for themselves and subsequently determined the course of the country's privatization. The all-encompassing corruption and criminal scheming that accompanied this was traced back to the weakness of the post-Soviet state. Russia plunged into a depression that rivalled the depths of the global economic crisis of the 1930s, and life expectancy fell to the level of a developing country. It was impossible for democracy to emerge under these conditions. Like the economy itself, it mutated instead into an oligarchy and finally, under Putin, into an authoritarian system.

The reforms in Poland did not get off to a great start either. The country's GDP fell by a total of 18 per cent in 1990 and 1991, far more than Balcerowicz had expected, and industrial production declined by nearly a third (this is indirect proof of just how severe the crisis was in Italy starting in 2009, when production fell by a quarter; more on this in the essay about *La Crisi*). Legions of people also found themselves out of work; in 1992, approximately 2.3 million Poles – or 13.5 per cent of the working population – were unemployed. Critics like Grzegorz Kołodko, a subsequent post-communist minister of finance, called this 'a shock without the therapy' and pressed for efforts to stimulate demand.[15] The experts from the IMF, by contrast, would have liked to see even more radical reforms. This fit with Polanyi's observations on the liberal economists of the nineteenth century, who also did not think liberalization had gone far enough in their own time.[16]

Economic growth picked up again in 1992, and Poland was the first former Eastern Bloc country to recover from the deep recession. As a result, the shock therapy was viewed internationally as a success, despite criticism within Poland itself and the defeat of the liberals in the 1993 elections. Poland's success story radiated to other post-communist countries and generated a neoliberal feedback loop in the West, like Chile had done previously. Balcerowicz's main American advisor, Jeffrey Sachs, praised the shock therapy at the time, as did Milton Friedman. So did the Harvard economist Andrei Shleifer and Californian political scientist Daniel Treisman, in retrospect. For the twenty-fifth anniversary of the transformation, Shleifer and Treisman published an article in *Foreign Affairs* entitled 'Normal Countries',[17] in which even Russia's development was portrayed as largely 'normal' despite the fact that Putin had already annexed Crimea by this point and was increasingly turning his back on the West (see the fifth essay in this book).

The success of the reforms, at least as measured by GDP and direct investments, was determined not least by factors mostly beyond the control of economic policy and thus neoliberalism. These factors were timing and geography. Countries like Poland and Hungary had already begun opening their doors to private entrepreneurs in the 1980s and were trailblazers in the reforms of 1989, so they had a significant head start. Poland also benefited from its strategic importance; as the biggest country in the former Eastern Bloc, it was essential for its reforms to succeed.

With this is mind, Western lenders in the early 1990s waived about half of Poland's old debts from the state socialist era. This jump start was very important, and Jeffrey Sachs was thinking of it twenty years later when he recommended waiving some of Greece's debt during the euro crisis. A similar approach will probably be necessary in Italy, too, where the loss of tax revenue and increased health spending during the coronavirus pandemic have driven up government debt in relation to GDP to levels last seen in Greece in 2011.

The West was less generous towards Hungary in 1989, even though the country had played a key role in opening the Iron Curtain. This came down to a combination of Western ignorance and Hungarian hubris. Hungary considered itself to be in the vanguard of economic reform, but servicing its debts overburdened the state budget. As a result, the post-communist government that had returned to power in 1995 was forced to adopt a drastic austerity programme. Like the Balcerowicz plan, Hungary's programme was named after the finance minister responsible for it: Lajos Bokros. Once the Bokros package was implemented, 30 per cent of Hungary's population fell below the poverty line. The post-communist Left thus lost its socio-political credibility, clearing the way for Viktor Orbán to win the next parliamentary elections and become prime minister for the first time. But then Orbán pursued a neoliberal programme as well, involving extensive privatization, which also covered pensions. This seems to confirm the central theory proposed by Ivan Krastev and Steven Holmes in *The Light That*

Failed, namely, that Eastern European politicians deliberately and obediently imitated the West.[18] However, which West did they strive to imitate and later repudiate? It is somewhat ironic that Trumpian America remained an object of orientation, and sometimes admiration, while the EU became a bogeyman, even as it continued to transfer huge sums of money to new member countries such as Hungary.

Geographical proximity to Western European markets was equally important to the economic recovery of the reform countries. Industrial companies tended to build new factories in the westernmost post-communist states rather than more distant ones. Only the former East Germany reaped few benefits from this, for reasons that will be explained in the essay on Germany's transformation. Considering this web of causalities, as well as the counter-example of East Germany and the many problems in Poland, it is simply not tenable to claim that shock therapy was the mother of all subsequent economic success.

Low wages and highly qualified workers were another lure for international investors in Eastern Europe. Industrial relocation could pay off quickly depending on a country's geographical position and political stability. This is not to say that targeted economic policy played no role, however. Romania, Bulgaria, Ukraine and other countries in which the post-communists came to power almost seamlessly and then ruled without a proper plan fared worse in the 1990s than the reform pioneers.

'Leaders' and 'laggards' were the terms used at the time, an indicator that neoliberalism was founded on an older kind of progressive thinking. At the end of the 1990s, the countries that had initially lagged behind put extra effort into proving themselves to be model students of economic reform. The political scientists Mitchell Orenstein and Hilary Appel aptly referred to this as 'competitive signaling'.[19] All post-communist states were in dire need of Western capital and technology to modernize their economies, so they tried to outdo one another in offering incentives to international investors.

International indices played a major role in this competition. In 1993, *The Economist* in the UK launched an Emerging Markets Index, a set of tables at the end of the magazine with major economic indicators. However, as its name revealed, this index equated countries with markets. Soon thereafter, neoliberal think tanks established the Open Market Index, Global Competitiveness Index, International Property Rights Index, Ease of Doing Business Index and Economic Freedom of the World Index.[20] The list could go on, but ultimately, all of the indices rewarded laissez-faire politics. Equally important were the professional journals for investors which consistently praised countries with minimal regulation and low taxes. This was in keeping with the political logic of neoconservatives in the USA, who insisted it was necessary to 'starve the beast'.[21] The beast they were talking about was the state, i.e., the commonwealth that was supposed to benefit all citizens.

These indices are evidence of both the triumph of econometrics (which had begun to take hold even earlier) and the global hegemony of neoliberalism. Competition for foreign direct investments also explains why 'laggards' like Slovakia and Romania, which were initially hesitant to privatize and liberalize, eventually also banked on radical reforms at the end of the 1990s.

But the relevance of economic policy is relativized once again when we look at the post-Soviet space. In the noughties, Ukraine and a few Central Asian countries achieved the highest growth rates in this region, some of them reaching more than 10 per cent annually. Their success was not entirely disconnected from their respective reform policies, but even outsiders like Belarus and Uzbekistan, which all but ignored the recommendations of the IMF and Western experts, did relatively well.[22]

Another new spin was put on neoliberalism around the turn of the millennium. In the first decade after 1989, the focus had been on privatizing state-owned enterprises and unbundling the state from the economy (a tactic Polanyi fundamentally rejected). The second decade, the phase of radical neoliberalism, was about curtailing the state's power over pensions, health care and education. In addition to (partially) privatizing these areas, all post-communist states introduced flat-tax systems which resulted in further cuts to social spending. This was followed by the deregulation of banks and the financial industry in the USA and globally – the main cause of the real estate bubble and stock market crash of 2008.

Even though it was often financed on credit, growing consumption legitimized neoliberalism from below. The long upswing that lasted from the early 1990s to the crisis of 2008–9 gave countries a good chance to catch up. For example, while Poland achieved only a third of the GDP of the EC per capita in 1989 and was considered the poorhouse of the Eastern Bloc, its per capita GDP rose over the following 25 years to reach two-thirds of the Western European average. In other words, Poland's economic distance from the West halved in a quarter of a century. This convergence, which also affected income, is extraordinary. The last time a country made up so much ground so quickly was when Germany caught up to industrialized England back in the nineteenth century.

While the German Empire of the nineteenth century used its new prosperity to establish a welfare state, the Eastern European countries of the twentieth century drastically cut their social benefits and barely increased them again even when they could afford to do so as their economies improved. This hurt children most of all, masses of whom grew up in poverty – a scenario we have seen in the USA and UK as well. In terms of system-immanent or even constructive criticism, neoliberalism's biggest problem was its lack of sustainability. In practice, this economic ideology weakened the very social resources it needed to fulfil its promise of prosperity and progress. This would become apparent all over again during the coronavirus pandemic, with lethal repercussions.

Social consequences of the neoliberal hegemony

Growth in all post-communist countries varied hugely from region to region. While the capital regions of Poland, the Czech Republic, Slovakia and Hungary surpassed the average GDP of the EU soon after the union expanded (adjusted for purchasing power parity, not in absolute terms), the villages, small towns and old industrial areas fell further and further behind. The poorest regions achieved a GDP just a fifth or sixth of that enjoyed by the front-runners in the same country. These regions are now the strongholds of PiS in Poland, Smer in Slovakia and Fidesz in Hungary.

There are obviously differences between the urban growth centres and rural areas of Germany, France, Austria, the Netherlands and Scandinavia, too. But the GDP gap is only about half as large in these countries as in the new EU member states, and government transfer payments greatly reduce income disparities as well. That said, the gap has been widening in Western Europe, and especially the south, for a good 30 years. Per capita GDP in southern Italy has fallen by more than 10 per cent compared to the EU average since 1995, and France's neglected provinces have recently become a breeding ground for the 'yellow vest' protests.

According to Branko Milanović's calculations, approximately one fifth of the population in post-communist Europe benefited from the radical changes there, while two fifths lost wealth.[23] These figures naturally differ from country to country. More people have certainly grown wealthier in Poland, but only a small sliver of the population has in Ukraine. The Czech Republic is an exception in many respects because the difference between its wealthiest and poorest regions is as small as it is in Germany (which might also explain the country's different voting behaviour; in the Czech parliamentary elections in 2021, the right-wing populists were soundly defeated). In South East Europe, by contrast, the social and regional divide is particularly deep.

This differentiated development in Eastern Europe is interesting in itself, and it is also enlightening to compare it to Western countries with a neoliberal slant. Ever since the Reaganomics era, the USA has developed much like post-communist Europe. The top fifth of the population has seen strong gains in income and wealth, while the lower three fifths have seen their income improve only minimally if at all, and many have actually become poorer.[24]

International economic advisors, financial institutions and the media were fixated on economic growth when assessing the 'performance' of post-communist countries. But even in economically pioneering countries like Poland, the high growth rates which lasted until 2008 tell us very little when we view them from a socio-historical perspective and dig into individual experiences. To mark the twentieth anniversary of 1989, the KARTA Center in Warsaw held a history competition to encourage young people to share their memories of the post-communist transformation. Although the availability of consumer goods had improved and some young Poles happily recalled getting their first car or other material acquisitions, many of the competition entries mentioned unemployment, social problems and the general sense of uncertainty after the transformation.[25] This is not what a happy childhood looks like – and even as adults, these Poles had never forgotten it.

Furthermore, the Baltic states, Romania and Ukraine occasionally achieved double-digit growth not just because their growth rates were low to begin with, but because they were the target of speculative investments. An Eastern European bubble formed in the early 2000s which paralleled the real estate bubble in the USA in some ways. Banks gave predatory credit to borrowers with little collateral, and they also imposed speculative foreign currency loans on people. The political scientists Dorothee Bohle and Béla Greskovits (whose work also draws on Polanyi) have shown that investments in the westernmost countries of the former Eastern Bloc focused on manufacturing, while foreign direct investments farther east and in the Baltic states flowed mainly into the financial and property sectors.[26]

When the Eastern European bubble burst in the wake of the global financial crisis of 2008–9, Latvia, Lithuania, Hungary, Romania and Ukraine stood on the brink of economic collapse due to excessive debt and drastic currency devaluation. This group of countries had to be 'rescued' through international aid programmes from the IMF and EU. But these rescue packages – which mainly benefited Western lenders – were tied to further social spending cuts. In combination with negative growth of up to 18 per cent and skyrocketing unemployment, these cuts led to an unprecedented wave of emigration. Latvia, Lithuania and Romania lost up to 10 per cent of their populations within the space of just a few years.

This had repercussions in the West. The UK was the most popular destination for economic migrants, and the country welcomed the cheap labour from Eastern Europe during the boom of the noughties. But after the global financial crisis, which hit the UK particularly hard on account of its inflated financial sector, these migrants found themselves in a society that was itself unsettled due to the deep recession and subsequent austerity measures. While Eastern European countries exported their social problems, the UK imported a political problem. And after the euro crisis, immigration from Southern Europe shot up as well.

The outcome of the UK referendum on EU membership was an expression of displeasure with the influx of migrants and fear of increased competition in the labour market. In this respect, the financial crisis was doubly responsible for Brexit: first, because banks and insurance companies were bailed out at the expense of 'ordinary people' (bankers in the City of London were already treating themselves to bonuses again while the Conservative government was cutting welfare benefits and even police funding), and second, because economic migration from Eastern and Southern Europe brought the consequences of the social upheaval in those regions to the UK.

Another problem familiar from post-communist Europe was the growing gap between the capital city and the rest of the country. Brexit received the most support in rural areas and the small to middling cities of central and northern England's declining industrial regions. The UK had been the deindustrialization forerunner amongst Western industrialized states since the 1980s. But no welfare state could cushion the blow of such a massive structural change, even disregarding the social spending cuts made by Margaret Thatcher and then New Labour under Tony Blair. Despite neoliberal ideas for mobilizing the unemployed, state benefits were barely enough for people to scrape by with poor food and a substandard education. The welfare system was not entirely dismantled, however, since even Thatcher would not touch the National Health Service.

Paul Collier, a British development economist, criticizes the very nature of these welfare benefits, which he says were like alms. In his opinion, while they covered minimum needs, they also robbed unemployed people and their families of their sense of self-worth due to a lack of reciprocal obligations.[27] This argument applies equally well to the former East Germany. The job creation schemes and early-retirement programmes that were created there in the 1990s worked like tranquilizers and prevented mass protests, but they also humiliated the approximately four million East Germans who had lost their jobs and prospects in the space of just a few years, and who certainly would have preferred to work than receive state benefits. No one wants to be thought of as a 'transformation loser' or live in a region that has been 'left behind'. Collier insists that more needs to be done for children and young people in particular, but it is doubtful whether the 'lean state' that was so often invoked in the 1990s would have been capable of this. Collier consequently proposes a massive regional and generational redistribution effort to support young people in disadvantaged regions and thus ensure the future of the entire country (though he focuses on cities like Sheffield and Stoke-on-Trent, many aspects of his findings are applicable to other regions and countries).

Polanyi always advocated a different relationship between the state and the economy, and above all a different function for the state. With respect to the nineteenth century, he noted critically that 'there was nothing natural about laissez-faire; free markets could never have come into being merely by allowing things to take their course. [. . .] Laissez-faire itself was enforced by the state'.[28] At first glance, Polanyi seems to endorse the traditional Marxist critique of the power cartel of political and economic elites in capitalist societies. It follows from this that we should name names when it comes to the period after 1989: the neoliberal order was created by the governments of the USA, the UK and even Germany and nearly every post-communist state, working in alliance with international financial organizations.

At the same time, Polanyi points out that the state itself made multiple attempts in the nineteenth century to mitigate the social impact of the industrial revolution and arrange for poverty relief. He believes it is the destiny of the state in later eras, too, to become a welfare state and thus a mediator between the interests of the market and society. He prioritizes social needs above the pursuit of profit, meaning that his book is based on a clear hierarchy of values.

This perception of the state is not without its contradictions, but it is far more complex than the anti-statism of orthodox Marxists, who famously wanted to replace the state with communism and violently opposed it before turning it into a monstrosity of economic planning and political surveillance under real socialism. Polanyi's view of the state also differs from the libertarian anti-statism of neoconservatives, for whom the state was an archenemy to be forced out of the economy because the free market could supposedly solve problems better and more effectively. The Chicago Boys fundamentally delegitimized the state by conceiving of it as just one actor amongst many, and as a representative of its own interests rather than an overarching authority dedicated to the common good. This is precisely what Polanyi demands of the state and corporations alike: that they should serve the interests of the people and not the other way around.

The need for social recognition is another Polanyian concept that deserves closer examination with respect to the period after 1989. Polanyi claimed that this need was especially prevalent amongst the déclassé unemployed and poor: 'Purely economic matters such as affect want-satisfaction are incomparably less relevant to class behaviour than questions of social recognition.'[29]

Essentials of neoliberalism: Mobilization through the threat of poverty

The lack of social recognition — its complete opposite, in fact — is reflected in linguistic changes and a raft of pejorative terms from the 1990s. In Poland, the term is *nieudacznik*, which literally means loser or failure. This word did not yet exist during the People's Republic; it began circulating after the end of state socialism, along with *biznesmen* and *menedżer*.[30] The analogous term in Germany, ever since the social welfare and labour market reforms under the social democrats and Greens, is *Hartzer* (in reference to the Hartz reforms developed by former VW executive Peter Hartz). And in the USA, the phrase 'white trash' has edged out the more Southern 'redneck'.

Where does this disdain for humanity come from? It has existed all along and can be found in every social class. There has always been a social pecking order amongst labourers and the rural population in Western societies, and also amongst the upper classes, as Pierre Bourdieu famously showed in his study of the fine distinctions in society.[31] But in the age of neoliberalism, social distinctions and punching down became systemic.

The thinking behind many of the reforms in 'emerging markets' and industrialized states alike was that the threat of poverty would force welfare recipients to be more active, flexible and mobile. The welfare reforms under New Labour in the UK and under the centre-left coalition that governed Germany from 1998 put increased pressure on unemployed people to take any available job. In abstract terms, this pressure came about because welfare benefits were no longer based on the traditional principle of entitlement – whereby contributors are entitled to receive certain services if required, which is why this is also referred to as social insurance – and were based instead on a principle of neediness. According to the rules of Hartz IV in Germany (there were a total of four major reform laws, hence the numeration), anyone who has not found a new job within a certain period of time must sacrifice the majority of their savings. This threat of impoverishment is supposed to motivate people to find a job as quickly as possible. Thanks to Germany's high standard of living, the impoverishment of Hartz IV recipients is relative. The bigger problem is their loss of socioeconomic status.[32]

In Western countries with less well-developed social welfare systems – such as the USA and UK, where Bill Clinton and Tony Blair introduced welfare reforms that cut social benefits and increasingly attached conditions to them – the everyday situation was actually worse for unemployed people than it had been before.

Mobilization through poverty had even harsher social and individual effects in the post-communist countries. It is this inherent disdain for humanity that is an essential component of neoliberalism.[33] Here, too, the responsible experts – who enjoyed long-term employment contracts and comfortable offices, unlike the people affected by their reforms – counted on the fact that the threat of destitution would be a good motivator.[34]

Their expectations were met to some extent, mostly in the form of labour migration on a massive scale. The East Germans were pioneers in the great East–West migration after 1989, with more than two million of them moving to western Germany in the following decade. They were followed by a similarly high number of Poles when Poland joined the EU, and then by an exodus from the crisis-stricken countries that had been 'rescued' from the global financial crisis and the shock waves it sent through Eastern Europe in 2009. This mass movement led to changes in the migrants' destination countries as well as in their countries of origin. Most of the emigrants were young and agile, and many were well educated. Had they stayed in their home regions, quite a few parliamentary elections in the eastern parts of Europe and Germany would have turned out differently later on.

International financial organizations had even more far-reaching goals in mind when they made recommendations to post-communist governments.[35] These governments were told to skimp on social spending so that the supposedly passive *Homo sovieticus* would become a *Homo economicus*. In countries like Slovakia and Poland, where wages of approximately two dollars an hour were common in the 1990s, the curtailment or abolition of welfare benefits (which were already meagre) made the unemployed truly destitute. It was almost impossible to find a job, especially for people with families to support, and for those who had to care for young children or relatives and could not simply move somewhere else. As a result, survival skills that had been acquired under socialism, such as subsistence farming in back gardens and at dachas, were put to use once again, though for different reasons after 1989.

In the USA, welfare reforms led to growing dependence on food stamps. Food stamps ensure that people can consume enough calories, but not that they can consume healthy food;

this fact, combined with a lack of education, means that the poor population is disproportionately affected by obesity, the new stigma of poverty. The abuse of illegal drugs and prescription medications also rose, one of the main reasons for the decline in American life expectancy even before the Covid-19 pandemic.

Increasing the margin between social benefits and wages was another argument for cutting welfare. This goal was expressed in the political slogan that it was important to 'make work pay'. In prosperous countries, regularly employed people may indeed be better off than those who receive benefits, but the starting point is different in countries with very low earned income. In these poorer countries, the margin between wages and benefits was increased by reducing benefits close to or even below the starvation threshold. The introduction of flat-tax systems further intensified the redistribution from bottom to top.

Populist revolts

Deterrence and punishment alone cannot be the sole basis of the socioeconomic order in a democracy; there have to be incentives as well. In the post-communist states, the incentive was the promise of a future with Western standards of living. This was supposed to justify the sacrifices of the present. Communists in the post-war period had used a similar argument to justify their own version of modernization from above. When this was no longer convincing, it was simply said that – in the words of Margaret Thatcher – there was no alternative. This anti- and apolitical reasoning was found in Germany, too, where the Social Democratic chancellor Gerhard Schröder was nicknamed the *Basta-Kanzler* – the 'that's that chancellor'. Angela Merkel used the word *alternativlos* (no alternative) at least as often as her predecessor, to the point that the

Association for the German Language declared it the *Unwort des Jahres* (Un-word of the Year) in 2010. Populists are appealing because they claim that an alternative does, in fact, exist; the Alternative für Deutschland (AfD) has baked this right into their party name.

The countless publications about right-wing populism and the crisis of democracy that have appeared since the *annus horribilis* might give the impression that these are relatively new phenomena. But people often forget that groups were already mobilizing against the great transformation in the second half of the 1990s on both the left and the right. In the following essays I look at individual precursors to Trump, Orbán and their ilk, but what I want to emphasize here is that such movements appeared early on in post-communist Europe. In all of the 'reform states' some of the population reacted to the supposedly unavoidable social cuts by simply not voting. Voter turnout in Poland was consistently below 50 per cent after 1993, much like in the USA.

The second reaction was a populist revolt – and once again, Poland led the way. When unemployment rose sharply in the early 2000s (partly for demographic reasons), three populist parties each received approximately 10 per cent of the votes in Poland's 2001 parliamentary elections, including PiS for the first time. The major winner was the post-communist Democratic Left Alliance (SLD), thanks in part to its own populist sociopolitical promises, which it was ultimately unable and unwilling to keep (I mention this as evidence that populism can certainly be part of the political mainstream, so it does little good for academics to treat it like a marginal political phenomenon). Voters punished the SLD for this in the 2005 elections, just as Western European social democrats who had shifted to the centre were punished later on. PiS came to power for the first time in 2005 and immediately tried to enforce authoritarian rule. The most important tool for doing so was zealous nationalism, which has only intensified since the party's electoral victory in 2015.

What do Poland and the new EU member states have in common with the UK and USA? All of these countries threw open their doors to globalization, but they had relatively undeveloped welfare systems which were further weakened after the financial crisis. The irony here is that it was the proponents of free trade, free capital flows and globalized markets who called for reduced government spending and social welfare cuts. Thirty years later, we know that the only way to achieve a lasting consensus for globalization is to couple it with social safeguards.[36] The same is probably true for European integration. Polanyi spoke of 'social protection' without going into detail on precisely what this might look like. If we take his predilection for cooperatives as a starting point, it seems most necessary to strengthen the self-organizational capabilities of socially disadvantaged classes so they can not only protect themselves ('protect' is a very defensive term) but also break out and harness new life opportunities and optimism.

From neoliberalism to antiliberalism

Rebellions and revolutions often have unintended consequences. We might have expected the global financial crisis of 2008–9 to lead to a renaissance for the Left, a 'Polanyian moment'. And for a while, it looked as if it had. Left-wing parties won elections, Occupy Wall Street took over squares and streets near the New York Stock Exchange, and hundreds of thousands of students and other young people took to the streets in Spain under the motto of *'Democracia Real Ya'*. But left-wing movements against austerity fizzled out. They managed to mobilize masses of young people through social media, but they failed to establish lasting structures.

The left-wing populist parties that came to power after the euro crisis faced tremendous disillusionment because there was little they could do to counter the existing austerity policies. In Greece, it was on the back of protests against the bailout conditions proposed by the 'troika' of the European Commission, the European Central Bank (ECB) and the International Monetary Fund that the Syriza party won the legislative election at the start of 2015 and a subsequent referendum, but the country still had to submit to the conditions of its international creditors. The newly elected prime minister Alexis Tsipras remained in power, but the left wing of his party split off, and he was ultimately only able to pursue a moderate course that supported the state. What was remarkable about this conflict surrounding the troika's austerity programme was not so much the behaviour of the German government, which stubbornly stuck to its conditions, but rather the line taken by French president François Hollande. Hollande was politically close to Tsipras in principle; both politicians were leftists (though the French socialists were originally allied with the socialist PASOK party in Greece, which was squeezed out by Syriza), and Hollande had previously provided rhetorical support to Greece on several occasions. But in the negotiations about cancelling the country's debt, Hollande left Greece in the lurch because he did not want to endanger the billions of euros that French banks had loaned to Athens. There was no question that these loans had been granted recklessly, but it was the Greek people and not the financial institutions themselves who ultimately paid the price in the form of an unprecedented recession and fast-rising unemployment.

President Obama also opted to overcome the financial crisis by siding with the institutions that caused it. If we include the family members of all the borrowers who lost their homes after 2008, then approximately 25 million Americans were directly or indirectly affected by this. The government's alliance with the stock markets, and the massive bailouts and capital injections that were provided to the financial sector, prevented a depression like the one in the 1930s. But as Adam Tooze points out,[37] they also sent a disastrous political signal that fostered conspiracy theories and practically invited voters to elect protest parties. Donald Trump took the opportunity in 2016 to rail against the establishment, even though he himself is obviously part of it.

Political scientists have repeatedly debated whether right-wing populism should be viewed as a conglomerate that borrows from various ideologies and employs new forms of political mobilization, or whether more emphasis should be placed on its ideological orientation. As a historian, I see it as a coherent world view that could be characterized as a bundle of promises of protection and security. Right-wing populists promise to protect the economy against international competition, which is why they have turned against free trade; to protect the domestic labour market from foreign competition, hence the smear campaign against 'illegal immigrants'; to protect society against crime, though crime rates have been falling for years, and against terror, which is seldom mentioned without the addition of the word 'Islamic'; and to preserve national values and the traditional family unit with its clearly defined gender roles. This is, overall, a resolutely antiliberal world view.

Naturally, there are variations between different countries and parties. Orbán, for example, does not oppose free trade to the same extent as Trump because export-dependent Hungary cannot afford it. Attitudes also differ regarding gender roles and the lesbian, gay, bisexual and transgender (LGBT) community. Perhaps the most pertinent difference is the stance of conservatives and moderate right-wingers and the extent to which they align themselves with right-wing populists, curry favour with them or even form coalitions with them.

The right-wing populists who have come to power in recent years certainly do not represent the interests of the common people, who often elect such parties out of a sense of helplessness and anger. These populists think primarily about themselves. Donald Trump, for instance, broke with the long tradition of American presidents who had kept their business interests separate from their elected office and who publicly released their tax returns. Trump cozied up to big corporations and the stock market even more than the Democrats before him. British conservatives probably do not even know what they want their country to look like after Brexit. Their initial plan was to make the UK a tax haven, but that would cause the party to lose most of the working-class voters won over by Boris Johnson's welfare promises.

Both Viktor Orbán and the short-lived coalition of conservatives and right-wing populists in Austria pushed through extensive social spending cuts, and the AfD has similar plans for Germany. The social and economic policies of right-wing populists therefore stand in continuity with neoliberalism almost everywhere (Poland is an exception). But by the time voters realize these policies might not benefit them as much as populists promise during their election campaigns, it will be too late.

Another continuity with neoliberalism can be seen in the rejection of critical debate, which is dismissed as 'fake news'. Since 2015–16 there has also been a rise in nationalistic propaganda which paints migrants and refugees as a grave threat and deliberately fabricates crises at borders and in migrant camps to attract public attention. This insistence on an ethnically defined nation, typically referred to by right-wing populists as a country's 'true' or 'real' people, has existed for a long time. Nationalism is woven into the fabric of European societies, just as racism is in the USA (racism obviously exists in Europe, too, but nationalism and racism should not be equated, any more than colonialism and imperialism). It is especially close to the surface in the new EU member states, which spent more than 40 years under the rule of a foreign empire and only regained full sovereignty after 1989.

I do not think that this is a counter-reaction to a two-decade process of over-adaptation to the West and the EU. This theory, which was put forward by Ivan Krastev and Steven Holmes, may work for Bulgaria or Hungary, but lumps all of the new EU member states together and portrays them almost as truculent children.[38] Polish politicians, at least, have clearly expressed their views in European debates concerning matters such as references to God in the Constitutional Treaty of the EU, involvement in the Iraq War, the 'Eastern policy' of the EU and many other issues, and they have sometimes managed to win over others.

Conspicuous nationalism (like the forests of flags that are so popular at official events and press conferences) serves a variety of purposes. An outwardly united front works like an internal bond and distracts from problems such as rampant corruption. The refugee crisis of 2015–16 was a good opportunity to ramp up nationalist propaganda. Viktor Orbán knew that most Hungarians were sceptical of both mass immigration and Muslims, and he ruthlessly exploited this in his political campaigns against domestic opponents and the EU. But this functional nationalism, which is geared solely towards maintaining power, can quickly turn into a hard, racist nationalism. After more than half a decade of forcing anti-European, anti-cosmopolitan and anti-Muslim propaganda down people's throats, Orbán and the Fidesz elite have probably come to believe it themselves.

While Donald Trump was in office, both the president himself and his advisors underwent a kind of auto-suggestive self-radicalization. This culminated in the myth of the stolen election, which Trump conjured up in the summer of 2020 and then repeated in increasingly shrill tones until even he was convinced by it. This is the deeper connection between Trump and his followers who stormed the Capitol. Scholars studying nineteenth-century nationalism have observed another effect of nationalistic tirades: the supporters of right-wing populist politicians, and party officials who aspire to higher positions, can best distinguish themselves from their peers by loudly voicing radical views. The self-referentiality of social media intensifies this effect, amplifying the people who make a racket and say or write what was previously unspeakable.[39]

Unlike the nationalism of the first half of the twentieth century, this contemporary nationalism rarely has expansionist aims. No one today wants to take over their neighbour's territory – other than neo-imperialist Russia, of course, or neo-Ottoman Turkey if its military and economy could afford it (see the fifth essay in this book). But the defensiveness of this new nationalism and its focus on an ethnically defined society make it no less dangerous. Its aggression is increasingly directed at minorities within countries and against people who think differently, as can be seen in the growing number of attacks by right-wing extremists.

Polanyi barely mentions the dangers of nationalism and racism, even though he had to flee from radical nationalists and antisemites twice in his life. This fault in his book stems from his Marxist background, which sensitized him to social issues but not to national conflicts or the racism of his time. Nationalism has always been such a powerful force in history because it plays on instincts such as the distrust of strangers, making it especially well suited to mobilizing the masses.

Trump and Orbán on the right and (prior to them) Slobodan Milošević on the left began their political careers not as notably radical nationalists or racists, but more as cynics who played with various ideologies for the sake of power. But over time, they all banked on nationalism and set their supporters against minorities and migrants.

In a literal sense, the term 'populism' suggests the instrumentalization of political programmes that are necessarily popular, meaning that they reflect the views of the people. There are two unspoken assumptions behind this. The first is that a country's people, or the voters who elect right-wing populist parties, are at least as nationalist and racist as their leaders, otherwise nationalist appeals would not make sense. The second is that these leaders are closely attuned to popular opinions and moods and are better able to respond to them than established political parties.

But once pure power has been attained, it cannot be an end itself in the long term. It is like a vessel that becomes filled with political content and ideologies. This explains why none of the right-wing populist parties and their usually charismatic leaders have moderated their nationalism once they have come to power, as generally happens with other campaign promises. Instead, they have ramped it up. It is not possible to develop a universal theory of right-wing populist power from this observation, but it does help explain why right-wing populists either start off as fervent right-wing nationalists or become so in the course of time.

Deliberate polarization gives rise to yet another ideologizing mechanism. Right-wing populists need bogeymen (as do left-wing intellectuals, for that matter), and the best way to create them is by drawing on national stereotypes and older forms of nationalism and racism. This is why old buzzwords like 'cosmopolitan' have suddenly appeared again, along with anti-migrant insults that seem to be taken straight from the fascist or Stalinist playbook.

Antiliberalism is older than this – since it already existed at the end of the nineteenth century – but it is also younger. Its current form can be traced back to the early 1990s, when neoconservatives in the USA managed to make 'liberal' a bad word. We have come full circle here, and the circle can only be broken by looking back to the great transformation after 1989. Liberal democracy was apparently a breeding ground not just for liberal democrats, but for increasingly powerful opposing forces. There is a comparison to be made here with neoliberalism, which auto-parasitically drains the social and economic resources it needs to survive in the long term. In light of this, our debate should not be about the 'bad' and morally condemnable right-wing populists, but rather about how we can make democracy resilient enough to withstand the recent movements of Polanyi's pendulum. If it continues to swing even more in the direction of right-wing populism and nationalism, it might make one of the main categories of this book obsolete: the West. This term was born in the Cold War (though its roots are much older, of course) and has been revived by the new, hot war in Eastern Europe. Regardless of how 'the West' is defined, it depends on a set of shared values, and they have been attacked most fiercely not from the outside, but from within.

2

Lost Social and Political Equilibrium
The USA after the Cold War

We do not yet know whether the storming of the Capitol Building on 6 January 2021 marked the inglorious end of a chaotic presidency or the beginning of a new American republic. Europeans are used to republics with consecutive numbers which change after wars, political upheaval and attempted coups; France is currently on its fifth republic, while Poland is on its third. Such numeration never bodes well. At most, it reminds us of the fragility of democracy and how counterforces have always tried to turn it into an authoritarian system.

While the prosecution of those responsible for this appalling assault on liberal democracy is still under way, the political reckoning appears to be a lost cause. A large majority of Republican voters still believe that the 2020 presidential election was 'stolen'. Donald Trump continues to spread this lie, proving himself to be a sore but politically effective loser. His delegitimization of the election is what motivated the attack on the political and intellectual centre of the world's oldest liberal democracy. And it was more than an attack – it was an attempted coup which was backed by the outgoing president himself.

The storming of the Capitol has done tremendous damage to the international prestige of the USA and the West in general, but its negative impact on the everyday workings of democracy must also not be underestimated. Congress can no longer be as accessible as it was when I was a student in Washington, D.C. I wrote my master's thesis in the Library of Congress in the spring of 1993, so I know the building from the inside. At the time, it was easier to get into the Library of Congress than into a local bank, and I marvelled at the openness of American democracy. The National Guard withdrew from Capitol Hill in May 2021, but there is nothing to prevent some peaceful demonstration in the future from devolving into another attack on Congress, or far-right assailants mixing in with the tourists. Just like the mob of 6 January 2021, such attackers will be white American citizens, not the kind of terrorists caught by immigration officials at international airports.

More police and security measures would change the atmosphere, of course, not just for visitors, but also for the servants of democracy who work in Congress and other government departments (this public servant ethos does still exist, though there is no guarantee that this will remain the case). Fear and defensiveness are toxic and make it hard for democracy to evolve. But such evolution is necessary, not least to counter internal and external threats and to cope with the technological developments that are shaping the media landscape and contributing to the much-lamented splintering of society.

Was this storm just an isolated squall or the result of a long-term change in the political and social climate? Historians will approach this question with a longer time frame in mind than the lawyers currently tasked with prosecuting the perpetrators. For example, Kevin M. Kruse and Julian E. Zelizer start their chronicle of contemporary American history in the turbulent 1970s and end it with Trump's presidency. The two Princeton historians delve deeply into the conservative turn under Ronald Reagan, who made the radical right and religious fundamentalism socially acceptable again. Kruse and Zelizer claim that the American divide is the product of intensified competition between the two main political parties and thus a consequence of the bipolar political system. Their argument is coherent in and of itself, but it is difficult to distinguish cause and effect here, making the fault lines seem somewhat tautological and almost inevitable.[1]

This essay strives to bring an external perspective to the debate about America, expanding it into something more than just an American debate. It centres on the period after the end of the Cold War, when the USA was at the peak of its power and international renown. In the 1992 presidential election, a centrist Democrat replaced a moderate Republican, which indirectly indicates that the deepest fault lines must have appeared sometime afterwards. In keeping with my own field of research, I focus less on the dysfunctional political system here than on the country's social history.

Because they are subjective, essays force writers to clearly define their position on a topic. My own position has been shaped by my deep shock about the storming of the Capitol. This was the darkest hour of American democracy after the Second World War. The violent end of the Trump presidency almost makes me long for the early 1990s, when the two parties and their voters still respected one another, and moderation was considered a value.

Nostalgia is a state of mind that can cloud our critical view of the past and present. A good example of this is the post-communist nostalgia that emerged in the 1990s, when many people – even former oppositionists – found themselves longing for the allegedly safe and predictable world of state socialism, which was illusory in any case. On closer examination, we can see that post-communist nostalgia was not primarily about the past, but rather about the present and all the uncertainty inherent in it.

The late cultural theorist Svetlana Boym noted that nostalgia often takes hold when a gap opens up between progressive thinking and lived experience.[2] The transformation that was envisioned after 1989 promised people a bright future in a free market economy and democratic society, but it first confronted them with post-communist tristesse and the immediate effects of shock therapy. This cognitive dissonance and the accelerated changes brought about by the transformation prompted people to retreat into an idealized past which had never really existed. The nostalgics of the time were well aware of this, but because communism had been delegitimized, it was all but impossible to highlight the achievements of state socialism and develop a forward-looking political programme based on them.

The liberal and social democracies of the post-war period and the democratic revolutions of 1989 are more promising in this regard. We can look back at their history without romanticizing it in order to recall the ideals of the time and use them as the basis for the political demands of today. In this sense – and as Svetlana Boym interpreted it – nostalgia can be a positive political force.

Will Americans soon feel a sense of nostalgia for liberal democracy? After his electoral victory, Joe Biden proclaimed 'America is back' almost like a mantra. But is there actually a way back? If so, where does the path lead, and is it even worth following?

Bill Clinton's election in 1992 after 12 years of Republican rule was undoubtedly a moment of democratic awakening. Samuel Huntington had published his book *The Third Wave: Democratization in the Late Twentieth Century* one year earlier, and the Western political order seemed to be prevailing in Latin America and Eastern Europe alike. Huntington was optimistic about Asia, too. The USA had won the Cold War and become a beacon of global democratization. Clinton confirmed his country's mission in his inaugural address when he pronounced the 'spring' of democracy around the world, and he gave encouragement to the proponents of democracy everywhere by claiming 'their cause is America's cause'.[3]

Clinton said nothing about the development of democracy in his own country, even though voter turnout for his victory had only been 55 per cent. This was actually an improvement over previous presidential elections. Turnout declined again in 1996, when nearly half of all voters gave democracy the cold shoulder and refused to participate in its most important practice. The same happened again in 2000. Did this perhaps have something to do with changes in the economy and the social fabric of American society?

Trade unions offer a good opportunity to participate in elections because their employee representatives are elected, as are the national representatives of the labour organizations themselves. But union membership (which also should not be idealized; more on this later) declined by more than a third under Reagan and Bush, and the trend continued under Clinton. Companies are notoriously hierarchical rather than democratic in their structure, so it is not accurate to say that the USA itself experienced a democratic spring at the start of the 1990s. There were interesting approaches to this in East Germany and Czechoslovakia in the first phase of the revolution, but they soon evaporated because economic hardship and the neoliberal turn quickly limited the possibilities of utopian thinking.

Clinton owed his victory above all to the economic situation and the election campaign he based it on. When he said 'it's the economy, stupid', he drew attention to the weak point in Bush's presidency. The economic cycle continued to work in Clinton's favour even after the election because the preceding recession meant there was almost nowhere to go but up. Clinton therefore had every reason for optimism (an American trait which we Central Europeans generally admire). The same applied to Poland, the first post-communist country to experience economic recovery.

It is a matter of good political custom in the United States for the population to take an interest in the inauguration of a new president. This public ceremony was especially impressive to us international students who had come from countries with smaller capital cities. We were fascinated right from the start by the extra-long black Cadillac that takes the new president from Capitol Hill down Pennsylvania Avenue to the White House. There were no stretch limousines in Germany at the time, much less throngs of people lining the streets to cheer a new president and wave flags. Even I was given a little flag for the occasion, as was the other German Fulbright student in Georgetown.

Thinking that we could wave our flags better from a height, we climbed up the tallest tree on Pennsylvania Avenue, right in front of the White House. Security measures would make such a thing impossible today, but at the time it gave us a great view of the approaching state car over the masses of people and TV cameras. Unlike the starchy George H.W. Bush, Bill Clinton was a good-looking, down-to-earth guy. He climbed out of the Cadillac a few hundred metres from the White House and walked the rest of the way to his future official residence. This drove the crowds wild, and they shrieked: 'We want Bill! We want Bill!' The sky seemed to be the limit for democracy that day.

This was certainly the opinion of the many students and educators from Eastern Europe who had either won a Fulbright scholarship, like I had, or were spending a semester or two in Washington with other programmes. These Poles, Slovaks and Czechs conversed with one another in a pan-Slavic mishmash, since Russian – the language they probably could have communicated in most easily – was frowned upon. Lacking money (the scholarships were meagre), we spent many an evening at kitchen parties, basically like you would do in Eastern Europe, and we all agreed that democracy was the future. We would toast this ideal, pour another round, toast again – and the rest is lost in the haze of time.

A quarter of a century later, the political hangover has kicked in. Since 2016, commentators and political scientists everywhere have fretted about the crisis of democracy, the threat of right-wing populists, the American divide and the decline of the West as a community of values and states – one which might not actually exist anymore (though the Russian attack on Ukraine has revived it, at least on the surface). This essay is a personal attempt to pick up the traces of post-1989 history in America. The opportunity to do so arose when I was invited to the USA again, this time as a visiting professor at New York University in 2018–19 (which already seems very long ago thanks to the pandemic). I focus mainly on the decade after the end of the Cold War here, partially for personal reasons, but mostly for intellectual and historiographical ones, since it was in this period that the groundwork was laid for the social and political upheavals of recent years.

Looking back on my years in the States (which included a post-doctoral fellowship at Harvard in 1997–8), I feel like I was a participant observer of the changes there. This was obviously not participant observation in the sense of social or cultural anthropology, since a research field cannot be transposed from a past period to the present day. But guided by my own memories and contemporary sources, I want to virtually revisit the East Coast of the United States and use what I find there as a matrix for the present. The advantage of a subjective view of the past is that it is often more direct, not mediated by data or the knowledge enshrined in secondary literature. Maybe this is why personally motivated research and books are so trendy right now. For example, in *Returning to Reims*, a book about revisiting his hometown, the French sociologist Didier Eribon delivers a clear-sighted analysis of the major social and political problems currently facing France. And the Berlin-based sociologist Steffen Mau uses his own hometown as a starting point for analysing East Germany's transformation and understanding the hardships associated with German unification.[4] Both of these scholars hark back to a much older method, however, one known in the USA as 'sociological imagination'.[5]

The deeper purpose of this approach is to take a more distanced view of the scientific claim to objectivity, and especially of the data on the 'booming nineties' in the USA. The usual figures for GDP, unemployment and consumption would suggest that the Clinton years were good. But different social groups experienced this socioeconomic transformation in very different ways, just as they did in post-communist Eastern Europe. This transformation was referred to as globalization in the USA, and its vision for the future was not as clear as the one in Poland or East Germany, with its telos of a 'double transition'. Globalization too promised prosperity while often having very different, negative consequences for the various social groups affected by this great transformation.

Bill Clinton's centrist shift

When Clinton became president, he had ambitious plans and the benefit of a solid majority in both houses of Congress. One of his primary goals was to introduce universal health care; the same applied to Barack Obama, who eventually carried through on the major reform effort in 2010. The American health care system is by far the most expensive in the world in relation to GDP, but it covers only a fraction of the population. I experienced this first hand while I was studying there, when I had to seek out a doctor for an acute illness. I was turned away the first time around because I did not have the right insurance documents with me, and the second time around because the hospital clerk was unfamiliar with the insurance scheme for Fulbright students. For every single treatment, you had to jump through multiple bureaucratic hoops before seeing a doctor, and then again to settle the invoice.

This bloated apparatus is responsible for some of the high costs in the US health care system, but others can be pinned on the stockholders who naturally insist on getting their 'shareholder value'. Problems are also posed by protracted illnesses which are treated too late because so many people have little or no insurance. This was already common knowledge in 1993, when health care costs swallowed up more than 12 per cent of America's GDP while accounting for less than 8 per cent on average in other Western countries.[6] Today the gap between the USA and the rest of the Western world is greater than 6 per cent. This is more than the entire defence budget, which is constantly held up as an argument for the supposed overextension of the American Empire. The USA does, in fact, spend much more on its military than its allies do, but what is most overextended is the capitalistic, bureaucratized health care sector. In this respect, Clinton's proposed reforms would have been a step in the right direction. But in hindsight, the question is whether the young, politically relatively inexperienced president and his team actually knew which direction to go.

The Democrats also pursued other reforms after coming to power, including a policy of equality for gay men and lesbians in the military – a question of identity politics, according to Francis Fukuyama.[7] Identity politics (as distinct from a sociopolitical agenda) can be defined as a political approach based on the interests of groups who define themselves by their cultural or sexual orientation, and often by their origin or skin colour. Before Clinton was elected, a soldier could be dismissed if it were discovered that he or she (there were not as many women in uniform at the time) were gay. Army investigators therefore often snooped around in soldiers' private lives, and while homosexuality was considered an offence, visiting a prostitute was not.

On just their fifth day in office, President Clinton and Vice President Al Gore summoned Colin Powell, Chairman of the Joint Chiefs of Staff, to a meeting to discuss a new regulation.

Gore, who had grown up in very privileged circumstances, asked Powell whether he thought there was a parallel between discrimination against Black Americans and discrimination against gays and lesbians (we know this because the notes from the meeting were declassified fairly recently by the National Archives). Powell, who had spent his youth in the 'ghetto' of the South Bronx in an era of open racial discrimination, rejected the comparison. Like so many Black Americans, Powell had enlisted in the army because it offered him a way out of poverty and promised a secure existence. He could have explained to Gore that there were huge differences between the two forms of discrimination, starting with the visibility of one's skin colour and the very scale of the issue. Black Americans account for more than an eighth of the population of the USA, and even more when you include the children of mixed-race marriages. By contrast, the proportion of gay men (who were the main topic of discussion both at the time and later on) was just a fraction of this.[8]

One of the generals present during these negotiations took a chance on open conflict and tipped off the press. This was fodder for conservatives, who hounded Clinton through his entire first year in office before the 'don't ask, don't tell' compromise was finally reached at the end of 1993. This compromise meant that gays would no longer be investigated by the army, but it also meant they could not talk openly about their sexual orientation. The solution offered no proper protection against discrimination, and over the next ten years nearly 10,000 gay men and women were dismissed from the army. The government could have achieved the same thing with a simple administrative regulation to govern its internal investigations.

It is hard to find discrete solutions to issues of identity politics, not least because the respective groups are concerned with public acknowledgement of their orientation and discrimination. The groups that can drum up the most support are the ones who get to have a say, leaving behind others who are less able to assemble a powerful lobby or PR campaign. Despite the obvious gulf between rich and poor, which is much larger in the USA than in Germany, this applies to every single socially disadvantaged group in America. Neither industrial workers, whose numbers have been shrinking for nearly half a century, nor the new service proletariat, who can barely live off their wages, are adequately represented in democratically governed Washington.

Incidentally, the same applies to the New York schools that my children attended during our stay in 2018–19. Our public elementary and middle school in the West Village had very active associations of gay and transgender parents, but there was no one to represent parents who were financially disadvantaged or flat-out poor. This is an indictment of the Democrats, who make record wins in the area but have apparently forgotten how to represent the lower classes. Their deficiency in this regard stems from the fact that most of the new political generation has been recruited from universities, not from the old or new working class. Political communication suffers as a result; the young Democratic representatives who were elected to Congress in 2018 out of protest against Donald Trump are perfectly capable of delivering solid lectures on diversity, but with very few exceptions (one being Alexandria Ocasio-Cortez) they probably know almost nothing about what everyday work is like at Amazon or any other retail or service corporation. Social diversity is a huge issue in general, but few people in politics or academia talk about this elephant in the room.

Sexual orientation was also a hot topic when I was at Georgetown University, and the concept of 'identity' was all the rage. One of the history professors, an openly gay former monk, put 'queer history' at the top of the syllabus for his foundational seminar in the master's degree programme. The seminar spent weeks focusing on the truly appalling discrimination against gays and lesbians, chemical castration and countless individual tragedies. But here, too, the question of proportion arose, because we learned much less about gender in the traditional sense and discrimination against women; we were taught almost nothing about social history in this seminar; and not a word was said about the history of the welfare state, even though this would have been a logical topic to discuss in light of the health care reforms that had been announced.[9] Our seminar probably faced the same problem as politics in general: you can't deal with everything at once; you have to prioritize.

Clinton's planned social reforms were not a frequent topic of discussion amongst the students at Georgetown, probably because they had almost no direct effect on us. The health insurance reforms which would have helped Black Americans and many others fell by the wayside on Capitol Hill in 1993. As a tangential anecdote, some of my fellow students in the foundational history class no longer wanted to read Marx because they were of the opinion that communism, and thus Marxism, had failed. But we all eagerly discussed the cultural turn, which felt like a revelation at the time. Another popular topic was postmaterialism, or the assumption that, thanks to the long post-war upswing and increased prosperity everywhere, cultural change would now take precedence over economic and social conflicts.

Attending lectures was a good way to get a sense of the popularity of a cultural versus social agenda. When Ronald Inglehart, founder of the World Values Survey, held a lecture in Washington, D.C., the auditorium was filled with hundreds of people. Social issues, by contrast – such as the rampant poverty in the capital – were 'out'. The residents of Georgetown had isolated themselves from this poverty in part by rejecting plans for a subway stop in their wealthy neighbourhood. More than half the city of Washington was branded a 'no-go area' at the time; there were shootings almost every day, and even armed carjackings at road junctions and in traffic jams. The high crime rate was another Achilles' heel for the Democrats. In early 1994, Rudolph ('Rudy') Giuliani was elected mayor of New York City with a motto of 'zero tolerance'. Meanwhile, a 'rainbow coalition' of Black Americans, Latinos, women's rights activists and gays failed to make inroads even in this Democratic stronghold.

The autumn of 1994 saw the worst defeat of a ruling party in the USA since the Second World War. In the mid-term elections, Republicans took the Senate and won 54 seats in the House of Representatives, the first time since 1952 that they had been the majority party there. The conservatives won by a landslide especially in the South and Midwest, and they made gains with white middle-class voters in New York and California as well. Many of the newly elected Republicans came from the party's right wing. They were ardent advocates of neoliberalism who wanted to pare the state down to a minimum and – like Ronald Reagan before them – viewed the markets as a panacea for all manner of economic and social problems. In 1995, the Republicans under Newt Gingrich allowed the debate about the federal budget deficit to escalate to such an extent that the government had to shut down for weeks.[10] Only the 2018–19 shutdown under Trump lasted longer, the difference being that the president and ruling party themselves were responsible for it that time. This says a lot about the talent that right-wing populists have for governing while pretending to be in the opposition.

Neocons and the rise of right-wing populists

Our terraced house in Georgetown was shared by three students and three young Congressional aides, one of whom was a Republican activist who had earned his political spurs as an intern on Capitol Hill. He was basically a nice guy, though before and after work he would endlessly and crudely insult both the Clintons. This was apparently the way to make a name for himself in his cohort. Such self-radicalization within one's own peer group is a key to understanding the political dynamics in Donald Trump's cabinet and in the orbit of other right-wing populists. Whoever badmouths their political opponents the loudest and condemns them wholesale gets the most attention.

Our housemate's ranting stood in strange contrast to his navy blue blazers and meticulously combed and gelled hair. We students just laughed off the 'angry young man', but in hindsight this was a misjudgement. He was a sign that there was already a young generation of neocons in the 1990s who were far more radical than mainstream Republicans. Not all of these young guns had a conservative background; our little Republican was rebelling against the protest movements of the 1960s – his father was a well-known presenter for one of the big liberal TV channels.

The Republican party took another step towards radicalization during the presidential election campaign of 1996. Journalist and commentator Pat Buchanan, who had spent a few years as Ronald Reagan's director of communications, railed against the establishment in Washington (where he himself had grown up and made a career), criticized the newly founded North American Free Trade Agreement (NAFTA) as a bad deal for the USA and pursued an openly nationalist and racist agenda. Buchanan agitated against minorities and claimed that mass immigration would lead to 'population replacement' in the USA. Right-wing populist and nationalist parties in Europe promoted similar theories in the mid-1990s, leading to their first major electoral successes in France, Belgium, Italy and Austria. Buchanan, who continues to be celebrated for his views by right-wingers in the USA, won more than 20 per cent of the votes in the presidential primaries, earning himself a respectable second place.

Many consider Buchanan to be a spiritual predecessor to Donald Trump. He does, in fact, have many adherents amongst Trump's followers, including one of Trump's most influential advisors: Stephen Miller. As a senior advisor on domestic and migration policy, Miller was the source of ideas such as the wall between the USA and Mexico, the Muslim travel ban and other measures to cut immigration and weaken asylum law (forgive me for recounting information that is probably old news to many Americans, but few people outside the USA are familiar with Miller, and it is important to know about the ideologues and strategists behind Trump). Miller also pursued a much farther-reaching goal, namely, to abolish the principle of *jus soli* for American citizenship. Though he failed to achieve this, the idea is out there now – and Miller, who was born in 1985, still has a political career ahead of him. If America's citizenship law were reformed in this way, the USA would no longer be a country of immigration, and what was once an open nation of citizens would become a closed society defined by ancestry.

To label Miller a right-wing populist would be misleading in two respects. First, it would suggest that Miller's radical anti-immigration agenda is genuinely popular with Americans, and second, it would underestimate Miller's ideological orientation and that of Trump's entire government. I should note here that political scientists such as Cas Mudde, Cristóbal Rovira Kaltwasser and Jan-Werner Müller argue that populism is not an ideology which can be clearly defined.[11] This may have been true at the start, but right-wing nationalism – which overhypes the nation as a value while simultaneously sealing it off ethnically from the outside – is obviously influential here. It has shaped governance in the USA as well as Hungary, Poland, Italy, Austria and every other country where right-wing populists have come to power in the past or continue to rule in the present. We should therefore consider right-wing populists to also be right-wing nationalists. This distinction is important for understanding their appeal and the mechanisms of their politics, and for anticipating what might lie ahead for liberal democracy.

It is hard to know what personally drives Stephen Miller. His radicalism, like that of our neoconservative housemate in Georgetown, can probably be traced back to a generational conflict. Miller grew up in the 1990s in a well-off household in multicultural southern California. Even as a teenager he rebelled against his liberal environment, fulminating against movements to make Spanish a second official language and complaining about bilingual loudspeaker announcements in his school. Looking at the history of nationalism (which Polanyi barely mentions – a shortcoming he shares with other Marxists of his time), this kind of chauvinism is nothing new. Miller then went to Duke University, another bastion of left-wing thinking, to study in the lion's den, as he saw it. He drew attention to himself at Duke by organizing provocative campaigns, writing articles in the student newspaper and inviting radical right-wingers to speak at the university. These deliberate provocations eventually scored him interviews on Fox News, which paved the way for him to join Trump's campaign staff and get into the White House.[12] Here, too, making a name for oneself in one's peer group clearly paid off. The antiliberalism promoted by Miller and his like-minded peers functions largely as a way of distinguishing themselves from an imaginary left-liberal America which has only ever existed at a few elite universities, if at all. The Clintons were another long-standing object of their hatred, which was followed by a more or less openly racist hatred of Barack Obama.

In the presidential election of 1996, Bill Clinton was lucky to have had a fairly unconvincing opponent in the person of Bob Dole, an old-school moderate conservative. Dole's defeat prompted the Republicans to double down on their strategy of moving even farther to the right, and they eventually succeeded in pushing the entire political coordinate system in that direction. After the Democrats' mid-term defeat of 1994, Clinton positioned himself even more as a centrist in support of equilibrium – a strategy that has been pursued by every

Democratic presidential candidate ever since, ultimately to the detriment of a clear socio-political profile for the Democrats. Clinton was elected for a second term, which is why his name is now often associated with the 1990s.

Deindustrialization, social reforms and the low-tax ideology

The decade after the end of the Cold War is generally thought of as a golden age in the USA, almost on a par with the early post-war years. The economy did, in fact, grow faster in the USA than in Europe (with the exception of Ireland and some East Central European countries later on). The upswing primarily affected states on the east and west coasts of the USA. New York City experienced a renaissance, and the economy boomed in California, Washington and other centres of software and computing.

This new wealth was barely noticeable in the respective cities, however, not to mention rural areas and the rest of the USA. This is what distinguishes the high-tech boom from earlier industrialization surges brought about the railways, the automobile industry, the oil industry or the aerospace industry. The tech boom led to growing regional inequality and greater social inequality in the cities housing high-tech companies. The reasons for this are varied and have to do with the type of production and the personnel needed for it. You do not need labourers or skilled tradespeople to make software programs; you need highly qualified specialists. No government can control this kind of technological change and all of its repercussions for the labour market.

But three factors combined in an unfavourable way in the USA. Deindustrialization was accompanied by a new view of government, which was no longer supposed to intervene in the economy, and which also cut welfare benefits. On top of this, the old industrial regions around the Great Lakes, in Pennsylvania and on the East Coast became increasingly irrelevant under Clinton's free-trade policy. This is when the Rust Belt – a term coined during the 1984 presidential election campaign – truly started to rust. Overseas competition and outsourcing were responsible for this, just as they were in Germany. But Germany profited in the long term because even though its industrial jobs moved east, demand for German products was high in Eastern Europe, and the countries there could now afford them. Free trade with China (and Mexico), by contrast, did not lead to greater demand for American cars, household goods or other industrial products.

The welfare states on the European continent responded to the coal and steel crisis by training unemployed workers for new jobs and actively supporting the establishment of new businesses and the structural change as a whole. Meanwhile, the pioneers of neoliberalism – the USA and UK – left their own transformation to the forces of the market. As a result, many deindustrialized cities fell into an economic and social downward spiral. Cities like Detroit and Sheffield, not to mention smaller monotowns that had been dependent on one or two industrial companies, more closely resembled places affected by the post-communist transformation than those affected by Western European structural change (a term which came to mean active divestment from heavy industry). In the USA, part of the blame for this could be placed on Clinton, who adopted the anti-government rhetoric of the Republicans and declared in his third State of the Union address that 'the era of big government' was over.[13]

The service industry somewhat compensated for the decline of industry, but most companies in that sector paid lower wages. In this respect, what was needed in the 1990s was a socio-political agenda with the new service proletariat as its target audience. Instead, the government cut welfare benefits and placed stricter conditions on them – proof, incidentally, that for all of its anti-government rhetoric, neoliberalism very much depends on a regulatory state. In 1996, sweeping welfare reforms were passed by a large majority in Congress. Like Tony Blair and then Gerhard Schröder later on, the Democrats in the USA wanted to demonstrate once again that they were no longer the party of the workers or of costly redistribution. In the 1990s, they mainly represented the interests of the middle class, suburban property owners and consumers.

Shopping – once a banal procurement activity – became a popular pastime, and many consumer goods grew ever cheaper thanks to outsourcing. But buying on credit became even more commonplace than it had been under Reagan. In this sense, the financial crisis of 2008 has its roots in this period, when people got used to taking on more debt to buy all manner of daily necessities. Rising consumption made the neoliberal order more socially entrenched and acceptable. This helps explain the resilience of the neoliberal order even after the global financial crisis. No government today would dare to raise taxes massively to give the state more room for manoeuvre – not just because taxes are unpopular, but because of an economic rationale: low taxes indirectly stimulate consumption.

Beneath the surface of the boom, the USA continued to live off its reserves in the 1990s and early 2000s. While Americans grew accustomed to the poor state of their footpaths, roads, bridges, motorways and railways, visitors from Western Europe were (and continue to be) shocked by the decay, more so than Eastern Europeans who were familiar with it from home. The specific reason for this decay is that less than 1 per cent of America's GDP was invested in public infrastructure, even under Clinton, despite the fact that twice as much is needed to maintain it. But the decline of America's infrastructure really began in the 1980s under Ronald Reagan. State spending programmes were taboo for Reagan and his main economic advisor, Milton Friedman, even though the arms race with the Soviet Union essentially amounted to the same thing. High military spending and tax breaks led to a huge budget deficit which only worsened under the elder George Bush due to the weak economy. In this respect, Bill Clinton did not have much leeway when he spoke of the renewal of America in his first inaugural address.

On top of this, after the mid-term defeat of 1994, the Democratic president had to contend with a Republican majority in Congress. The Republicans at the time were largely fiscal conservatives who, after years of debt management (under their own presidents Reagan and Bush, one might add) now insisted on a balanced state budget (just like German finance minister Wolfgang Schäuble twenty years later). In the party's right wing, and now in the mainstream, this austerity policy was ideological. In keeping with the motto of 'starve the beast', the Republicans wanted to famish the governments in Washington and the individual states.[14] Their approach to this in the early 2000s involved paring back government revenue through tax giveaways to such an extent that future governments would have no choice but to slash welfare programmes. Even the food stamp programme that enables the poorest of the poor to eat is a thorn in the side of radical Republicans.

These fiscal anarchists have not yet achieved their aim. The USA still has the remnants of a welfare system, a state pension programme (which provides minimal security) and federal health insurance for pensioners and people with disabilities (Medicare). Anyone 65 or older can visit a doctor or be admitted to hospital and undergo even expensive surgeries like knee and hip replacements for free, all because good money can be earned from it. This, in turn, drives up costs and is another reason for the high level of health care spending in the USA. Despite this, average American life expectancy is appoximately two years less than in Germany or France – a very big difference for an industrialized country. Furthermore, life expectancy started declining back in 2015, well before the Covid-19 pandemic. This is due largely to the abuse of illegal drugs and the addictive painkillers that were approved during Clinton's second term in office. In this respect, neoliberal deregulation not only affected the stock markets, it had ramifications for every last corner of society.

After the younger George Bush waged two costly wars in Iraq and Afghanistan, there was no more left for public spending in the 2000s than there had been in the 1990s. Even in the wake of disasters like the collapse of an interstate bridge over the Mississippi in Minneapolis in 2007, which claimed the lives of thirteen people, America's infrastructure continued to crumble. Towards the end of his time in office, George W. Bush lacked the political energy and means to make any significant investments in this area because the government was using every available tax dollar to bail out banks and insurance companies. It remains to be seen whether Joe Biden's investment programme will improve the dilapidated state of America's roads, bridges and railways. The fundamental problem is that it will take a long time to make up for thirty years of underinvestment.

Clinton's concessions to the Republicans and Wall Street make sense when we look at his staff. Robert Rubin, Clinton's highest-ranking economic policy advisor and Secretary of the Treasury from 1995 to 1999, had previously served as co-chairman of Goldman Sachs, and several other members of the National Economic Council also came from Wall Street. This close alliance with the stock markets was entirely in keeping with the Democrats' move to the centre. Bill Clinton and German chancellor Gerhard Schröder after him symbolically communicated their proximity to the business world by smoking thick cigars and wearing expensive suits. Power thus shifted even more to corporations, which no longer needed lobbies to directly influence the government. There must be a biographical explanation for this behaviour on the part of Schröder and Clinton (Tony Blair was more reticent in this regard). Both men came from families of limited means, and both were fierce strivers. They could have used their experiences to do something about the declining social mobility in their respective countries, but their politics were ultimately shaped more by their high office than the memory of their own past.

Fiscal policy role reversal

The Democrats' solid fiscal policy did not pay off in the next election, however. In 2000, Al Gore – who could at least claim some credit for the upswing of the 1990s – narrowly lost to George W. Bush. All eyes were on Florida at the time, but the Republicans had also flipped Ohio and nearly took Wisconsin as well. Like his boss's wife sixteen years later, Gore was unable to sufficiently mobilize Democrats in the Rust Belt states. Working-class voters had gotten little to no benefit from the boom of the 1990s, so they logically opted not to vote Democrat again – or not to vote at all. No one was talking about a crisis of democracy at the time, or if they were, it was only in reference to the vote count debacle in Florida. Bush took the lead there by just a few hundred votes, which ultimately handed him the presidency. But the real problem was the high percentage of people who did not vote. Voter participation in the US elections in 2000 was not even 50 per cent, as low as Poland and other post-communist countries.

The change in government in 2001 was followed by a fiscal policy role reversal between Republicans and Democrats. Until then, the Republicans had largely pursued a policy of frugal and sustainable budget management, at least as long as they were in opposition. The Democrats, by contrast – like the socialists in France and social democrats in Germany – had the reputation of frittering away money and raising taxes. Secretary of the Treasury Robert Rubin in the USA, Chancellor of the Exchequer Gordon Brown in the UK and Finance Minister

Hans Eichel in Germany were determined to achieve a balanced state budget in part because they wanted to cast off this negative image and make the moderate left more attractive to the middle classes. But strangely, their fiscal policy no longer referred back to their parties' origins – namely, the unions and cooperatives which had always had to budget carefully and use their members' fees sensibly.

Cuts to the welfare state, as embodied in Germany by the Hartz reforms (see the next essay about unified Germany), pushed the social democrats into a political field and sphere of competence that had been occupied by liberals and conservatives since the 1980s. The Democrats in the USA and social democrats in Europe thought they could compensate for the loss of their core working-class voters by making gains with the middle class. This political calculation paid off for a good number of years, but it also created a political vacuum that was later exploited by populists of various stripes.

This fiscal policy role reversal from the turn of the millennium was carried over the finish line by Donald Trump. In 2016 he claimed to represent the interests of ordinary American workers, which won him voters in the Rust Belt states. Trump's sometimes blatant racism was like the inverse of a rainbow coalition. Instead of appealing to a wide spectrum of voters, he banked everything on white (which is, admittedly, what you get when all the colours of the spectrum are combined). The fact that Trump had plundered the state coffers for the benefit of the rich and not the poor was not even an issue in the 2020 elections. On the contrary, the economic upswing – financed by debt and ultimately cyclical in any case – made him popular. And now, once again, a Democratic successor has to grapple with the problem of ailing state finances after the end of a Republican presidency.

This problem was faced previously by Barack Obama, who inherited both the worst post-war economic crisis and a huge budget deficit from his predecessor George W. Bush. The reason for this was that even Bush was not a classic conservative in his approach to the budget (Trump was not the first in this regard). Instead, he followed the playbook of his party's radical neoliberals and anti-statists and pushed the national budget deep into the red through massive tax breaks for companies and the rich. As a result, power continued to shift from the government to business. Bush's goal was to stimulate investments and the economy, though to do so he actually needed to strengthen the purchasing power of the masses, not just the top 1 or 2 per cent of the population. In the mid-2000s, a number of experts were already warning that Bush's debt policy and the huge trade deficit with China – which was entirely in keeping with the logic of focusing on cheap mass consumption – would not be sustainable in the long term.

When disaster finally hit, it was not due to high government debt or a currency crisis, as had been expected (and as will probably happen in the future), but rather because the real estate bubble burst. Though many a Republican would have happily done away with the government prior to this, it was the government that conquered the crisis by pumping 235 billion dollars of fresh capital into the failing banks and insurance companies and taking on deficiency payments in the amount of 396 billion dollars.[15] While some bank managers were already approving high bonuses again by 2009, more than nine million Americans lost their homes because they could no longer repay their loans. The foreclosures were particularly hard on the lower middle class, the Democrats' traditional pool of voters. The bank bailout could have been arranged 'from below' if the government had deferred the loan repayments of desperate borrowers, but this was never seriously considered by Obama's Treasury secretary, Timothy Geithner (who later became president of a private equity firm), or his top economic advisor, Larry Summers (who was instrumental in deregulating the banks as Clinton's last Treasury secretary). Although the two men certainly deserve credit for having prevented the crisis of 2008–9 from descending into a scenario like Black Friday of 1929, the Democrats' pact with Wall Street provided the perfect ammunition for Donald Trump in his election campaign. The economy had recovered by 2016, at least on paper, but growth was uneven as it had been in the 1990s, and it barely reached the rural South, the Midwest or all the other regions devastated by real estate foreclosures. This stoked the anger that many Americans and Trump supporters felt for the politicians 'out there' in Washington.

Fiscal policy role reversal is not a purely American phenomenon. We saw it in the early 2000s in Italy (first under Berlusconi, though not to the same extent as Bush, and then again in 2018–20 under the co-governance of the right-wing populist Lega party led by Salvini), and more recently in Poland. This is a declaration of bankruptcy for conservatism, as fiscal conservatives now make up a small minority of Republicans and only call the shots in a few think tanks and university economics departments. Despite this, the Democrats and social democrats are the ones who have been hurt by the role reversal, not the Republicans and right-wing populists. Trump lost the 2020 election not on this political front line, but largely because of his mismanagement of the Covid-19 pandemic.

Rip-off America

The emotional bias against Washington and the complaints about high taxes which launched the 'Reagan revolution' are misplaced in any case. Big corporations are the ones increasingly exploiting Americans through price agreements. I could cite market concentration studies and other statistics here, but really just spending a few weeks in the USA is enough to justify the heading of this sub-section.

Denizens of the postmodern world rely on smartphones to transfer money, buy train tickets and, since 2021, prove their

Covid vaccination status. But mobile phone contracts in the USA currently cost about three times as much as they do in the EU (the opposite was true in the early 1990s, when it was far cheaper to make phone calls in the USA), and internet service is even more expensive by comparison. It is a mystery to me how people living in poverty are supposed to afford monthly basic costs of at least 100 dollars for a telephone line and internet connection. You certainly can't pay for it with food stamps.

Apparently, there are cartels even for ordinary consumer goods like rubbish bags and toilet roll in the USA, because these also cost three to four times as much as they do in the EU. Online shopping is no better since Amazon is so dominant that shipping is much worse and more expensive than in Europe. The growing dysfunctionality of the market economy is rarely addressed in the American media or political discourse, however. Unfortunately, very few Americans can afford to travel to Europe to compare prices and services on both sides of the Atlantic for themselves. This is hardly even possible on the internet, because big corporations serve national markets, so consumers cannot simply order cheaper items on a foreign platform and have them sent to their own country. Amazon's profits reflect this development; they rose in 2020, partially as a result of Covid-19, to reach 24 billion dollars (that's 72 dollars per inhabitant of the USA, or 24,000 dollars per employed person).

President Trump contributed to this huge profit increase by saving big businesses more than 1.5 billion dollars in taxes with his 2017 tax reform. The idea here – the same one held by Republicans under George W. Bush – was that the money would spur investment, giving rise to new and better-paid jobs. But corporations used more than half their tax savings to buy back shares on the stock market. This led to rising prices and rising bonuses for managers. The industrial renaissance that had been promised never materialized, but Trump voters did not chalk this up to the president himself.

Insufficient tax funds are also causing social problems to pile up in the cities that house high-tech firms and internet companies. This is especially true in the property market, where cut-throat competition has grown increasingly fierce. States like New York and California also invest too little in their public infrastructure, meaning everything from streets to schools. Teachers in the Los Angeles school district went on strike in 2018 because the average number of students per classroom in public schools had risen to nearly forty. In New York City, the subway is in such a poor condition that employers complained because their staff were often showing up to work late and unnecessarily stressed (the Covid pandemic eased the situation somewhat, but it also further exacerbated the financing problems for public transport).

But corporations do not want to pay higher taxes either. This is a good opportunity to recall the conflict surrounding Amazon's plans to build a second corporate headquarters. New York City submitted a bid to host the site; the Democratic mayor and state governor at the time were considered pro-business and were prepared to grant three billion dollars in tax subsidies, despite Amazon's eye-watering profits (Amazon is known for demanding tax benefits and pitting potential sites against one another). When opposition was voiced and the residents of Queens organized local protests out of fear that they would be forced from their homes, Amazon immediately withdrew its plans for New York at the start of 2019, as if the company wanted to punish the New Left for its opposition to big business. Alexandria Ocasio-Cortez's constituency is nearby, and the Republicans promptly used the quarrel with Amazon to decry the supposed anti-business stance of the Democrats.

Antitrust proceedings would be one way of cracking down on the market power wielded by Amazon, phone companies and internet providers. When the telephone corporation AT&T was broken up in the early 1980s (one of the good deeds done by the Republicans under Reagan), it led to much cheaper prices for consumers. I was a student at the time and had the impression that the market and capitalism functioned much better in the USA than in Europe in many ways. Now the opposite is true, because the American government has taken hardly any action against monopolies and oligopolies since the 1990s.[16]

Microsoft is more concerned with its image than Amazon. The company offered 500 million dollars to the city of Seattle, where it has its headquarters, to fund an affordable housing programme there (homelessness is skyrocketing in Seattle, just as it is in the Bay Area around San Francisco). But there were two catches. First, Microsoft would only provide the money as a loan, and second, it was a one-time offer. When the Seattle City Council passed a head tax for large employers in 2018 (the tax would have amounted to 275 dollars a year per employee, or just 22 dollars a month), an alliance of big businesses spent 300,000 dollars on a campaign to oppose it – another example of the marketization of politics in democracies. Amazon even implied that it would pull its own headquarters out of Seattle. In the end the city repealed the tax, and in return, Amazon promised to make higher voluntary payments to non-governmental organizations (NGOs) supporting homeless people. The outcome of the conflict boiled down to charity instead of taxes. It demonstrates how big business dominates politics, and it takes us back to the 1990s, when Bill Clinton, Tony Blair and Gerhard Schröder argued that civil society should take on the tasks of the allegedly excessive state.

The problems in the housing market – the consequences of which are apparent at every turn these days – are also evidence of the failure of the neoliberal Chicago School. Milton Friedman wanted to create a nation of property owners and was opposed to public housing because he thought it distorted the power of the market and led to fewer new houses being built. The number of homeowners in the USA did, in fact, rise by more than 20 million from the time of Reagan's presidency. This was the heart of the American Dream, which was still functioning quite well under Bill Clinton. But property prices have exploded since the global financial crisis because of how the crisis was managed. The low interest rate policy was supposed to make national debts tolerable while incentivizing higher investments and stimulating consumption. But the side effect was sectoral inflation that mainly affected the property industry. As a result, young people and families with modest or low incomes can barely afford to buy their own home now, or they have to get up to their ears in debt to do so. Contrary to Friedman's intentions, the number of renters in the USA rose by about 10 million between 2009 and 2019. They have few protections compared to renters in most European countries, and house price inflation indirectly affects them through their rental rates. As a result, where and how you live are determined not just by your income but increasingly also by your social origins. And where you live, in turn, determines the quality of the schools available to you and thus the opportunities available to the next generation.

In addition, more and more young people are ending up on the streets. My own children saw this in New York in 2018–19, when their mile-long walk to school in the affluent West Village took them past at least three or four clusters of homeless people every day. These people would lie under scaffolding to shelter from the rain and snow, or on metal plates which were warm from subway exhaust air and wasteful household heating systems. Many of them would hang around in doorways or at the edges of the only public park in the area, where they spent their day. Now and then we would see young white men and women who had lost their homes, but an overwhelming majority were people of colour. The inhabitants of New York and other large American cities might be long-accustomed to the sight of homeless people, but our nine-year-old daughter was afraid of them. This might have been in part because she was just four feet tall at the time and therefore much closer to the faces and gazes of the people sleeping on the streets. She would cross to the other side of the road or run away, and she never wanted to walk along the dark side paths in Washington Square Park.

There was a simple reason for her behaviour: she had grown up to that point in Vienna, a city with a functioning welfare system. Vienna has many homeless people, too, a growing number of them now from Hungary, Romania and other eastern EU member states. They have mostly fled from the miserable conditions in their home countries and cities (the USA also has its share of poverty-driven migration, with people moving to New York City because conditions there are still better than in the Republican-governed states of the South). But in Vienna, the homeless are usually gathered together in the evening and taken to emergency shelters, which are permanently open throughout the winter and temporarily open in the summer. This is why Viennese children rarely see anybody living on the streets as they make their way to and from school, which they are allowed to do on their own even at a very young age, because it is safe enough to walk through the city.

The issue of race is also always an issue of class. This is obviously not a new insight. Thousands of intelligent and well-meaning people of all backgrounds have tried to improve the situation of people of colour in the USA. Political condemnation of racism has led to many changes, and racism was addressed better at my daughter's primary school in New York than in Vienna, where people are less accustomed to racial diversity. Much progress has been made since my time in Washington in the early 1990s, when a South African Fulbright student remarked that he had never seen a city with such stark racial segregation. You see many more diverse couples in the USA today, and Trump's blatant racism is likely to have contributed to his defeat in 2020. But the social divide in America has deepened in many places on account of the decline of industry, a sector in which many people of colour had been employed. On average, Black Americans have suffered more from the great transformation triggered by global and national laissez-faire capitalism after 1989. This is what my daughter saw on the streets of New York, and since then I have wondered how racial reconciliation can ever occur as long as class divisions reinforce racial ones.

What would Karl Polanyi have said about this problem? He makes almost no mention of housing shortages or homelessness in his book, which is surprising when you consider the scale of these problems even during his lifetime in Vienna. Following the logic of his arguments, the problem could be solved by not leaving all basic human needs to the powers of the market. Polanyi referred to 'the soil' here, which he considered to be a part of nature and thus a finite resource (he was prescient in realizing that, in a totally free market economy, nature goes to rack and ruin). While soil may be finite, the number of houses is not, because more can always be built. But the laws of supply and demand have long ceased to determine their price. Other forces are at work now, above all the monetary policies of the central banks. Families with many children, young people without an inheritance and the majority of the now near-mythic middle class in the USA need more than this – they need a housing policy based on the principle that housing is a basic human necessity.

Polanyi also revealed how an overemphasis on the free market had led to social and political counter-reactions in the past. This is precisely what has happened since 2016 – but the Left is not leading the protest, because right-wing populists have hijacked it. After four years of Trumpism, we know that it does not work politically to point fingers at Trump and a radicalized Republican Party. The liberals and the Left have to put their own house and the Democratic Party in order. Only then will true change be possible – a New Deal, and hopefully a green one.

Will this be feasible with a Republican majority in the House of Representatives after the midterm elections in 2022? The likelihood of such a New Deal has diminished after the recent elections. Nevertheless, it is sometimes worth reviving historical myths, especially if they still have positive connotations and can acquire a new meaning.

3

The Price of Unity
Germany's Shock Therapy in International Comparison

Germany has been considered a model of economic success in both the USA and Europe since 2009 because it overcame the global financial crisis faster and better than other countries. Its unemployment rates are lower than any other EU member state, its federal budget and social security funds have been in surplus and incomes were rising significantly until the outbreak of Covid-19. But looking back at the late 1990s reveals just how quickly a country can fluctuate between boom and bust. In 1999, Germany was referred to as the 'sick man of the euro' in *The Economist*, and the federal republic seemed to be stuck in a vicious cycle of slow growth, rising unemployment and government debt.[1]

The economic situation was particularly dire in Berlin, where I was living at the time. You could tell by the decline in commuter traffic, especially in the early hours of the morning (Berliners today can only dream of such a thing). There were no commuters because nearly all the big industrial enterprises in the former East Berlin had closed, and tens of thousands of jobs had disappeared in the former West Berlin when it stopped receiving subsidies from the federal government. The only things booming there were the new shopping centres, symbols of the transition from an industrial to a service economy. But it was a bad sign that the shopping centres were busy even in the morning, filled with people who could not buy anything because they had lost their jobs. The contrast between the colourful merchandise and the people who couldn't afford any of it, between surplus and lack, was striking. These contradictions of postmodern consumer society are one of the long-term reasons for the rise of right-wing populists in Germany and elsewhere.

The economic crisis of the 1990s never had a soubriquet like the 'euro crisis' or the 'refugee crisis' later on. But in historical hindsight we should refer to it as the 'unity crisis' because it related directly to the way in which Germany was unified. For a long time it was hard to have any critical discussion of this issue, or of the economic reforms in East Germany. After unification, the political elite reflexively blamed the defunct German Democratic Republic (GDR) for all the problems, even though it was common knowledge that West German politicians were behind both the reform policies and the Treuhandanstalt (commonly known as the Treuhand, the agency responsible for managing and privatizing East German enterprises).[2] But the recent electoral successes of the nationalist and right-wing populist Alternative für Deutschland (AfD) in eastern Germany and the departure of the key political figures of 1990 have opened up new opportunities to debate Germany's transformation.

This debate is important because it could spark new ideas for reviving the stagnant federal states in the east. These states are still unable to stand on their own two feet and depend instead on transfer payments from the west. When we talk about the mistakes of the past, it is not to imply that we know much better now. The key players in Germany's unification often had to make decisions under extreme pressure for various reasons: because there was only a small window of opportunity in which to act (one that might have slammed shut again after the putsch against Gorbachev in August 1991 at the latest), because the trickle of people fleeing East Germany turned into the first major East-to-West exodus after the fall of the Berlin Wall, and because policy is rarely based exclusively on economic calculations.

The Federal Republic of Germany and the West as a whole viewed the outcome of the Cold War as confirmation of the superiority of their own system. West German political and economic elites did not express this post-Cold War triumphalism very conspicuously because they knew it would be a huge undertaking to get the former East Germany up to a Western level of prosperity. The majority opinion, however, was that this would be accomplished in the foreseeable future. In keeping with the 'convergence theory', even many experts and social scientists thought that the East would quickly catch up with the West.

Theo Waigel, the German finance minister, and Wolfgang Schäuble, one of the architects of the Unification Treaty, were not followers of the neoliberal Chicago School of Economics. They were old-school conservatives who still clung to the concept of the social market economy and were influenced by Christian social teaching. But apart from social cushioning measures, heavier state regulation and a system of collective bargaining agreements, the reform concepts for the former East Germany were largely consistent with those for other post-communist states.

Radical economic reforms can be pushed through most easily when the economy in question is close to collapse. This was certainly the case in the last year of the GDR. The exchange rate between the East German mark (the Ostmark) and the West German mark (the Deutsche Mark, also known as the D-Mark) dropped to 7:1 in the autumn of 1989 and plunged even deeper that winter. The decline of the Ostmark meant that East Germany could no longer pay its high external debts, nor could it afford to import oil, gas, coffee or other common consumer goods. The GDR was on the brink of bankruptcy, and insiders in the Socialist Unity Party (SED) under the party's last premier, Hans Modrow, knew it. The massive environmental damage that had been wreaked in East Germany and the miserable state of the country's pre-war urban buildings were further evidence that the GDR was running on empty.

The power asymmetry between West and East was apparent to anyone who watched TV and saw the hulking Helmut Kohl alongside the diminutive Lothar de Maizière, who became East Germany's last premier in the Volkskammer elections of March 1990 and was subsequently responsible for negotiating the treaties on German unification. Reunification was not carried out on the basis of Article 146 of (West) Germany's constitution, known as the Basic Law, even though this article was formulated for just such a scenario. The negotiators opted instead for a faster process under Article 23, whereby the five 'new states' in the East simply 'joined' the existing ones in the West. Unification thus entailed the enlargement of West Germany, not a union of two equal states.

The collapse of the Ostmark was a reflection of East Germany's economic problems and poor prospects for the future, but the currency's devaluation had begun long before. While East Germany officially insisted on the parity of the Ostmark and D-Mark in the 1980s – and forced visiting West Germans to exchange a certain amount of money at this rate for each day of their stay – the foreign trade bank of the GDR halved its internal clearing rate for the D-Mark in the same decade. In 1988, its strictly confidential exchange rate was just 4.40 Ostmarks for one D-Mark, because it was only at this cheap rate that the GDR could sell its goods.

Illegal moneychangers in the back streets of East Berlin and Leipzig paid roughly the same rate, and the East Germans who had long used the D-Mark as a substitute currency knew this. The black market was therefore a much better indicator of the economic situation than the official exchange rates. When the Ostmark declined after the fall of the Berlin Wall, it led to the further devaluation of East German salaries and wages, which were already low. Just like in Poland and Czechoslovakia, a broken washing machine or expensive car repair could throw off a family's entire budget. The economic crash and general uncertainty of the time explain why the original revolutionary slogan of '*Wir sind das Volk*' – we are the people – morphed in the autumn and winter of 1989–90 into a new slogan: '*Wir sind ein Volk*' – we are one people.

Another slogan started making the rounds in the spring of 1990: '*Kommt die D-Mark, bleiben wir, kommt sie nicht, geh'n wir zu ihr!*' – 'If the D-Mark comes, we'll stay here, if not, we'll go to it!' The second half of this phrase hinted at the threat that even more East Germans would flock to West Germany if the economic situation did not improve soon. The open inner-German border and right of abode for East Germans were special factors in Germany's transformation which differed from all other post-communist countries. In the East German election campaign of 1990, the Christian Democratic Union (CDU) offered an obvious way out: quick reunification accompanied by an economic and monetary union with West Germany. The CDU kept this campaign promise, and on 1 July 1990, the D-Mark – an icon of affluence – became the official currency of the GDR, to great jubilation in Berlin, Leipzig and other cities in the East. But considering how rapidly the Ostmark had declined after the fall of the Wall, why was it valued at an exchange rate of 1:1 with the D-Mark?

The Bundesbank, the central bank of the Federal Republic of Germany, warned that excessive appreciation of the Ostmark would be economically risky, so it advocated a rate of 2:1 (this rate was, in fact, implemented for savings deposits of more than 4,000 marks). Representatives of the GDR's state bank argued for a 7:1 exchange rate, which they said was an accurate reflection of the country's economic power and would have enabled the East German economy to compete with West German industry.[3] But Chancellor Kohl ultimately made a political decision. The threat of mass migration from East to West was the argument put forward again and again, and it distinguished the situation in Germany from that of every other post-communist state.

Germany's special path

Distracted by their zeal for national unity and traditional focus on the West, elites in the Federal Republic of Germany tended to overlook what was happening in their immediate vicinity when they conducted internal and public debates. Czechoslovakia had been one of the most prosperous Eastern Bloc states alongside the GDR, but its currency also declined dramatically in the winter of 1989–90. The official exchange rate fell to the level of the black market rate, which was three times lower, or about 15 koruna for one D-Mark. Unlike the West German government, however, the Czechoslovak government put up with this devaluation. Finance minister Václav Klaus, like his counterparts in Poland and Hungary, hoped that the cheaper national currency would boost exports and keep wage costs low, thus preserving the big enterprises of the socialist era and curbing unemployment. This strategy worked quite well until 1996, when bad loans and corruption in the privatization process led to the Czech banking crisis.

While the devaluation of the koruna made Czechoslovakia's exports cheaper by a factor of about three (taking the official exchange rate as a reference point), the German monetary union made East German exports four times more expensive than they had been in 1988. It was therefore inevitable that East German products would never be able to compete with Czech goods – a Wartburg car, for instance, would never compete with a Škoda – and Western industries looking for new production sites would generally pass over East Germany (the Czech Republic benefited the most from this; industrial production now accounts for more of its GDP than any other EU member state, which is in keeping with the country's historical role as the industrial centre of the Habsburg Empire).

The monetary union was followed by a second shock for the East German economy, namely, the rapid liberalization of foreign trade. The accession of the five new German states to the Federal Republic of Germany – and, simultaneously, to the European Community – eliminated all trade barriers with Western Europe, a step generally in line with the Washington Consensus. But the East Germany economy was not up to the competitive pressure. Proof of this could be found on the supermarket shelves of the former GDR, which were soon devoid of products once produced in the East (at least until they experienced a renaissance driven by *Ostalgie*, or 'eastern nostalgia').

The fact that memories of East Germany were so tied up with consumer goods says as much about late-stage state socialism as it does about the unified Germany. Western German companies were thrilled by this new market with its 16 million consumers. It was lucrative in the first three years after 1989 and somewhat protected Germany from the recession that struck the USA and other Western countries in 1991. Even the significant eastern enlargement of the EU in 2004 was driven in part by the lure of new sales markets for Western companies – with consequences similar to those faced by East Germany in 1990.

A third special factor in Germany's transformation was radical privatization, which disregarded a fundamental market mechanism. The Treuhand was intermittently in charge of 12,534 companies with a total of over four million employees. More than 10,000 enterprises were sold by the end of 1992, in the space of just two years.[4] When so many companies are thrown into the market all at once, their sales price will inevitably plummet. Some enterprises could only be sold with massive state aid and investment commitments. As a result, instead of the expected profit of about 600 billion Deutschmarks, the Treuhand made a loss of 270 billion, or more than 15,000 Deutschmarks per East German citizen.

At the end of 1994, the German federal government proudly announced that the Treuhand was being dissolved because the privatization process was complete. But most of the privatized companies simply ceased production. Marcus Böick has calculated that only a quarter of the jobs in the companies sold by the Treuhand were retained. Mid-size cities in particular, whose prosperity had depended on a few large factories, have still not recovered from this structural rupture. It was also a rupture in the lives of millions of people who lost their jobs, had to retrain, often struggled to find another permanent position and were finally forced into early retirement. The German social state ensured that those who had lost out in the transformation could at least get by financially and were much better off than the Poles, Czechs and Slovaks who had no 'big brother' in the West to help them. But unemployed East Germans compared their own situation either with that of their richer West German counterparts or with their own lives prior to 1989.

These critical comments about Germany's shock therapy – which was never actually referred to as such in Germany, as it was in Poland – prompt the question of whether any other options were available at the time. Such a thought was out of the question in the early 1990s, when it was generally said that there was 'no alternative' to the reforms. A more realistic exchange rate for the monetary union would have disappointed many East German voters and resulted in an even larger wage, salary and pension gap between East and West. But would this really have driven even more people to migrate from East to West Germany, as politicians feared at the time? It is impossible to answer this question after the fact. In any case, despite the social cushioning effect of the reforms and the transfer payments made to the East, more than two million people moved from East to West Germany in the 1990s.[5] In this respect, the wider objective of the monetary union – namely, to keep people in East Germany – was not achieved.

Although these German labour migrants sent money back home, their departure had a negative overall effect on their regions and societies of origin. The many people who moved away left behind voids, not least in a political sense. We can assume that the outcome of the 2017 Bundestag election in Saxony, when the AfD became the strongest party in this federal state, would have been different had all the people who emigrated to West Germany and other European countries after 1989 instead stayed where they were. Most East German labour migrants were young or middle aged, and only the most agile members of the population were able to leave their homes in search of better-paid jobs. When I worked at the university in Frankfurt an der Oder between 2002 and 2006, I witnessed the repercussions of this migration, which were apparent in both the population statistics and everyday life. This East German border city had only approximately 60,000 inhabitants in the early 2000s, as opposed to the 90,000 who had lived there prior to 1989. As soon as commuters started boarding trains to Berlin again, the city felt dead, and prefabricated high-rises in the suburbs emptied out and were torn down.

Emigration had a less dramatic impact on the overall population in Poland, but after Poland joined the EU, a good two million people moved to Western Europe (initially to the countries that immediately opened their labour markets after the EU's expansion: England, Ireland and Sweden). The global financial crisis triggered a third exodus from Eastern Europe starting in 2009, which hit Romania, Bulgaria, Lithuania and Latvia particularly hard. After the collapse of the Eastern European bubble, which bore some similarities to the real estate bubble in the USA (a high inflow of speculative capital, inflated profit expectations and excessive lending leading to debt overload), these countries had to be bolstered by 'rescue packages' from the IMF and EU, which involved austerity measures and further cuts to already dwindling social benefits. As a result, these Eastern European countries lost up to 10 per cent of their population in just a few years.

Returning to Polanyi, it is worth noting that these countries – like East Germany before them – experienced mass migration instead of a 'double movement' in the form of lengthy strikes or protests against austerity. The people who stayed behind in the regions drained by migration are, on average, older, more conservative and more dependent on welfare. And just like in East Germany, these regions are now bastions of right-wing populism. However, it would be too simple to attribute the success of the AfD in eastern Germany leading up to the Bundestag election of 2017 solely to the people who lost out in the transformation. As Philip Manow has shown in his comparative study of populism, many members of the middle class also voted for the AfD, especially in Saxony.[6] According to Manow's interpretation of the situation, memories of past unemployment and the accompanying existential insecurity make people receptive to the promises of protection made by right-wing nationalists. Another less frequently discussed reason is apparently the weaker bonding force of the Left and the German political party of the same name (Die Linke), which in its previous incarnation (as the Party of Democratic Socialism, or PDS) had given a voice to social protest.

There were certainly alternatives to the Germany's 'special path' when it came to privatization, too. For example, Poland and the Czech Republic initially kept large, strategically important companies under state control, only selling them at the end of the 1990s or later. This did not mean that the companies continued to operate at a loss as they had before 1989, however. They were expected to be profitable, and some of them managed this quite well, including the Polish shipyards which put strong pressure on the German shipbuilding industry until the early 2000s. The shipyards in Szczecin and Gdynia ultimately went bankrupt during the financial crisis in 2009 because the

EU prohibited the provision of state aid to keep them afloat. This policy has given rise to all manner of conspiracy theories in Poland today, which benefit and are further propagated by the ruling PiS party. One advantage of East Germany's privatization was that it took place under the rule of law, because West Germany's systems were rapidly implemented in the former GDR. This did not prevent horrendous losses, but it did limit corruption.

Competition from Asia also contributed to the bankruptcy of Poland's shipbuilding industry. In China, key sectors such as shipbuilding and heavy industry in general are supported by the state. New sectors like the electronics industry, by contrast, have largely been left to private companies. The same coexistence of state and private sectors would not have been possible in Germany or the EU. Additionally, China's large combines have survived by paying their workers very low wages. No shipbuilders from Poland or East Germany would have worked under such conditions for any length of time.

On top of this, the old EU states wanted to prevent too much competition from Eastern Europe. The competition watchdogs of the European Commission prohibited state aid even though, in the case of the shipyards, it might have been smarter to think more about competition from outside Europe than inside it. But with the exception of cases like Airbus, Europe as a whole has never really developed its own industrial policy. The national interests of its individual member states usually stand in the way – though, admittedly, it was the European Commission which recently prohibited the planned merger of the rail divisions of Alstom and Siemens. In any case, considering the different paths taken elsewhere, it is incorrect to say that there were no alternatives to the neoliberal economic reforms after 1989. China's mixed system was also not a viable model in Europe because of its political implications; if state industries had continued to exist, it would have kept the old cadre in power. Most people in East Central Europe were against such a thing, especially the population of the former East Germany (notwithstanding any temporary electoral successes enjoyed by the Party of Democratic Socialism (PDS)).

Liberalizing foreign trade and opening the East German market may have been the only policies for which there really was 'no alternative'. They could probably not have been delayed unless a separate customs area or special economic zone had been established with different import restrictions. China and Vietnam took this approach in several regions, but it would have been hard to implement in the EU. Furthermore, a special economic zone in East Germany or at least parts of it (such as the Lusatia region which was battered by the economic crisis, or the tri-border area around the town of Görlitz) would have posed tougher economic competition for the old federal states – and no one was interested in that either.

The swift opening of the East German market hurt the very group that was most likely to have spurred a bottom-up economic recovery: the self-employed. Unlike Czechoslovakia, East Germany had small niches for self-employed workers in retail, manual trades and service professions (after the Iron Curtain opened on the Hungarian–Austrian border, the first East German citizen who hurtled through it with his family on a trip to Passau in August 1989 was a hairdresser). After German unification, long-standing self-employed workers in the East were joined by new, small-scale entrepreneurs, some of whom started their own businesses because unemployment was on the rise, others because they wanted to seize the opportunities offered by the newly open economy (it would be an oversimplification to view neoliberalism only as an ideology or imposition, as it also required the participation of certain segments of the population).

But even the former East Germans who took the plunge into self-employment fared worse on average than other professional groups or the new entrepreneurs in Poland and Czechoslovakia. Many of the self-employed experienced downward social mobility or, in the worst case, went bankrupt.[7] This was often due to a lack of capital reserves and assets which would have helped them withstand the difficult periods after the recession of 1993 and again in the early 2000s.

The professionals least affected by the economic upheaval in the former East Germany were civil servants – with the exception of those who lost their jobs because they had been Socialist Unity Party officials or worked with the East German secret police. Thanks to the monetary union and the expansion of Germany's labour legislation to cover the five new federal states in the East, public officials in East Germany saw their salaries rise significantly. This was especially true for the many West Germans who were sent east with bonus payments as an incentive. But aside from this, the federal government seemed to have little idea of which social classes and elites could be counted on to carry the former East Germany forward.

The problem was tricky, not least because it required a more nuanced view of East German society and perhaps some concessions being made to the mid-level leadership in the economy. Another pressing issue was the lack of social recognition, to use Karl Polanyi's term. When East Germans (and not just unemployed ones) criticized the reform policies of the 1990s, they were accused by the Western-dominated media of doing nothing but moaning. In an interview in 2003, the former chancellor Helmut Schmidt berated East Germans for their constant complaining, which he said he found 'sickening'.[8] He made no mention of how many of them had retrained or moved to find a job, or had made other efforts to adapt to the new economic situation.

The price of this lack of a social vision, combined with national self-centredness and Germany's specific shock therapy, was an unprecedented economic slump. By the mid-1990s, East Germany's industrial production had fallen to just 27 per cent of what it had been in 1988. No other post-communist country – not even the war-torn former Yugoslavia – experienced such a dramatic decline. As a consequence, approximately 1.4 million East Germans had emigrated by 1994 alone. Almost exactly the same number of new businesses were founded in Czechoslovakia, a country which had nearly as many inhabitants as the GDR, making it a fairly good comparison in this regard. In Poland and Hungary, too, large numbers of people took the leap into self-employment (not all of them entirely voluntarily – some did it to avoid unemployment). In the first five years after 1989, a total of about four million companies were founded in the four (as of 1993) countries of the Visegrád Group.[9] This entrepreneurial boom was not as pronounced in the former East Germany.

The collapse of East Germany's economy strained the federal budget, and especially the social insurance system which had to directly or indirectly support the millions of people without jobs. Early retirement costs were shouldered by pension funds, and health insurers also made high transfer payments. But using social benefits to pacify East German 'transformation losers' was not a financially feasible tactic in the long term.[10] Social insurance contributions, taxes and government debt continued to climb in the 1990s at the expense of Germany's growth as a whole. Unified Germany had reached a dead end, and Chancellor Kohl was accused of creating 'reform bottlenecks' and was voted out after 16 years in office. The self-dubbed 'reform chancellor' Gerhard Schröder of the Social Democratic Party (SPD) won the 1998 elections, but he bided his time during his first two years in office. Germany was coasting on the global economic boom, and the SPD chairman was unsure of the political risks he might face if he introduced far-reaching reforms.

Schröder therefore initially fell back on Germany's old, consensus-based policies and corporatist structures. Soon after coming to power, the chancellor convened an Alliance for Work (Bündnis für Arbeit) consisting of employers' associations and trade unions who were supposed to negotiate strategies for making German industry more competitive while protecting jobs. This was an urgent task considering the systemic crisis mentioned earlier and the wave of companies moving their production to Eastern Europe and Asia.[11] The Alliance for Work did not get good press at the time, and historians have largely overlooked it ever since, not least because its talks ran aground after just three years and it was officially disbanded in 2003. But the employers' associations and unions did reach a consensus, one which had already begun to take shape in the mid-1990s and could be summarized as job retention through wage restraint. In the long run, modest wage agreements made German industry more competitive and led to increased exports. This compromise by corporatist Germany probably contributed to the country's subsequent economic recovery, as did the radical social and labour market reforms which are often cited by prominent economists as an explanation for Germany's upswing after the crisis of 2009.

One drawback to the pact between employers and unions was that real wages, which were stagnant at best, negatively affected domestic demand. This had an impact on the overall mood, especially when two recessions started in quick succession, one after the collapse of the dot-com bubble in 2001, the other in the winter of 2002. High unemployment and a general lack of prospects created a breeding ground for xenophobia, aggression and crime. The police defined these criminal offences as *Rohheitsdelikte* or 'acts of brutality', and they hovered at approximately 70,000 cases a year in Berlin.[12] The mutual recriminations also intensified between Germans in the east and west – after all, someone had to be blamed for the misery.

Reform backlogs and co-transformation

In the early 2000s, Germany's 'red-green' coalition (the Social Democrats and Green Party) adopted various social and labour market reforms which had previously been implemented by post-communist states in the 1990s.[13] These included the partial privatization of pensions and liberalization of the labour market. For a time, there was even lively discussion of a flat tax or some other vastly simplified tax system[14] (flat tax systems were introduced in all post-communist states in the early 2000s, but they were abolished again in many countries after the crisis of 2009), as well as flat health care contributions instead of income-dependent health insurance. With regard to post-communist Europe, we could say that a kind of co-transformation began in East Germany and spread to the rest of the federal republic, modelled in part on the social reforms under New Labour in the UK. Social benefits were cut, and after a short-term shock, the trinity of liberalization, deregulation and privatization was supposed to bring about a long-term boom, as had been expected in 1990. The unique aspect of Germany's red-green labour market and social reforms was that they hit West Germans just as hard as East Germans, though the latter suffered more on account of high long-term unemployment rates.

The reforms severely exacerbated social inequality in Germany, which climbed from nearly Scandinavian levels in 1999 to reach the level of post-communist countries like Hungary and Poland by the 2009 economic crisis. Based on the Gini coefficient (the international standard for measuring income inequality), inequality rose from 0.25 to approximately 0.29 between 1999 and 2009.[15] This development cannot be attributed to a single factor like Hartz IV, but there is no doubt that the social and labour market reforms increased the fear of downward social mobility. This was intentional; the threat of poverty was supposed to motivate people to accept more poorly paid jobs which required a longer commute. This *negative mobilization*, which was even more consequential in the poorer countries of East Central Europe, may well have contributed to Germany's 'job market miracle', but it also led to insecurity in wide swathes of society.

The fundamental problem in both Germany and the entire EU is that the current economic order primarily benefits countries, regions and social groups which are already well off. Structurally weak regions – such as parts of eastern Germany, the Mezzogiorno and areas along the eastern border of the EU – and people with fewer qualifications are left behind with poor prospects for the future. This divergence is clearly visible in Germany's big cities, and it becomes even more apparent when you leave metropolitan areas like Cologne, Hamburg and Leipzig and head about 30 miles into the countryside.

In some respects, the Hartz reforms were a reversal of the strategy adopted in 1990. While the goal of the monetary union was to rapidly align East Germany with the West, the Hartz IV programme and the low-wage sector (another idea that can be traced back to the Chicago School) brought West German labour costs into alignment with the wages typical in Poland and the Czech Republic at the time. This, too, was part of the co-transformation of the entire Federal Republic of Germany.

The Hartz reforms did not do much to alleviate the misery of the five new federal states. This was partially because it did little good to mobilize job-seekers (as the unemployed were now called) for the labour market in regions where there were simply no jobs to be found. The government's only real options were to provide financial support to the unemployed, force them into early retirement or put them to work through job creation schemes. This continued to be a costly problem; net transfer payments in the quarter century after German unification amounted to 1.6 trillion euros (net, in this case, meaning that the return flows from East to West, for example, and payments made into the German national budget by East German taxpayers are taken into account).[16] In peak years, the German government spent up to 100 billion euros on infrastructure modernization, privatization (in the early 1990s) and, above all, social benefits.

Despite this flow of money, the new federal states only generated about two thirds of West German per-capita GDP even 25 years after unification.[17] The Czech Republic, which had to get by without the support of a 'big brother' in the West, has achieved nearly the same level of economic power. Granted, the standard of living is lower in the rural areas of the Czech Republic and its former centres of heavy industry and mining than it is in the east of Germany, due in part to far lower wages. But having never depended on transfer payments like East Germany, it is presumably easier for Czech society as a whole to take pride in what the country has achieved on its own.

Germany's history since the fall of the Berlin Wall raises all manner of critical questions about the neoliberal reform concepts of the early 1990s and early 2000s, and about the effectiveness of state development programmes. Regardless of the outcome of this discussion, we can pre-emptively say that eastern Germany's current economic and political problems can no longer be pinned on the former GDR. The anniversaries of the fall of the Berlin Wall and German unification are good opportunities to debate the long-term consequences of the tremendous uncertainty created by mass unemployment, mass migration from East to West and cuts to social spending.

We saw these consequences in 2015–16 when parts of German society in the east opposed Germany's acceptance of Middle Eastern refugees. Cultural factors played a role in this, just as they did in the neighbouring Czech Republic and Poland, where people are less accustomed to encountering foreigners, especially Muslims. But there is also connection here to the unification crisis, the Hartz reforms and the general uncertainty caused by the transformation, which continues to resonate even though the labour market has improved.

The differing economic conditions in East and West Germany are also a key to understanding why the allocation of social benefits is a sensitive topic. Many opponents of Germany's *Willkommenskultur* ('welcoming culture') objected to the idea that refugees should essentially receive the same benefits as Germans. They pointed out that Germans had paid into the country's benefits system for a long time (which is only partially true for those who were previously unemployed), and they found it unfair that refugees who had never contributed would be treated as equals (which is absolutely untrue in many cases, such as pensions). This has been called 'welfare chauvinism',[18] though for a somewhat more neutral term we could refer to the English social historian E.P. Thompson and his 'moral economy' of the citizens of welfare states. Fears of future spending cuts probably also play a role here, and these fears have been exploited by right-wing populists and deployed mercilessly against refugees and labour migrants. The arguments are different in the new EU member states, which do not necessarily want to endanger or share their newly found prosperity. This is a thorny political problem, because a hard core of right-wing voters will not even accept the drastic reduction of welfare benefits for refugees – a strategy adopted by Austria's conservative and right-wing populist coalition in 2017–19. In this respect, populist right-wing policy has once again led to nothing but discontent all around. Nonetheless, it is important to recognize why such a policy became popular in the first place, at least in certain parts of society in both East and West.

To understand this facet of Germany's transformation, it is helpful to return once again to Polanyi's *Great Transformation*. In a later chapter of his magnum opus, he writes that once social deprivation has been experienced it is never forgotten. Even when someone's situation subsequently improves, the scars and fears of another decline always remain.[19] It is not easy for historians to confirm this, because oral history interviews generally reveal how people feel *now* when they think about their experiences back then; it is difficult to reconstruct how they actually felt *at the time*. Despite these limitations, interviews (particularly when conducted soon after the fact) and other ego documents can tell us a great deal about the time of transformation. There are striking differences between the official rhetoric around German contemporary history – which claims that the project of reconstructing East Germany was, all in all, a success – and the actual experiences of many people who lived through it. This cognitive dissonance, too, is fertile ground for right-wing populists and nationalists. They are a strong force in the east of Germany, but still weaker than comparable parties in neighbouring Poland and other post-communist countries. This is another argument for taking a comparative view of the respective shock therapies in these countries, with all of their political and social repercussions.

4

La Crisi

Italy's Decline as a Portent for Europe

In the 1980s and early 1990s, when Italian governments seemed to change as fast as the seasons, a popular witticism in Italy was that a bad government was no match for a good economy. Thirty years later, we know this was a fallacy. Italy amassed a mountain of debt in this decade and a half, which proved to be a huge burden during the euro crisis of 2011 and grew even larger during the Covid-19 pandemic. Italy is a founding member of the European Community, and if its excessive debt ever forced it out of the eurozone, this would be an even harder blow for the EU than Brexit. This debt is usually treated as a fiscal problem, but it is first and foremost a political one.

Italy is a prime example of how populist politics can run a country into the ground. It also shows that the crisis of democracy and triumph of right-wing populism, which have been bewailed since 2016, actually started back in the 1990s. Silvio Berlusconi, often ridiculed abroad and highly controversial at home, was ahead of his time in a sense. He dominated Italy's domestic policy for nearly 20 years and was the first right-wing populist to govern a developed Western industrial country. He achieved a total of three major electoral victories, which should be a warning to the USA and any other country that believes Trumpism ran its course after four chaotic years. Italy proves that worse scenarios are possible, too. Like a political roly-poly toy, Berlusconi kept popping back up and returning to power in alternation with the moderate Left, which is much weaker now than it was 30 years ago.

When Italians elected Berlusconi as prime minister for the first time in 1994, right-wing populism was not yet a widespread concept in the media or social sciences. In general, it is worth noting that there tends to be a subtle discourse of exclusion around the concept, one which ultimately helps right-wing populists position themselves against the 'big shots' or allegedly liberal elites. I have never encountered a colleague or student at any university who would have self-identified as a right-wing populist, which indicates that the term has negative connotations (unlike 'neoliberal', a term embraced by Milton Friedman and other economists for a time; see the first essay in this book).

Berlusconism

Berlusconi won elections mainly by promising Italians the moon and making people feel good. As a former crooner (he earned good money as a student singing on cruise ships) as well as the founder of multiple television channels and owner of a large media corporation, he had the business of promises and illusions down pat. Considering his lack of ideological substance, there is a good argument to be made for initially interpreting Berlusconi's right-wing populism as a *form* of politics based largely on orchestration and communication. Berlusconi was a very compelling speaker and always cut a *bella figura* with his permanent smile and bespoke suits. He was so successful at this that even left-wing and liberal media outlets and historians referred to him as *Il Cavaliere*, a nickname that literally means 'The Knight' and played on his carefully orchestrated projection of masculinity. When he founded Forza Italia, Berlusconi created a collective movement and political party tailored entirely to himself. All of this corresponded to the type of charismatic leadership described by Max Weber back in 1919, at a time when liberalism and the economic foundations of the middle class had been seriously weakened and fascism was emerging as a political movement in Italy.

Forza Italia was established four years after the upheaval of 1989, but it cloaked itself in the traditions of the Cold War. In his 1994 election campaign, Berlusconi adopted some of the rhetoric of the past, using anti-communist slogans much like the Christian Democrats did in Germany with their 'red socks' campaign. This seemed paradoxical at first glance because the Italian Communist Party (Partito Comunista Italiano, PCI) had ceased to exist by then, and the Socialist Party was collapsing under the weight of a huge corruption scandal. Nonetheless, memories of the Cold War lingered, and distancing oneself from 'the lefties' was a successful tactic. All the same, Berlusconi was not a right-wing nationalist like his political heir apparent Matteo Salvini, or like Giorgia Meloni, the winner of the most recent parliamentary elections. Berlusconi occasionally criticized the bureaucrats in Brussels, but he did not play up conflicts with the EU. He tried to curb migration across the Mediterranean and signed a corresponding pact with Gaddafi (an agreement that Italy's centre-left government renewed with its new Libyan partners in 2017), but he did not harp on about the migration issue for campaign purposes, as Salvini would later on. In this respect, we have to flip the famous quote by the young Karl Marx that history repeats itself as farce. Berlusconi, Salvini and now Meloni show us that history can start as farce and continue as the fight for the soul of a nation.[1]

Ever since the *annus horribilis* of 2016, it would be negligent to view right-wing populism primarily as a *form* of politics. Instead, it is important to look at its ideological substance, as difficult as it may be to grasp. The drawback to this dynamic, contemporary definition of right-wing populism, with its focus on ideological rather than formal criteria, is that it is not as clear-cut as a political science model based on a set of fixed characteristics. But the fundamental disadvantage of any social scientific model is that it can be too static, making it difficult to incorporate external and internal dynamics and understand changes over time (which is one of the basic tasks of a historian). We can use Trump as an example here once again: in 2016, no one – especially not Trump's moderate Republican supporters – could have imagined how his presidency would end in January 2021.

It is a time-honoured tradition in social and cultural anthropology for authors to position themselves with respect to their object of study (economists and other 'hard scientists' famously eschew this, claiming that they and their research are objective). So I should say here that, like most avid young travellers who grew up north of the Alps in the 1980s, I was an Italophile. Italy represented a cool lifestyle, better food and fashion, and every German and Austrian knew what *dolce vita* meant. The Italian economy was also growing faster than the German one at the time. This essay is not based on disappointed Italophilia, however, but rather on my understanding of Italy's history and language. I first acquired this understanding through reading and then continually expanded it, including during my time working at the European University Institute in Florence from 2007 to 2010, when Berlusconi won his third election – to the incomprehension of most people outside of Italy.

Right-wing populism as a form of politics was also a cultural phenomenon to begin with, but we have to look more closely at Italy's social and economic history to understand it. The country's three-decade tragedy (which will hopefully not end as such) is significant not just to Italians but to everyone in Europe and the West, because it is a cautionary tale of what can happen when right-wing populists remain in power for a long time. In general, when analysing this political current, a much clearer distinction needs to be made between right-wing populism as a political movement and ideology, and right-wing populism as a form of self-radicalizing governance (more on this in chapter 6).

Berlusconi governed for nearly 10 years in total, longer than any other post-war prime minister. His lengthy tenure was made possible by the weakness of his political opponents: the social democrats, the successor parties to the PCI and the left wing of the Christian Democrats who were inspired by Catholic social teaching.[2] These three strands form the core of the Partito Democratico (PD), which was dismally defeated in the 2018 parliamentary elections (and previously in the constitutional referendum of 2016). In this case, too, Italy's tragedy transcends the country itself. The self-inflicted defeat of Matteo Renzi and the quarrelling PD marked the end of reform-minded social democracy in Europe in the tradition of Tony Blair and Gerhard Schröder. That said, we must be cautious when proclaiming an end to something, because as the young Marx noted in his essay on Napoleon III, history can move in a circle. (To carry the historical analogy even further, we could view Napoleon III as an early example of a right-wing populist who invoked the grandeur of the nation and, with a single electoral success and his own charisma, managed to destroy the liberal republic that had been created in 1848.)

Historians have not given much thought to Berlusconi as a predecessor to our current right-wing populists, presumably because not enough time has passed yet.[3] Referring back to Polanyi's *Great Transformation*, we can better see the contours and underlying causes of Italy's tragedy. It is important to make a distinction here between the political, socioeconomic and fiscal dimensions. Berlusconi's political career has its origins in the party-political and ideological vacuum left after the fall of the Berlin Wall and end of state socialism, not just in the former Eastern Bloc but throughout Western Europe. The exclusion of communists from the corridors of power in Rome during the Cold War led to a deformation of Italy's democracy. Although most Italian governments were in office for a maximum of one or two years, there was never any real change of power in the country. The long reign of the Christian Democrats, in coalition with the Socialists from 1979, facilitated widespread corruption. This came to light in Milan in 1992 in a huge scandal known as *Tangentopoli*, or 'Bribesville', when it was revealed that companies had been forced to pay one-off bribes and even revenue-based kickbacks in order to be considered for public contracts. These 'political costs' amounted to between 5 and 13 per cent of a contract's value depending on the sector and region, and the money was used for party financing, election sweeteners for party members and personal enrichment.[4] The only party with relatively clean hands on a national level was the PCI, but the communists were too ideologically disoriented and self-absorbed after the collapse of the Eastern Bloc to present a real alternative to the corrupt bourgeois parties.

The plundering of the state contributed to the growing budget deficit, causing Italy's debt-to-GDP ratio to rise from almost 54 to more than 100 per cent between 1980 and 1992.[5] Both governing parties were totally compromised by the *Tangentopoli* scandal, enabling Berlusconi to rake in the votes, particularly on the right. His Forza Italia party promised an end to the corrupt *partitocrazia* and a new beginning. Berlusconi claimed that his great wealth made him immune to corruption, and he declared that he would run the rotten state as effectively as he ran his corporate empire.[6] (Subsequent right-wing populists, like Trump in the USA and Andrej Babiš in the Czech Republic, have also invoked their supposed skills as business tycoons. While it applied to Berlusconi, it was famously a fabrication in Trump's case, and Babiš proved to be an incompetent manager during the Covid-19 pandemic – more on this in chapter 7.) With his broadsides against excessive bureaucracy, Berlusconi affirmed Italians' traditionally sceptical view of the state. He was also in sync with the Chicago School of Economics and the US Republican party, who demonized the idea of 'big government'. Berlusconi's claim that he would step back from his business interests as prime minister turned out to be one of many lies, as he took multiple opportunities to foster his media empire. In 2013, the former prime minister was convicted of tax evasion and abuse of power.

Even during his first term in office, however, Berlusconi proved to be a poor manager of the state's finances. Though he cannot be blamed for the mountain of debt he inherited, Italy's total debt-to-GDP ratio grew by another 6 per cent to 117 per cent under his government.[7] And just like in the 2000s and after Berlusconi's final resignation in 2011, the ones left holding the bag were his successors, who had to adopt drastic austerity measures in response.

Detour into Italy's economic history

Berlusconi was able to build on the boom of the 1980s because the recession of 1993 was brief and not too severe. In 1987, Italy had proudly overtaken the UK – Europe's former leading economic power – in per-capita GDP, placing it fifth amongst Western industrialized countries.[8] The UK finance minister refuted these figures at the time because they indirectly called into question the success of Thatcherism. Italy owed its upswing to its mixed economic structure, its resourceful entrepreneurs and its strong position in growth sectors such as the electronics and computer industries.

One of the companies emblematic of this upswing was Olivetti, a typewriter manufacturer that began producing personal computers in 1982 and released a laptop soon afterwards. In the following years, the Piedmont-based firm was second only to the global market leader IBM in terms of market share in Europe, and the company expanded into Germany with the acquisition of Triumph-Adler, a long-established office equipment manufacturer. But problems began piling up in the early 1990s because Italy was unable to compete with the USA, Japan and Germany in the production of computer chips, and its labour costs were higher than those of Asian manufacturers. Olivetti stopped developing new PCs in 1995, and it ceased all computer production two years later (Siemens, which had previously acquired Nixdorf, met the same fate in 2005 – so Italy was not the only EU country to struggle with competition).[9] Instead of focusing on the high-tech sector, Olivetti shifted its attention to traditional markets and acquired a 50 per cent stake in Telecom Italia when the company was privatized. In more abstract terms, this could be viewed as a transition from productive capitalism to rentier capitalism. Today Olivetti still has a good 500 employees at its main site in the city of Ivrea, and its defunct industrial facilities were designated a UNESCO World Heritage Site in 2018. This is nice, but it does not bode well when a city's prospects for the future depend on it becoming a museum of the past.

Italy's automotive industry followed a similar trajectory. In the 1980s, Fiat specifically and Italy as a whole were in a strong position internationally. Thanks to Fiat's dense network of licensees in the Eastern Bloc (the Soviet Union and Poland), Southern and South East Europe (Spain, Yugoslavia, Turkey), and South America (Argentina and Uruguay), Italy's largest industrial concern was primed for global expansion just like VW.[10] But its market share declined continually in Europe in the 1990s, and its activities in Eastern Europe were limited to the construction of a large Fiat factory in Poland and another in Serbia later on. Unlike Olivetti, Fiat suffered from the fact that it was still a family-run company and it was poorly managed.

Sergio Marchionne joined the board of Fiat in 2003. He made the company profitable again, and even expanded into the USA after the global financial crisis. But ever since its merger with Chrysler, Fiat has no longer been purely Italian.

The company moved its headquarters to Amsterdam in 2014, meaning that in legal terms it is actually Dutch. So much for the effects of globalization – not to mention the European integration which made the move possible in the first place. Fiat's employees are understandably worried, and the company's 2021 merger with Peugeot will only lead to further job losses. This will inevitably set Polanyi's political pendulum in motion again – though neither the left-wing nor right-wing populists have a formula for how Italy should handle these challenges as a centre of industry.

State-controlled companies were a pillar of the Italian economy after the Second World War,[11] and their development followed the pattern seen in other EU states. The government began privatizing them in 1991, usually by converting them into stock corporations. This is how shares came to be sold in Enel (the national electricity board), Eni (oil, natural gas, petrochemicals), state-controlled banks and insurance firms, and companies in the state holding corporation known as IRI (which was founded by the Fascist regime and is an example of the long-lasting effects of dirigisme). Very few of the privatized companies remained global players like Enel. Instead, following the logic of global financial capitalism, many of the companies that were formerly controlled by IRI were sold on, broken up or at best restructured. Italy's profile as an industrial centre did not benefit from this; despite having much lower wages than Germany, more and more production moved to Eastern Europe and Asia from the 1990s.

The motivation for privatizing these companies was not ideological in Italy, as it had been in the UK, but rather fiscal. State companies were sold primarily to bolster the ailing state coffers. We can therefore make a distinction here between British neoliberalism by conviction, as put into practice under Margaret Thatcher and maintained in a weakened form by Tony Blair, and situational neoliberalism. This typology is important if we want to avoid turning neoliberalism into a cudgel, which is good for bashing policy but useless for analysing it.

Though the pressure on Italy increased with the strict deficit rules of the Maastricht Treaty and the introduction of the euro, Berlusconi's successors finally managed to overhaul the budget. The centre-left governments under Romano Prodi, Massimo D'Alema and Giuliano Amato from 1996 transformed the deficit into a primary surplus (before interest payments) and reduced total debt by 12 per cent to reach 105 per cent of GDP by the end of the decade, enabling Italy to join the eurozone. But beyond this success, Italy's centre-left governments were lacking in vision and joint projects. The government reform that was urgently needed fizzled out in a parliamentary commission, and the budget overhaul left no money for developing Italy's welfare system and infrastructure. It was only in education that the government was able to make a mark; vocational training reforms lowered the notoriously high rate of youth unemployment, which once again became Italy's biggest social problem after the global financial crisis.

The Italian historian Guido Crainz cites another reason for the weakness of the Left in Italy: its failure to culturally renew itself in the 1990s.[12] This was most apparent at the grassroots level. For example, the social and cultural centres known as *case del popolo* ('houses of the people') were a great achievement on the part of the Italian Left. They can be found in all the districts and neighbourhoods of Italy's larger cities and were once sure sources of votes for the PCI and Socialists. They were places where party members, trade unionists and passers-by would meet after work for film screenings, political discussions, card games and chats over a glass of wine. It was all more about socializing than politics. When I lived in Italy, the *casa del popolo* in my Florentine neighbourhood was only sporadically open. Other 'houses' were more lively, especially on holidays such as May Day, including the one in the nearby community of Fiesole, a stronghold of the PCI and its successor parties. The cultural programme on such occasions involved a choir that would sing workers' songs dating from the nineteenth century to the *Resistenza* era, as well as older music from other parts of the world. I once dared to ask whether there weren't any more contemporary songs. But the post-war accomplishments of the Italian Left – universal health care, paid sick leave, free schools and universities, protection against unfair dismissal and the general expansion of the social state (as limited as it may be in Italy) – are probably hard to set to music. I had the impression that the cultural vacuum and dissolution of post-war social milieus are what caused the *case del popolo* to stand empty most evenings, frequented only by a few old party members.

Il Cavaliere won the next election in 2001 thanks to a mixed bag of promises and his media influence. He pressed ahead with privatization, though the sale of shares did not mean that much changed in the respective companies. In the long term, however, companies that were converted into stock corporations tended to focus more on profits and thus on cutting jobs (prior to their conversion, Enel, Eni and IRI together employed approximately 690,000 people). Privatization did not spark more competition, as its adherents claimed it would, but instead led to cartels and monopolies with the attendant inflated prices. (My own experience backs this up: when I moved to Italy in 2007, the privatized electricity, gas and phone companies demanded sometimes absurdly high connection fees and basic charges; only the municipal refuse collection service, which was still run by the city, was much cheaper than in Germany.) In his second and longest period of governance (2001–6), Berlusconi made no effort to combat illegal collusion or the hefty price hikes that followed the introduction of the euro. The resulting high inflation hurt the population's purchasing power. This, in turn, impacted consumption and economic growth, which fell to an average of just over 1 per cent during Berlusconi's second term. So even before the global financial crisis, Italy was trailing far behind the rest of the EU.

Stagnation prompted even Italy's business associations to criticize Berlusconi, but the TV mogul was able to fall back on his media machinery in the parliamentary elections of 2006. Considering that Berlusconi now controlled not only his own channels but also public television, Italy was already dealing with a 'crisis of democracy'. Berlusconi conducted yet another polarizing, partisan election campaign (just like Trump and other right-wing populists after him). In addition, prior to the election he had changed Italy's electoral law to grant a majority prize, in the form of a large number of extra parliamentary seats, to the party with the most votes.[13] This rule also applied to the upper house of parliament, the Senate, where seats are awarded on a regional basis. This trick allowed Berlusconi to oust the centre-left coalition under Romano Prodi, which had narrowly won the election in 2006. Prodi's coalition had only the slightest majority in the Senate; Berlusconi blocked it on important projects and then claimed once again that the Left was unfit to govern. It was partially because of this that a later successor, Matteo Renzi, wanted to diminish the power of the Senate. However, Renzi lost the constitutional referendum in 2016 that would have enabled him to do this.

The power-grab tactic – a hallmark of right-wing populists everywhere – paid off. With the Left mired in infighting, not least on account of their lack of political clout, Berlusconi won the snap parliamentary election of 2008. The history of Italy's changing governments after 1989 demonstrates that once right-wing populists have attained power, they will resort to legal manipulation to hold onto it. There are some parallels here with Hungary, where Viktor Orbán won two thirds of the seats in parliament in 2014 with barely 45 per cent of the national vote, and also with the USA, where the Republicans have used bureaucratic tricks in a number of states to make it difficult if not impossible for certain social groups which have traditionally favoured the Democrats (such as poor Black Americans) to vote at all.

Italy is also another example of the fiscal role reversal mentioned earlier in the essay about the USA. All of its centre-left governments since 1995 have followed a frugal and rational budgetary policy – so this policy cannot be blamed solely on the introduction of the hard euro. In 2007, during Romano Prodi's second term, Prodi managed to reduce Italy's total debt to below the threshold of 100 per cent of GDP. This was evidence that liberal democracy still had budgetary and political reserves which could be put to good use if necessary by a competent government (this was no longer the case after the global financial crisis and euro crisis). Berlusconi, by contrast, was an extravagant spender who catered especially to his constituencies in southern Italy.[14] The Left therefore took on the role of liberals and conservatives in terms of their budget policy, a move which gained them the approval of experts and international finance organizations, but not their voter base. Under Berlusconi, the majority of workers in Italy began voting for the Right.

After the euro crisis, this meant voting mainly for the Lega, whose rise can also be traced to Berlusconi. In 1994, Berlusconi appointed five ministers from that party (still known as Lega Nord at the time) to his first cabinet. It was a risky move because the Lega's leader, Umberto Bossi, was a political rabble-rouser who had threatened the violent secession of 'Padania' (the Lega's name for a theoretically independent northern Italy) and repeatedly insulted Berlusconi.[15] Bossi let the coalition fall apart after less than a year, but he allied himself with Berlusconi again after the latter's second electoral victory in 2001, when Bossi himself was appointed to the cabinet. The Lega thus acquired a sheen of respectability under *Il Cavaliere*, and the party was normalized despite having what is, in many respects, a radically right-wing programme. The Lega lost government power in 2011 and seemed to be done for in 2012 when it emerged that Bossi had siphoned off party funds for himself and his two sons. But despite this fraud, the

Lega under Matteo Salvini became the third-strongest party in Italy's 2018 election and even achieved a relative majority in the European parliamentary elections of 2019. The various scandals around Bossi and Berlusconi clearly did no lasting damage to the right-wing populists. They actually benefited Berlusconi indirectly (at least until he was convicted) because the public paid more attention to his personal antics than to his politics.

Berlusconi's career as prime minister ultimately ended because of a coincidence: he returned to power at the wrong time. Shortly after his third electoral victory in 2008, the global financial crisis erupted and Italy felt the full force of it. The country experienced negative growth of 5.2 per cent in 2009, the worst economic slump of any Western industrialized country. This was partially because the government coffers were bare; unlike the USA or Germany, Italy could not afford a spending programme to counter the recession. On the contrary, Berlusconi's long-time finance minister, Giulio Tremonti, prepared an austerity package in 2010 to prevent the Greek debt crisis from spilling over to Italy. The package mainly hurt schools and universities, which were already neglected. Even deeper cuts amounting to 54 billion euros followed in 2011, but they further strangled the economy and triggered a downward spiral. Most disastrously, the state stopped paying its bills, and by 2013 its outstanding debts to companies amounted to nearly 100 billion euros.[16] This caused an unprecedented wave of insolvencies and is one of the reasons the government's budget crisis had such a huge impact on the economy. One million jobs were lost, and industrial production fell by more than 25 per cent – nearly as steep a drop as in Poland and Czechoslovakia in 1990–1.[17]

In the face of such a major crisis, Berlusconi's old tactic of making people feel good and sweeping problems under the rug no longer worked. International lenders and the European Central Bank did not trust him to get the state's finances under control. This was no surprise, seeing as Italy's mountain of debt had doubled from one to two trillion euros since Berlusconi's first term in office.[18] In order to refinance expiring government bonds and take on new debt, the Bank of Italy had to pay higher and higher interest rates (a huge redistribution programme for the benefit of Italian banks and those Italian citizens who could still afford to buy government bonds – another example of rentier capitalism). In the second half of 2011, the interest rate rose to over 7 per cent, in part because the German government refused to introduce joint bonds for the eurozone known as Eurobonds.[19] Berlin did not want to share liability for Berlusconi's policies, nor did Paris. *Il Cavaliere* clung to his high office, not least to continue enjoying immunity and drag out the legal proceedings that had been brought against him. But when the interest rate spread between Italian and German government bonds rose to 5.74 per cent in November 2011 (*lo spread* became a loan word in Italian – more evidence of how international financial capitalism had become the measure of national fiscal policy) and Italy faced a debt crisis on the scale of the one in Greece, Berlusconi had to throw in the towel. He resigned not because of a democratic vote, but solely because of pressure from the international financial markets, his EU partners and some domestic elites.

The social consequences of Berlusconism

Italy's post-2008 recession lasted for nearly six years on and off, much longer than in any other developed economy. The crisis in Italy is a demonstration of how the first right-wing populist to govern a large Western industrialized nation drove his country into the ground. It would be wrong to focus only on government debt here, however. Fiscal policy became an obsession in the age of neoliberalism, one that grew even more intense during the euro crisis. What Italy really needs is for a new economic dynamic to emerge from society itself. But this seems unlikely at the moment, because Italian society has been hobbled by long stagnation and the financial crisis. This makes it even more susceptible to right-wing populist demagoguery than it was in Berlusconi's time.

It is not possible to write a complete social history of Italy over the past 30 years in the space of an essay. The country's north–south divide, which has only deepened on account of the crisis, would also need to be taken into account. I can therefore only look at a few aspects in more detail, just as I did in the previous detour into Italy's economic history. My points of reference are the books by the social historian Paul Ginsborg (1945–2022), who moved to Italy from England at a time when so many northern Europeans dreamed of doing just that. Starting in the 1980s, he published a number of essential works on Italy which provide insights into social changes 'from below' by looking at the importance of family, shifting mentalities and the effects of Berlusconism.[20]

Increased television consumption was one of the direct consequences of the Berlusconi era and his activities as a media tycoon. From 1988 to 1995 alone, the time that Italians spent watching TV each day rose from an average of two-and-a-half to more than three-and-a-half hours.[21] This was due above all to new private channels serving up an endless stream of quiz shows, prize draws, talk shows and soap operas. The standard of public television also declined dramatically under Berlusconi; RAI, the national public television station, now mainly broadcasts cheap entertainment during prime time. And the division of roles between the oily moderators and the scantily clad, overly made-up assistants is a blow to gender equality – something Berlusconi rejected, as do other right-wing populists.

While the media has been dumbed down, the education system has been neglected at the same time. Italy has long lagged behind Germany and France in terms of the proportion of young people who attend academic secondary schools or universities. The country was catching up until the 1990s, but the gap widened again under Berlusconi. In 2018, Italy had by far the lowest proportion of college graduates of *all* EU member states (just 26.8 per cent of 25- to 34-year-olds). By contrast, the proportion of young Italians who only complete the compulsory level of schooling is nearly 35 per cent (this was also the youth unemployment rate in 2018 – the connection between the two is a well-known problem). In terms of education spending, Italy trails far behind every other OECD state.[22]

This has to do with the austerity measures following the financial crisis. In the first austerity package of 2010, finance minister Tremonti cut approximately 8 per cent of the already meagre budget for universities and schools[23] – and their infrastructure shows it. When I visited the closest primary school on the outskirts of Florence for one of my children in 2009, the damp that had penetrated the roof was visible to the naked eye. Since the roof was made of reinforced concrete, like so many buildings constructed in the post-war boom, it needed to be laboriously renovated or completely replaced to prevent it from collapsing. A similar roof had collapsed shortly before in Piedmont, burying several children, so I was sensitive to such water damage. Accidents like this happen almost every year in Italian schools and kindergartens. The spectacular collapse of the Polcevera Bridge in Genoa, which killed 43 people in August 2018, finally drew international attention to the problem. The bridge has since been rebuilt, probably the greatest achievement of the centre-left government under Prime Minister Guiseppe Conte, who governed Italy from the summer of 2018 to the start of 2021. In terms of internet infrastructure and digitalization, too, Italy has lingered near the bottom of the list of EU countries for years.[24]

Italy clearly needs an extensive investment programme which would create jobs on the side. In lieu of this, the left-wing populist Five Star Movement (M5S), which came to power in

2018, followed through on one of its campaign promises and introduced a *reddito di cittadinanza*, or universal basic income (a pet subject of the global Left). But this basic income requires huge bureaucratic effort to manage and is not nearly as unconditional as promised. Because the programme was so costly, the government had to place more and more constraints on it, meaning that only about one million people received any payments.[25] This simultaneously reveals the limits of national social policy in the framework of the EU.

Poor conditions in the labour market from the mid-1990s led to the 're-familialization' of Italian society. Rising youth unemployment made Italian teenagers and college graduates even more dependent on family networks when they wanted to enter the labour market.[26] Furthermore, young Italians were increasingly unable to afford to cut the cord to their parents. In 1993, half of Italian men under the age of 30 still lived in their parental home. This triggered a debate about so-called *mammoni* ('mama's boys') and the question of whether their behaviour was a consequence of the difficult labour market or something gender-specific, seeing as only about a quarter of women of the same age were still living with their parents in the mid-1990s. Stagnation and the financial crisis protracted and heightened this dependence on the family. According to more recent data, two thirds of all Italian men and women between the ages of 18 and 34 were still living with their parents in 2018, with the statistics for women largely in line with those for men.[27]

A glance at Italy's income statistics immediately explains why family ties have become so important again. After the euro crisis, Italians under the age of 35 earned an average taxable income of just 540 euros monthly.[28] Even subtracting the unemployed from this statistic, this is about as much as the statutory minimum income in Germany and Austria (Hartz IV with a housing allowance in Germany, and basic income with allowances in Austria; this is essentially a kind of social basic income, but no one dares to call it that because it would sound too socialist). The miserable starting salaries in Italy – which often barely top 1,000 euros even in well-paid sectors – mean that young Italians generally cannot afford their own place unless mama and papa help out. Their parents are also indispensable as soon as these young Italians have children themselves, because childcare and kindergarten places are rare and expensive. This is another argument in favour of expanding the social state in combination with an education initiative.

In society as a whole, however, there are limits to the solidarity of older Italians. The financial crisis caused youth unemployment to double to more than 42 per cent between 2008 and 2014. At the same time, the employment rate for over-55s rose from 33 to more than 40 per cent.[29] This generational crowding-out has to do with the fact that young workers are easier to dismiss. Even though I use neoliberalism as a critical interpretive lens for contemporary history in this book, neoliberalism cannot be blamed for this particular development. Ultimately, it comes down to how society distributes opportunities and risks between the generations (I discuss this problem in more detail in chapter 7, which deals with the Covid-19 pandemic).

Many young Italians have all but given up on themselves; about one fifth of Italians between the ages of 15 and 24 do not work or attend school or any other educational establishment (in international statistics, they are referred to as NEET: not in education, employment or training). The *reddito di cittadinanza* has not reduced their dependency because there are especially strict conditions on paying this basic income to people under the age of thirty. In general, one of the weaknesses of an unconditional basic income is that it is primarily a budgetary solution. But state fund transfers and cash for welfare recipients will not solve Italy's problems, especially not in the ailing Mezzogiorno.

This was already apparent under Berlusconi, who, until the crisis of 2009, funnelled sums in the double-digit billions to the south each year through Italy's fund for underdeveloped regions (*fondo per le aree sottoutilizzate*). But economic growth in the south was half a per cent lower on average than in the north from 1995 onwards. As a result of accumulation over the years, southern Italy's per-capita GDP had already dropped from 79 to 69 per cent of the EU average even before the financial crisis.[30] After the crisis, the Mezzogiorno fell behind Poland in its GDP (adjusted for purchasing power); within the EU, only Romania and Bulgaria are poorer. Historians are not trained to propose solutions, and certainly not to act as political consultants. To tackle the complex problems of the Mezzogiorno and other structurally weak regions (though it is important to distinguish here between agrarian and post-industrial areas), what is needed is a development economics for the developed world, and a different kind of welfare state designed not around payments but around employing people in a planned and purposeful way, especially in kindergartens, schools and social hotspots (this corresponds more to the Nordic model of the welfare state than the southern European model).

Italy's tragedy probably has something to do with the fact that it has been part of the developed world for only a relatively short time. Aside from Lombardy, Piedmont and parts of Emilia-Romagna and Tuscany, Italy was a poor and structurally weak country even into the 1960s. Its wealth grew rapidly in the following three decades, especially in the northeast and central Italy. But this means that only a single generation has enjoyed the high standard of living largely taken for granted in Germany and the Netherlands, for instance. This might be one of the reasons Italians fell back into old behavioural patterns after the boom ended. Family ties and clientelism grew more important again, and the role models for men and women became more regressive.[31]

Labour migration has always been one potential response to poverty and a lack of prospects. According to Eurostat, the

EU statistical office, emigration from Italy nearly doubled in the decade after the global financial crisis. Until the outbreak of the coronavirus pandemic, about 150,000 people left their homes in Italy each year and headed north. The number of Italian immigrants in the UK tripled between 2009 and 2016, and there is a large Italian diaspora in London.[32] Many of these immigrants are highly qualified academics. Even in Berlin, Munich and Vienna, you see more and more Italians on the subway, in cafés and at playgrounds with their children. Right-wing populists are using this exodus to propagate their far-right 'population replacement' theory, contrasting 'good' Italians with 'bad' immigrants from elsewhere.

The loss of so many agile young people is socially and economically draining for Italy itself. Labour migration from Italy is still low compared to Eastern Europe, but it is a constant topic of discussion amongst academics in particular. Almost everyone knows someone who has moved away (and unlike the guest worker migration starting in 1955, many women are now also seeking jobs abroad). This contributes to the gloomy mood of those who stay behind. Even if they have a job, low wages make them wonder if they, too, should leave.

Joseph Schumpeter, a contemporary of Polanyi who also started his career in the Habsburg Empire, but who enjoyed an illustrious academic career in the USA, proposed the oft-cited theory that capitalism tends towards 'creative destruction' and continually renews itself through crises. Schumpeter developed his theory primarily in terms of the economy and companies, not capitalist states and societies. In this respect, it is only partially applicable to Italy and the longer-term decline of a whole country. What is relevant, however – particularly to Italy, but perhaps also the entire EU – is his warning that, through the formation of monopolies, focus on entrepreneurial rents and waning innovation, capitalism endangers its own existence. Schumpeter assumed that history would someday end in socialism, while Polanyi believed that either socialism or fascism was possible. In Italy, *la crisi* has yet to unleash any creative impulses; instead, it has paralysed society. This is just as true for big companies, causing productivity to stagnate since the mid-1990s. Such a development is unique amongst Western industrialized countries, and it means that, from the perspective of employers, there is little or nothing left to distribute. In this respect, the crisis goes even deeper and is far more than just a fiscal problem.

The pendulum swings to the right

Why did the 'Polanyian moment' fail to materialize after Berlusconi's fall? The crisis and general exasperation with the *partitocrazia* initially benefited the left-wing populist Five Star Movement in 2013, which hit the ground running with a quarter of the votes. The social democratic PD did not fare particularly well in the elections, but it became the strongest party ahead of the leaderless conservatives.

A coalition between the two left-wing parties would have been the logical option considering the majority situation, and it would have enabled a fresh political start. But the destructive rhetoric and authoritarian style of M5S leader Beppe Grillo ruled this out. The international financial markets and other eurozone countries would also have been wary of such a coalition in 2013, and Italy would have been punished like Greece. The Partito Democratico therefore opted instead to continue Mario Monti's reforms in a more socially responsible way as part of a grand coalition.

The centrist shift was based on an alluring calculation: the young head of the PD, Matteo Renzi, who had ousted the old guard in an internal party referendum, figured that he could attract centrist voters and some of the bourgeois camp which found itself leaderless after Berlusconi's conviction. The bankruptcy of right-wing populism would thus be followed by a renaissance of reform-minded social democracy. This calculation panned out for a while, and in the 2014 European Parliament elections, Renzi – who had since become prime minister – achieved a record result of over 40 per cent of the vote for the PD. He portrayed himself as a 'wrecker' (*rottamatore*) of the crusty old Italy and passed a fundamental labour market reform bill. However, he also upheld Mario Monti's pension reform, which had adjusted the retirement age based on increased life expectancy (an overdue but unpopular step in light of Italy's ageing population).

Three factors then led to Renzi's downfall. First, he overestimated his power and made a bad call with the constitutional referendum. The referendum would have simplified Italy's government administration and deprived the Senate of much of its power. These were logical reforms considering the previous deadlocks, but they would have vastly expanded the power of the prime minster. The opposition sensed an opportunity to take down Renzi, and enemies in his own party who had been publicly humiliated in the past seized the chance for revenge. In the end, nearly 60 per cent of Italian voters rejected the reform.

The second and deeper reason for Renzi's defeat was that his social and labour market reforms did not bring about any rapid improvement. One core reform eased the rules that protected workers from unfair dismissal, a change that was bitterly opposed by trade unions (just as their German counterparts had opposed the Hartz reforms). The measure was supposed to motivate companies to hire more new employees whom they could dismiss again as needed. This expectation was met to some extent, but the liberalization of the labour market brought almost no benefit to structurally weak regions. Meanwhile, youth employment fell only very slowly, and most new jobs involved fixed-term contracts and were still dismally paid. In more abstract terms, we could say that, on account of the grand coalition, the political pendulum did not swing very far after the end of Berlusconism, and it ultimately got hung up on Italian domestic policy.

The third reason for Renzi's failure was the inaction of the EU and its leading power, Germany. The crisis saw Germany achieve an unprecedented position of power in the EU and eurozone, but Angela Merkel's European economic policy focused on ensuring compliance with the deficit limits for the euro. This was the modern equivalent of the gold standard, which Polanyi wrote about in such detail in reference to the nineteenth century and the 1920s. On top of this, the grand coalition in Germany saw to it that the 'debt brake' for a balanced budget was written into Germany's constitutional law. What the German debate overlooked was that the crisis had started as a speculation crisis (to which German banks had been major contributors) and not as a government debt and budget crisis. These latter crises only emerged in the course of the euro crisis, from which Germany indirectly profited. The growing interest rate spread between Germany and the countries in Southern Europe meant that Germany could issue government bonds with increasingly favourable terms. Although the German federal government could have invested in the country's long-neglected infrastructure (the cause of many delayed trains, crumbling motorway bridges and slow rural internet) more cost-effectively than ever before, it instead bet everything on breaking even and reducing its debt.

At first glance, Italy could be viewed as an argument in favour of this fiscal conservatism. The mountain of debt it accumulated from the mid-1990s had disastrous repercussions, not least continued stagnation and the particular contours of Italy's financial crisis. It is hard to escape a debt trap; even though Italy achieved a primary surplus, before interest payments, every year since 1992 (with the exception of 2009 and some downturns under Berlusconi), its total debt continued to rise in both absolute terms and in relation to GDP.[33] This benefited institutional investors and Italy's upper middle class, which was wealthy enough to buy the government bonds with their good interest rates. In this regard, an egalitarian argument could be made against a policy of debt management, since this contributes massively to social inequality.[34]

But fiscalism – or focusing solely on government debt – also just leads to stagnation. After 2009, it was out of the question that Italy would be able to reduce its government debt, which shot up to over 130 per cent of GDP by 2013 on account of the recession, which was exacerbated by austerity policies. Consequently, the actual problem is weak growth, not the high level of debt per se. Renzi logically refused to continue Monti's strict austerity policy, and he exploited the deficit limit of 3 per cent as much as possible to stimulate economic growth. But much like Germany in the first years after the Hartz reforms, it was already clear in 2015 that Italy's economic recovery would be sluggish.

It was at this moment (which was not, however, a Polanyian one) that Italy's European partners should have come to its aid. The EU Commission tried to do so with the Juncker Plan, but this consisted only of investment guarantees of 21 billion euros which were supposed to be a lever for actual investments. Unsurprisingly, this financialization worked better in northern EU countries than southern ones, where the banks still had to stomach an unprecedented wave of corporate bankruptcies and loan defaults.[35] The European Central Bank provided more effective support to Italy. By purchasing Italian government bonds, ECB president Mario Draghi kept their interest rate low, which indirectly relieved pressure on the national budget of his home country.

Why did Italy's reform government not receive more decisive help from the country's EU partners – Germany above all – and the European Council? (The EU Commission and even the ECB were more constructive, which speaks in favour of the Commission as a *supranational* institution and against the Council as an *international* one.) This question will probably have to be answered by future historians when they gain access to the respective files, or by social scientists who conduct interviews with experts. My own attempt to find answers would lead me up the garden path of counterfactual assumptions, and it is not the job of historians to claim to know better after the fact. Essentially, a whole range of structural factors come into play here, one being the bond between democracy and the general public of the nation-state. No one can win an election in Germany by taking on the concerns of desperate Italians.

The euro crisis only intensified fiscal nationalism and the pride in breaking even and then achieving a budget surplus. Such surpluses partially came down to the spread (because EU countries with lower credit ratings paid higher interest), but countries on the losing end of this deal paid more attention to this than the big winner, Germany. Looking back at history since the First World War, it almost seems to be a rule that in times of crisis and threat, internationalism fails and national egoism wins out over solidarity. But it would have been rationally and perhaps even emotionally appropriate for a country as economically dependent on global free trade and European integration as Germany to come to the aid of the governments of Mario Monti (who was highly regarded by Angela Merkel) and then Matteo Renzi.

There were plenty of opportunities to do so, both symbolically, through more state and parliamentary visits, and tangibly, by providing funds for renovating schools, expanding internet access, helping Italy move more quickly to solar energy – the list could go on. It is impossible to know after the fact what the political implications of a greater commitment to Italy would have been. Demagogues à la Salvini would probably have distorted even the most well-meaning measures. Furthermore, Italian politics are at least as self-indulgent as those in Germany and France (aside from Italy's nervous obsession with *lo spread* and international ratings). The power struggles and intrigues in Rome have always played out with no consideration for Italy's international reputation. But the bottom line is that Angela Merkel and her finance minister Wolfgang Schäuble played a major role in causing Italy's traditional admiration for well-ordered Germany to curdle into envy and resentment.

For a long time, the proponents of European integration placed great hope in the development of a European public. And while national media outlets do now provide much more in-depth coverage of election campaigns and political developments in other EU countries, the emphasis is always on mutual differentiation – and not just in social media channels, but even in quality European newspapers. The press coverage of Italy in 2018–19 by everyone from *The Guardian* in the UK to the *Frankfurter Allgemeine Zeitung* in Germany largely consisted of regurgitating Salvini's provocations. There were certainly more than enough of them; during his time as minister of the interior and deputy prime minister, Salvini tweeted an average of ten times a day, surpassing even Donald Trump. This kind of 'Twitter politician' was a new phenomenon in Italy at the time. Salvini and his ilk posted banal pictures of beaches, cafés, bowls of pasta, etc., in an attempt to project a human side while attracting attention with provocative messaging. This kind of content is cheap fodder for social media outlets and established print publications alike. More balanced voices rarely get heard, as demonstrated by the international fixation on the names of right-wing populists. The real news about Salvini and other Twitter politicians (though all of them tweet now, so we can probably ditch the term) was that he was neglecting the actual job of a minister, namely, to govern. *La Repubblica* newspaper calculated that the interior minister spent a grand total of 17 days at his actual place of work in the ministry between January 2019 and the European elections in May – or not even four days a month.[36] This didn't hurt Salvini, though; he won the European elections in 2019 with a considerable lead over M5S and the social democrats.

Salvini's antics, like those of Berlusconi, hurt Italy's international prestige. But external criticism was usually not taken well – except by the practically masochistic left-wing and liberals, who felt that it confirmed their own critique of the two right-wing populists. Meanwhile, Italy's long economic decline and the country's dependence on the monetary policy of the ECB and the ratings of international agencies have been a blow to the country's self-confidence. Aside from the kind of demonstrative national pride trumpeted by Salvini and more recently Meloni, the reaction to this has mainly been self-pity. The accusation heard again and again is that the EU, and Germany especially, left Italy alone to deal with its most urgent problems.

Is this true? The impression is not misleading when it comes to migration policy, and it points to a structural problem with the EU – namely, that the EU influences many policy areas but lacks the ability to take action in emergencies or crises. Italy was initially only tangentially affected by the 'refugee crisis' of 2015–16 because most refugees went to Germany or Northern Europe. But when the EU (or essentially Angela Merkel) established a refugee agreement with Turkey, the flow of refugees and migrants was redirected to the Central Mediterranean route and thus to Italy. This was predictable, but the EU offered neither financial nor logistical support to Italy's centre-left government of the time (Renzi had already fallen and Paolo Gentiloni took over as prime minister). Since the EU did not assist him, Gentiloni entered into an agreement with the Libyan government, which was supposed to hold back refugees and migrants with the help of warlords on the coast (Berlusconi made a similar deal with the Libyan dictator Gaddafi in 2008). The number of refugees declined, as intended, but the PD was unable to shake off the impression that its migration policy was ineffective, and Salvini mercilessly exploited this in the campaign of 2017–18. In the long term, however, voters were more concerned with the minimal and belated effects of the social democratic economic and social reforms. The reforms were not amiss with respect to inter-generational equity and equal opportunities, but in the end they achieved too little and took too long to create new jobs. This dilemma of reform-minded social democracy cannot be solved, and it cost Emmanuel Macron – who, admittedly, now positions himself not as a moderate leftist but as a liberal – his parliamentary majority in the most recent French elections.

In the Italian parliamentary elections of the spring of 2018, M5S became by far the strongest party because many voters drifted away from the PD, just as they had done in 2013. The election's biggest loser did not want to enter into a coalition, so Salvini got his chance; his Lega party had achieved 17 per cent of the votes, prevailing over Berlusconi in the right-wing voting bloc. The subsequent development of Italy's pan-populist coalition is of general interest because it once again proves the rule that, when left-wing and right-wing populists compete, the right-wing apparently always comes out ahead (this was the case in Poland and Germany, too; Greece is the only exception to date). The second lesson from this experimental coalition was that it took no time at all to wreak havoc on the government budget and Italy's entire economic development.

In addition to introducing tax breaks for small businesses – Salvini's gift to his northern Italian electorate – the new coalition adopted the basic income that had been promoted by the M5S. Neither measure was financially feasible, so the budget deficit rose sharply, the economic mood immediately turned, and Italy's already weak growth dropped to below zero in the second half of 2018. High government spending caused the spread between Italian and German government bonds to rise by nearly 2 per cent at times. Expiring government bonds constantly need to be refinanced, which led to an additional burden of about 5 billion euros in the 2019 fiscal year alone. Budget experts predicted further interest costs of 9 billion euros in 2020 – before the Covid-19 pandemic threw every calculation overboard.[37] The government wound up spending more on the higher interest for new government bonds than it ever spent on the *reddito di cittadinanza*, and the money budgeted for the basic income evaporated in the international financial markets. This prompts the question of just how much even a medium-sized industrialized country like Italy can still exert sovereignty today – and such questions are grist for the mill of right-wing and left-wing populists.

On account of unfulfilled and unfulfillable socio-political promises, the Five Star Movement lost nearly half of its voters in the European elections of 2019 compared to the parliamentary elections of March 2018. The Lega, by contrast, doubled its votes to 35 per cent, while the PD only slightly recovered in comparison to the national elections, meaning they were only able to win back a small portion of M5S voters. We can draw two conclusions from the election platforms and election campaigns of the competing parties: first, that Salvini's pointed criticism of the EU (though less biting than it was in 2018) was apparently more attractive than the scepticism of M5S towards the euro, and second, that the xenophobic right-wing nationalism of the Lega has a different punch than the left-wing critique of capitalism.

But like Berlusconi in his first short term in 1994–5, Salvini then made a strategic mistake. Riding high on his victory in the European elections, he made a grab for full power in Rome and quit the coalition with the M5S to try to force a new snap election. Instead, the left-wing populists allied themselves with the PD, and prime minister Giuseppe Conte pulled off the feat of remaining in power despite the formation of a new government coalition. This configuration was not stable, however, because even as the government was being formed, Matteo Renzi broke with the PD and founded a centre-left party by the name of Italia Viva.

An ongoing point of contention in the left-wing-populist/social-democratic/reformist coalition was whether Italy should avail itself of low-interest financial assistance from the European Stability Mechanism (ESM). In purely fiscal terms it was foolish not to, but the left-wing populists argued that it would make Italy even more dependent on the EU, and that there might be conditions on the loans. It ultimately came down to how much each party trusted the EU and the question of fiscal sovereignty. The Lega has always had a clear answer to this question: the motto of the so-called *sovranisti* (souverainists) is to have as little to do with the EU as possible. The Italian Left therefore came out looking like what many of its supporters have long suspected it of being: a squabbling heap.

To avoid new elections in the middle of the Covid-19 pandemic, Italy's president Sergio Mattarella (a Christian Democrat by political origin) called for the formation of a government of experts – and history repeated itself in Italy once again. Back in 1995, Berlusconi's defeat and his first coalition with the Lega led to the appointment of a cabinet of technocrats. After Berlusconi resigned again in the wake of the euro crisis, Mario Monti governed for a year and a half. He helped to rebuild trust in Italy's public finances and set some social reforms in motion. This made him a good antidote to Berlusconi's showmanship, but when he tried to run for prime minister again with a newly founded centrist party, he achieved just 10 per cent of the votes.

Italy's most recent (caretaker) prime minister, Mario Draghi, was the third technocrat in the past three decades. He enjoyed high prestige as the saviour of the euro, and he managed to form an all-party coalition including everyone from the Lega on the far right to the M5S on the left. Draghi governed Italy remarkably well through the second and third waves of the Covid-19 pandemic and secured a 191 billion euro reconstruction package from the EU. He put the EU funds to good use domestically, creating a foundation for strong economic recovery in 2021 with GDP growth of 6.5 per cent. This made him hugely popular and earned him the nickname 'Super Mario'.

But in the end, all of his efforts to build a grand national coalition were to no avail. The M5S fell apart over conflicts about how to deal with the Russian war against Ukraine, and a right-wing coalition ranging from Berlusconi to Salvini eventually toppled Draghi – because a successful centrist is the biggest threat to right-wing politicians vying for middle-class voters. Draghi could have tried to found his own political party, like Monti did, but he would have had to switch from the habitus of an expert and caretaker to that of a campaigning politician. In the end, he failed not only because of the usual scheming in Italian politics, but because of the internal contradictions and political limits of a technocratic government. The only party that stood unanimously behind Draghi was the Partito Democratico – more evidence of how social democracy has transformed into a beacon of technocracy.

Power was once again up for grabs in Italy, and it was eventually won by Giorgia Meloni, another right-wing populist and nationalist who has less baggage from past political intrigues than Salvini. Meloni and whoever else governs Italy in the future will have to contend with a mountain of debt which grew even faster during the pandemic than it did during the economic crisis. Even before the pandemic, Italy's total debt-to-GDP ratio was higher than after the Second World War. This figure shot up by more than 20 per cent in 2020 because of greater spending to support health care measures and prop up the economy, and the deep recession due to the pandemic.[38] Draghi subsequently stabilized Italy's debt-to-GDP ratio, but interest rates for the government's debt depend heavily on bond purchases by the ECB and thus ultimately on the trust of Italy's partners in the eurozone.

In the history of the twentieth century, there were two classic ways of resolving such a debt crisis: inflation or currency reform. In Greece and Latvia, the IMF and EU prescribed drastic austerity programmes in their support packages after the global financial crisis. This essentially amounted to 'internal' devaluation and made it possible for these countries to remain in the eurozone. But such a strategy would be unfeasible and economically counterproductive after the many hardships of the pandemic. The IMF proposed a new tactic during the euro crisis in 2013: a one-off capital levy in the amount of 10 per cent to be implemented in the entire eurozone. This was supposed to push the government debt ratio below the threshold of 60 per cent of GDP again.[39] The young Federal Republic of Germany employed a similar measure after the Second World War in the context of its Equalization of Burdens Law (Lastenausgleichsgesetz), and in principle it would be possible in Italy, too. But the IMF proposal quickly sunk without a trace because it would have unleashed a political earthquake.

Polanyi barely mentions Italy in his magnum opus, perhaps because he felt the Mediterranean country was too peripheral to global capitalism. Economically speaking, Italy is not at all peripheral to the EU, despite its decline since the 1990s. The common currency means that Italy's development will play a major role in shaping the future of the EU. The country's recent history does not allow for much optimism, however, especially if an essentially Eurosceptic populist and nationalist right-wing coalition governs in Rome. In crisis-ridden Italy, Polanyi's pendulum has more often and profoundly swung to the right than to the left, and there is no way to predict how a populist, nationalist right-wing government will deal with its European partners and the decreasing confidence in debt management. I refrain from making predictions as a historian, but one thing is clear: if Italy has to pay higher interest rates for its mountain of public debt because of the growing political risks and the recent rise in inflation, then the euro and the entire EU will be in a shambles as well.

5

The West, Turkey and Russia
A History of Estrangement

The military museum in Istanbul is an oasis of calm in a metropolis of 15 million people. It is just a few minutes away from hectic Taksim Square, the centre of the city, of the secular Republic of Turkey and of the protest movement against President Recep Tayyip Erdoğan in 2013. The garden of the former Ottoman military academy is filled with large cedars, palms, rose bushes and silent cannons. But every afternoon, the silence is broken by the *mehter* military band performing traditional Ottoman marches in historical garb. Played on big kettledrums and piercing zurnas (double-reed wind instruments related to the oboe), these marches struck fear into half of Europe from the fifteenth to eighteenth century, as did the Ottoman cavalry and artillery. Anyone who hears a *mehter* marching band will immediately understand why Haydn and Mozart were fascinated by Ottoman military music and instruments, and immortalized their sound in the Surprise Symphony and various works 'alla turca'.

When I was child in Turkey in the late 1970s (my parents spent a few years there for professional reasons), the attendants at the military museum often provided a kind of political-historical accompaniment to the displays. I enthusiastically tagged along whenever visiting relatives went to the museum, where the attendants would lead them unbidden to the rooms with exhibits from the First World War. The attendants would give me a squeeze, clap the German visitors on the back and say with a smile: *Türkiye – Almanya – Arkadaş* (Turkey – Germany – friend). They were referring to the brotherhood-in-arms between the German and Ottoman Empires, and to the Battle of Gallipoli, when the Ottoman Army repelled the British attack on the Dardanelles and Istanbul with German help. Gallipoli was a decisive battle in the First World War; had its outcome been different, Istanbul today might be a Greek city called Constantinople. Any reasonably educated Turk at the time therefore knew about the alliance between the Kaiser and the Sultan.

This historic brotherhood-in-arms underpinned Turkey's orientation towards Europe in general and Germany in particular, which had welcomed two million Turkish guest workers by the late 1970s. When these workers returned home, they brought washing machines, TVs and cars back with them to the old country – symbols of prosperity and progress. These *almancı* (literally 'Germaners') were considered nouveau riche and were not particularly popular, but their wealth stoked Turkey's admiration for far-off *Almanya*. You could sense this all over Turkey, even in rural areas, and this sentiment in combination with Turkey's traditional culture of hospitality led to countless invitations to people's homes.

My family was suspicious of Turkey's cult of the military and strong national pride (students would sing the national anthem after the last lesson every Friday afternoon, a replacement for the Islamic ritual of Friday prayers). Their discomfort was rooted in Germany's National Socialist past and the Second World War. Turkey had not experienced the same rupture in its history because it learned a lesson from the First World War and remained neutral in the second one. The consistent avoidance of revanchism is a great achievement on the part of the republic founded by Atatürk, one that is all the more notable when compared with the Weimar Republic.

Turkey's insistence on neutrality indirectly strengthened the political power of its armed forces, although the military backed the transition to democracy in 1946. The country's new electoral law brought about a multi-party system. In 1950, the military accepted the defeat of the Republican People's Party (CHP) which had ruled to that point, enabling a peaceful transfer of power (the CHP still exists and is currently the strongest opposition to President Erdoğan). This made Turkey – alongside Italy and unstable Greece – one of the only democracies in Southern Europe in the early post-war period. The country's further democratization did not run smoothly, with the military staging coups in 1960 and 1971 because it perceived risks to either the secular order or its own position of power.[1] Not long after my childhood visits to the military museum, the Turkish army bared its teeth once again. In 1979, violent civil unrest between left-wing and right-wing extremists claimed the lives of more than 3,000 people,[2] and Taksim Square became the site of frequent shootings. I sometimes heard this gunfire on my way to school, and a bullet once hit a German teacher's car.

The parents of some of my schoolfriends were almost relieved when the military seized power again in 1980 and restored public order. One of its popular measures was to get rid of the masses of stray cats and dogs in Istanbul which had been another side effect of the growing anarchy. But we knew from German newspapers and private conversations with Turks that the military was also taking brutal action against left-wing intellectuals, Kurdish activists and others in the opposition. Thousands of people were arrested and thrown in jail, just as they were in 2016 after Erdoğan's counter-coup – which was, in turn, a response to an amateur coup attempted by a few members of the armed forces.

The coup of 1980 led to an exodus of left-wing intellectuals and Kurdish activists, with a good 50,000 Turkish citizens applying for asylum in West Germany. The Western NATO countries reacted by introducing a visa requirement for Turks. This was hardly a declaration of commitment to democracy in Turkey, and it also violated the Agreement of Association with the European Economic Community (EEC) of 1963 and the Additional Protocol of November 1970,[3] which had promised that Turkish nationals would be able to settle freely in the European Community between twelve and twenty-two years after the agreement came into force (meaning 1986 at the latest).

Turkey had a population of 30 million in 1963 (compared to 85 million today), so any future immigration from the country must have seemed manageable at the time. The purpose of the association agreement and the promises that went with it was to tie the NATO country – which was just as strategically important then as it is today – more closely to the West and the EC. The Turkish government (the military had quickly ceded power to civilians after the coup of 1980, just as it had before) denounced the breach of the agreement. But these complaints were no more effective than its protests in the early 2000s when first Cyprus (in 2004) and then Bulgaria and Romania (in 2007) breezed past Turkey to become EU members, even though the latter two countries were poorer as measured by per-capita GDP, and Turkey had a much longer history as a market economy. Another chance for rapprochement arose in 2016 with the refugee agreement orchestrated by Angela Merkel between the EU and Turkey (which Erdoğan capitalized on domestically). But the EU did not keep its promise to abolish the visa requirement, probably out of fear of mass immigration – though contractual protections could have been put in place to prevent this.

These repeated affronts and broken promises are a partial answer to the question of why Turkey has become so estranged from the West, and why this probably would have happened even if someone other than Recep Tayyip Erdoğan were president. Russia has also obviously turned away from the West, to the point of starting a war against pro-Western Ukraine in 2022. History in Eastern Europe has thus, for the time being, come to a very different end than the one predicted in 1989. Even into the early 2000s, Russia and Turkey were expected to voluntarily westernize and gradually transform into liberal democracies and free market economies. There were similar expectations for China, where it was hoped that globalization and growing wealth would 'liberalize' the country. In light of this, it was self-evident to the EU that it should call the political and economic shots for its Eastern neighbours and define the accession criteria for joining the union. This assumption makes it all the harder for the West to understand why Russia and Turkey have gone their own way for many years now and rejected a Western model of modernization. But considering the strength of the Western hegemony until the global financial crisis of 2008–9, it was only logical for Turkey and Russia to polemically reject and resist it. Putin made this clear in his famously incendiary speech at the Munich Security Conference in 2007, when he openly broke with the West. Erdoğan has imitated him in his own verbal sorties.

Domestic policy is another driving force behind the bad-mouthing of the EU and the entire liberal West by Putin and Erdoğan. The two authoritarian presidents need nationalistic bogeymen to distract from the massive social and political problems in their own countries. Russia's economy has stagnated since the 2009 crisis, and by the time Turkey slid into recession in 2019, it was already suffering from the dramatic depreciation of the lira, growing inflation and declining real income. Based on recent economic developments, one might conclude that their apparently defensive but actually highly aggressive nationalism does not 'pay off'. But this nationalist stance is not just about material considerations or rational calculations; it is about bruised egos, complexes and a tangible show of strength. The EU currently has little way to counter this, as doing so would require greater trust in its own strengths – in the ideal of the European project and its power of attraction.

Despite the primacy of domestic politics in Turkey and Russia, their nearly simultaneous rejection of the West raises a question: is there an issue with these two countries specifically, or is there some connection to Western and especially German politics? To answer this question I will, once again, turn the lens on the West. This will accomplish more than pointing fingers at others, because ostracizing Erdoğan and Putin also serves as a kind of political self-affirmation for Germany, France and other EU countries. Russia's attack on Ukraine marks the start of a new chapter in East–West relations, but the justified outrage at this war of aggression should not stifle critical discussion of Western policies towards Turkey and Russia prior to 2022.

Relations with both countries are hugely important to Germany not least because a good five million residents of Germany come from these two countries, and some are still Turkish or Russian citizens.[4] Critically assessing the history of Germany's relations with these nations is a step towards better integrating these population groups and limiting external political influences.

How far does European history reach?

It is easy enough to write 'external' without giving it too much thought, but it indirectly says something about what we consider to be 'internal' or part of us. Ever since the expansion of the EU in 2004, it has become common practice for the Western media and sometimes even academia to equate Europe with the European Union. There has been a corresponding development since the 1990s in Russia and Turkey, where *Yevropa* or *Avrupa* is often mentioned as if it were somewhere else entirely, far from these two countries. Similar parlance can be found in England, where 'Europe' is said to start on the other side of the English Channel; in this respect, Brexit had a long pre-history in the mental mapping of the British Isles and the Continent.

This sense of distance is not new. Even nineteenth-century Russian intellectuals were ambivalent about Western Europe, which they often admired but sometimes also scorned. All the same, they did not fundamentally question whether Russia was part of Europe. It is telling that the Eurasian movement, which considers Russia to be its own unique civilization, first developed in the 1920s amongst Russians in exile, not within Russia or the young Soviet Union. The country's orientation towards Europe even withstood the Cold War, and in the late 1980s Gorbachev always spoke of a 'common European home' in his efforts to reach a new détente. It remains a great historical achievement on his part to have resolved the Cold War – partially out of necessity, due to the deteriorating economic situation in the Soviet Union, and partially out of the conviction that the East–West confrontation would lead nowhere.

But these times are long gone. In 2007, Putin declared the EU to be an enemy just like NATO, and his government has nurtured the new Eurasians in Russia, fostering an intellectual break with Europe. Surveys from before the most recent war against Ukraine show that barely half the Russian population considers Russia to be part of Europe. Far more than half the German population shares this view, forgetting the countries' cultural similarities.[5] In this respect, while inner-European walls and borders disappeared after 1989, Europe as a whole also began to drift apart.

What would a comparable survey in Turkey reveal? Most Europeans probably know that a small part of Turkey and most of Istanbul lie on the European continent. But countries like Germany and France reject the idea of Turkey being part of Europe, just as they reject the idea of Turkey's EU membership. This perception of Europe and its borders is culturally reinforced, and the humanities as an academic discipline play no small part in this. Nearly every German and Austrian university with a big history department has a chair for Eastern European history, but the history of the Ottoman Empire and Turkey is almost always covered by a philological faculty.[6] This might not seem particularly objectionable at first glance, since experts are addressing the respective countries in either case, and the philological connection can be useful for learning the language. But assigning these subjects to different faculties also expresses a hierarchy: European countries (including Russia) have a history, while non-European cultures (Turkey, but also China and India) do not. This classification is not as strict in the UK on account of the country's tradition of empire and greater openness to the world – but even there, a clear distinction is made between European and non-European history.

Moreover, Ottoman rule is remembered as the era of the 'Turkish yoke' in South East Europe to this day. By harbouring this attitude, countries like Hungary, Romania, Serbia, Bulgaria and Greece are somewhat overlooking the fact that, in certain cases, it was their own elites who summoned the Ottomans (as some Hungarian nobles did after 1526 to prevent the rule of the Counter-Reformational Habsburgs). But this has largely been forgotten, while memories of the struggle for liberation are kept alive. The countries in South East Europe could be a bridge to Turkey – geographically, historically and economically – but the opposite has been true for the past 200 years, and walls are built instead.[7]

In the nineteenth and twentieth centuries, differentiating oneself from 'the Turks' was also an expression of European Orientalism, which deliberately defamiliarizes and devalues 'the East'. During the Cold War, the same attitude was expressed towards the Soviet Union, such as when German Chancellor Konrad Adenauer spoke of the 'Asiatic hordes' and 'Asiatic Russia'.[8] Soviet soldiers were stationed along the Iron Curtain in the middle of Europe in the post-war period, so there could be no doubt that the Soviet Union was a major European power – but this was precisely the situation used to dispute that 'the Russians' were part of Europe.

The Ottoman Empire and Turkey in European history

A good hundred years ago, the question of whether South East Europe was part of the West was not nearly as clear-cut as it might seem today, considering that Bulgaria, Romania and Greece are all members of the EU. Before the First World War, when conflicts over Ottoman territories on the Balkan Peninsula escalated between the great powers and the states in South East Europe, the issue was referred to by British, French and German experts as the 'Eastern Question'. The 'East' was thus closer back then than it is today, and it included parts of South East Europe.[9] But we need to go further back to determine the extent to which the Ottoman Empire can be considered a part of European history.

Any historian working in Vienna will eventually encounter the sieges of 1529 and 1683. They still play a formative role in the city's identity and are present in the cityscape – see the Türkenschanzpark ('Turkish entrenchment' park) in the Währing district, for instance, or the Leopoldsberg hill in the Vienna Woods, where Vienna's liberation by the Poles is commemorated. The first siege was largely a military demonstration of power which consolidated Ottoman rule over Hungary. From there, the Ottoman Empire expanded to the northeast and even conquered territories belonging to early modern Poland, as well as the entire Black Sea coast. Considering this expansion, there can be no question that the Ottomans were a major European empire.

After losing the Battle of Vienna in 1683 and subsequent defeats in the Great Turkish War, the Ottoman Empire gradually shrunk, but it was still one of the largest territorial states in Europe until 1878. Once the immediate threat had passed, cultural exchange increased. Coffee and elements of Ottoman clothing and music were adopted and spread through Central and Eastern Europe. The Ottomans, in turn, appointed painters and musicians like Giuseppe Donizetti (1788–1856), brother of the famous opera composer, to the sultan's court. There were limits to this westernization, however. For example, the Ottomans never managed to secure their conquests through dynastic connections. This had to do with the religious differences between the Muslim Ottomans and Christian dynasties, as well as the rules of inheritance at the sultan's court – where, from the fifteenth century, it was customary for a deceased sultan's successor to have his brothers and potential rivals killed. This rule prevented dynastic wars and the fragmentation of the Ottoman Empire, but it also limited the possibility of marrying off children or cousins to other European dynasties, as the Habsburgs and Romanovs did. Whether religion would have fundamentally precluded this is debatable; after all, one of the early Ottomans married the daughter of a Byzantine emperor in the mid-fourteenth century.

Despite the lack of family ties, the Ottoman Empire and other European states frequently formed alliances. France, in particular, entered into a pact with the Sublime Porte to wage war against the Habsburgs. But the Ottomans' military might waned in the eighteenth century, causing the empire to lose its status amongst the great powers. At the Congress of Vienna in 1815, neither the sultan nor his envoys sat at the negotiating table. The weaker the Ottoman Empire grew, the more it became a factor in the balance of power and a central element in pre-1914 European history. The rivalry between Austria-Hungary and Russia in the Balkans and the regional imperialism of the nation-states in South East Europe ultimately led to the First World War.

The Ottoman Empire was one of the defeated powers, and the Treaty of Sèvres (one of several treaties named after Paris suburbs) called for it to be partitioned so that it would continue to exist only as a small rump state in Anatolia. This was essentially comparable to Hungary's fate after the Treaty of Trianon, though with an added colonialist element. But the Turks, who had only just amalgamated into a modern nation during the Balkan Wars and First World War, resisted subjugation by the European colonial powers. The remnants of the Ottoman army reassembled under the command of Mustafa Kemal Pasha, later Atatürk, and defeated the Greek army which had invaded Asia Minor in 1919 with British support. The subsequent expulsion and forced resettlement of all Christians from Anatolia was a continuation of the genocide committed against the Armenians and Assyrian Christians in 1915–16, but it was sanctioned by the League of Nations as an 'exchange of populations' in the Treaty of Lausanne of 1923. According to this agreement, which set a fatal precedent for other ethnically mixed regions in Europe, all Christians were supposed to leave Turkey and, in return, all Muslims would leave Greece. Only Western Thrace and Istanbul were exempt from this.

Western media and politicians once again blamed 'the Turks' collectively for the suffering associated with these expulsions. But the idea of homogenizing entire states was first proposed by Central and Western European intellectuals and experts, and it was promoted in Lausanne by Lord Curzon, the British Foreign Secretary and chief negotiator. The homogeneous nation-state embodied the European ideal of the time. France, Italy and the other victorious Western nations naturally declined to commit themselves to protecting minorities in the Paris Peace Conference treaties, but they demanded such guarantees from the newly founded and enlarged states in Eastern Europe.

The violent foundation of the state of Turkey after the First World War (which dragged on in subsequent conflicts in Eastern Europe until the early 1920s) followed a broader European pattern. The nineteenth-century foundation and expansion of the nation-states of South East Europe had also been based on the persecution and expulsion of minorities, first and foremost 'the Turks' – a term applied indiscriminately to Muslims regardless of their nationality (another product of European Orientalism). Ever since coming to power, Erdoğan and the ideologues of the AKP have tried to offset the Armenian genocide (which they reflexively deny) against the expulsion of Muslims from South East Europe. There is, in fact, a connection here: most of the leaders of the Young Turks – the movement responsible for organizing the genocide during the First World War – came from families who had previously been expelled from the European part of the Ottoman Empire. This trauma in no way excuses the Armenian genocide, but it explains at least some of the repugnant violence attributed to 'the East' or 'the Turks' by contemporaries. Acknowledging the mistakes of modern Europe and admitting that the foundation of nation-states in Central and Eastern Europe was an extremely bloody affair might have made it possible to resolve this point of contention with Turkey during its period of rapprochement with the EU. And Germany could have taken the lead in debates about these darkest hours of history, since German military officials were involved in planning and carrying out the Armenian genocide.

Its violent birth was a burden for the Republic of Turkey, particularly economically, but it also enabled far-reaching reforms. Atatürk was continuing a longer tradition here, one which ultimately went back to the European Enlightenment. In the mid-nineteenth century, the sultans Abdülmecid (r. 1839–61) and Abdülaziz (r. 1861–76) implemented the Tanzimat reforms, which particularly aimed to bring the tax system and economy of the 'sick man on the Bosphorus' (a phrase stemming from this period) up to a Western standard. The reforms ultimately failed because the Ottoman Empire was repeatedly attacked from the outside and the great powers in Europe increasingly interfered in its internal affairs, and after the empire's sovereign default of 1875 there were no funds left to modernize its administration. Added to this was the strain of accommodating a total of approximately four million refugees from the Caucasus and Balkans; this tradition of acceptance may help explain why Turkey tolerated the influx of more than three million Syrians largely without complaint.

Instead of reforms, the last long-reigning Sultan Abdülhamid II (r. 1876–1909) pivoted to autocratic rule and promoted Islam as a unifying bond. The devout monarch shuttered the parliament which had been convened in 1876, persecuted his opponents using the police and a system of informants, and rejected Western influences (it is no wonder that Erdoğan reveres this sultan and celebrates him in expensive TV series produced for the state broadcaster TRT). This Islamization, together with ongoing unrest in the Ottoman Empire from 1876, seemed to confirm Orientalist European prejudices about the 'Turkish yoke'. But autocracy and the religious legitimation of it were not unique to the Ottoman Empire; the Russian Empire went in a similar direction under the last Tsar Nicholas II. The result in both cases was growing violence, conflicts between different ethnic groups and religious communities, and corruption.

The similarities between the two empires do not end there. Social and political tensions led to the first Russian Revolution in 1905, which, in turn, inspired the Young Turks' revolution of 1908. The nation-states in Eastern Europe were not just 'founded' after 1918; they were the product of national revolutions. In this respect, there are parallels between the two Russian Revolutions and the founding of the Republic of Turkey, which took place during a war. There are also connections between the revolutionary upheaval in both countries. The Bolsheviks initially sympathized with the Turkish republicans and sent them weapons and money in a critical phase of the Turkish War of Independence. The republican-nationalist revolution was longer lasting, however; Turkey still exists today, while the Soviet Union fell apart in 1991.

Like the Soviet Union, the Republic of Turkey was founded as a democracy, though it was actually a developmental dictatorship in its first two decades. This was the only way Atatürk could push through his bold reforms, ranging from the abolition of the caliphate (lest Istanbul become the Rome of Muslims, which the head of state did not want) to writing reforms and new clothing laws. The young Turkish republic ruthlessly persecuted its national minorities, but this violence pales in comparison to the Soviet Union, where collectivization and the Great Terror at the end of the 1930s claimed around six million victims. Both states were pioneers in granting equal rights to women; women in Turkey were allowed to vote and stand for election locally in 1930, and they achieved full national suffrage in 1934. It was another ten years before France – the republic that served as a model for Turkey – granted women universal suffrage, and it took even longer in Turkey's neighbouring states in South East Europe.

In light of these developments, it was logical for Turkey to align itself more closely with the democratic West after the Second World War. The republic received aid through the Marshall Plan, joined NATO at the same time as Greece in 1952, and entered into the previously mentioned Agreement of Association with the EEC in 1963. Considering this, it is easy to understand Turkey's expectation that it would be accepted into the EC and then the EU, and its disappointment at continually being passed over. This development, too, happened in stages, starting with the introduction of the visa requirement (German Chancellor Schmidt said in internal discussions in 1980 that Germany should not become 'some Turkish province'[10]), followed by the violation of the Agreement of Association in 1986, and the repeated deferment of EU membership during the EU's expansion in 1995, 2004 and 2007. The opening of accession negotiations with

Turkey in the early 2000s had sparked new hope but ended in disappointment once again.

Just as Romania and Bulgaria were being accepted into the EU, French president Sarkozy declared that Turkey was not part of Europe.[11] This made headlines in the EU for a day, but in Ankara and Istanbul it left the impression that, no matter how much Turkey adapted to Western standards and values, it would never be part of the exclusive club. Sarkozy's comments were rooted in French domestic politics; the acceptance of more and more new EU members was unpopular in France, and most French citizens had voted against a European Constitution and thus a deepening of the union in 2005. An honest response to Turkey's accession request would be to say that the EU is incapable of expanding for the foreseeable future.

Instead of showing humility, the French president resorted to sloganeering, proving once against that the borders between right-wing populism and the conservative political mainstream are blurry (others have also doubled down on dissociating themselves from Turkey and specifically Erdoğan in recent years, including Dutch prime minister Mark Rutte, German politicians and both the conservative Austrian People's Party and the right-wing populist Freedom Party of Austria). Such comments can have serious consequences, particularly when a country lacks self-confidence – something the Turkish state tries to conceal by propagating nationalism instead. In the years that followed, the insulted Erdoğan turned away from the EU and lost interest in joining it. Some European politicians were initially relieved, but the repercussions were disastrous for Turkish domestic policy.

These observations are not intended to be a belated plea for accepting Turkey into the European Union. Aside from Erdoğan's dictatorial rule and all the political problems associated with it, it would be difficult to accommodate a country which has a larger population than any other EU state. For the foreseeable future, the European Union will be busy grappling with Brexit, the tensions following the 'refugee crisis', the rule of law in new member states and other internal conflicts. But the EU's inability to absorb new members is a problem that has nothing to do with democratic, political or any other deficits on the part of Turkey.

In Germany, pointing fingers at Turkey has also contributed to the alienation of many Turkish citizens who are second- or third-generation residents of the country. There are a number of reasons for their limited integration, not least that the guest workers and their descendants lost out in the socioeconomic shifts of the past decades: the structural changes in German industry since the 1980s, production moving to Eastern Europe since the 1990s and new competition in the labour market from East Germans and immigrants from Eastern Europe. A lack of social permeability in the German education system has exacerbated the problems. There are, of course, also group-specific reasons for the problems in the labour market and schools, including discrimination against women and girls, which is clearly apparent in education statistics and cannot be attributed to the German school system.[12]

In the 2000s, public debate in Germany about the complex problems of integration was driven by one thing above all else: Thilo Sarrazin's book *Deutschland schafft sich ab* (Germany Is Doing Away With Itself). Sarrazin, Berlin's former finance senator, made bold claims for someone with absolutely no expert knowledge of the Turks living in Germany or any other (post-)migrants. In essence, Sarrazin's book was deterministic, biologistic, insulting and misogynist to boot. Sarrazin described girls and young women of Turkish origin as *Kopftuchmädchen* ('headscarf girls') who had too many children and raked in welfare benefits. The response to the book in Germany was largely negative, but the insult could not be undone.

Sarrazin's theories were not new. Back in 2002, Hans-Ulrich Wehler (1931–2014), Germany's most prominent post-war historian, spoke in multiple interviews and articles about the *Türkenproblem*, or 'Turkish problem'. He evoked the Turkish Wars as the 'incarnation of antagonism', associated the presence of a Muslim minority with the terrorist attacks of 11 September 2001, stoked demographic fears (because the Turks living in Germany supposedly had so many children) like Sarrazin would later on, and denied that the Turks living in Germany were capable of integration.[13] Wehler also equated Turks with Muslims, as did Sarrazin. It never occurred to either of them that not everyone from a predominantly Islamic country is necessarily devout. This conflation almost inevitably forces Turks living in Germany (and the refugees from the Middle East who have arrived since 2015) to identify with Islam. There is no denying that Turkey's growing Islamization has an effect on the Turks living in Germany, as more people in both countries are committing themselves to religion and religious values. But the Republic of Turkey was founded by a convinced atheist, a fact that the current ruling party (the AKP) uses to vilify Atatürk as a Freemason, drinker and immoral person. This secular legacy exists, too, and it could become more significant again as the generations change, just as Islam has since the 1990s.

An essay is not long enough for an in-depth sociological analysis of the people of Turkish origin living in Germany and other EU states. Suffice to say that, compared to Austria or France, Germany is not doing so badly. Over time, a German-Turkish middle and upper class has developed which accounts for more than a quarter of this population group and has a median household income that is above the German average. Five per cent of people with family ties in Turkey (please forgive the vague formulation, but along with Sunni Turks there are many Kurds and Alevis) are very wealthy, earning more than 150 per cent of the German median income.[14] They include Uğur Şahin and Özlem Türeci, who developed the Covid-19 vaccine at BioNTech and were immediately co-opted by German politicians as representatives of a successful immigrant society.

After all the praise heaped upon them by the German chancellor, the president and the heads of the federal states, they probably do not feel rejected or discriminated against by the majority society. But surveys show that most German Turks do feel this way, even if they say at the same time that they are individually very satisfied with their lives. This discrepancy, the alienation of a part of the minority from German majority society and Erdoğan's electoral successes amongst Turks living abroad (who can vote in Turkish elections as long as they are still citizens) are enough to continually reignite debates about the integration of German Turks and the treatment of Turkey and the Turks living in Germany. In recent years, however, this integration debate has been conducted mainly with the representatives of religious organizations, which once again has to do with the traditional conflation of Turks and Muslims. Meanwhile, secular associations and stakeholders, like the German-Turkish societies that can be found in every big German city, have been pushed into the background, as have all the descendants of guest workers who only tenuously identify with Turkey, along with Kurds, Alevis and other small groups. As a consequence, even the majority society has wound up externally promoting identification with Islam instead of nurturing the potential of the post-migrants who arrived in Germany long ago and have had more positive experiences in the country.

This dialogue with Turks living in Germany and with Turkey itself needs to be conducted with a long-term perspective in mind, with an eye to the time after Erdoğan, who is already approaching 70 (Putin is ahead of him by two years) and whose party lost the important municipal election in Istanbul in 2019. The president will do his utmost to ensure that the anniversary of Turkey's foundation in 2023 is celebrated in accordance with his vision – and he undoubtedly envisions Turkey as an Islamic republic. The massive support for this vision has to do with Turkey's difficult relationship with the EU as well as past and present debates about the Europeanness of Turkey. But the state was founded as a European republic, and this legacy is not easily extinguished.

Russia in contemporary European history

Unlike Turkey, Russia's place in European history is indisputable. This applies to the Soviet Union, too, even though the Cold War was occasionally waged with civilizational arguments and the majority of Russian territory lies in Asia. After 1991, the 'Russian question' became, in some respects, a counterpart to the 'German question' of the nineteenth and early twentieth centuries. Russia is too big to be integrated into the existing European order, but it is too economically weak to exist on its own. This is true even if, like Putin, we conceive of the 'Russian world' (*russkiy mir*) as an expansive imperial project encompassing all Russian-speaking minorities in the Russian Federation's neighbouring states. This ethno-cultural understanding of a nation, as embodied by the term *russkiye* (meaning ethnic Russians), is very dangerous; the term *rossiyane* (meaning citizens of Russia), which is found in the name of the state itself – *Rossiya* – represents a more open, citizenship-based concept of the nation.

Much of Russian society views the end of the Soviet Union as a defeat, and President Putin referred to the collapse of the empire as the 'greatest geopolitical disaster of the 20th century'.[15] Russia did indeed lose control of nearly all the territories it had acquired during its long westward expansion starting in the seventeenth century. Most painful was the loss of Ukraine, the conquest of which was once used by the Russian Empire to demonstrate its status as a great power.

But parting with an empire, like Turkey did after the First World War and Germany did after the second, always presents an opportunity. Gorbachev loosened Russia's hold on the Eastern Bloc because he realized that the Soviet Union was overstretched and, between unsustainable military spending and discounted gas and oil supplies, it is a drain on resources to dominate so many countries. The loss of the outer Soviet empire was not planned, of course, but rather the result of the democratic revolutions of 1989. When Boris Yeltsin dissolved the Soviet Union, and thus the inner empire, in 1991 after the coup against Gorbachev, he was also striving for consolidation, as the cohesion of the Russian Federation was threatened, especially in the Caucasus by the Chechen independence movement and other separatists.

The transformation of the 1990s plunged much of Russia's population into destitution and misery. Economic statistics show that the situation was as dire as it had been in the early 1930s in Germany or the USA, and Russian life expectancy dropped to the level of a developing country (under 60 years for men).[16] Widespread alcoholism and Russia's own elites were largely to blame for this, but the Western advisors who recommended rapid privatization and liberalization – thus contributing to the rise of the oligarchs – also played a part in Russia's social and economic catastrophe. Capitalism had always been viewed as a Western concept in Russia, and Soviet propaganda demonized it as such. In this respect, it was predictable that Russia's transformation would damage relations with the West and result in a Polanyian 'double movement' – in this case, a nationalist counter-movement.

Taking a longer historical view, the 1990s could be compared with the *Smuta* or Time of Troubles in the early seventeenth century, when Russia was also at risk of collapsing. Modest Mussorgsky's opera *Boris Godunov*, the Russian national opera *Ivan Susanin* (Stalin's favourite opera) and a number of plays and novels deal with this period. The topoi of the disintegration of the state and exploitation of Russia's vulnerability by devious Westerners (Poles play this part in *Boris Godunov* and

Ivan Susanin) are just as deeply ingrained in Russian identity as the desire to someday enjoy a life as orderly and prosperous as in Western Europe. The first Russians to fulfil this desire were the profiteers of privatization: the oligarchs.

Even though everyone knew the oligarchs had acquired their fortunes through criminal schemes during the privatization process and by exploiting their workers, they were welcomed in London, Vienna, Switzerland and all of Europe's finest resorts. Ordinary Russians, by contrast, had to put up with demeaning procedures when applying for a visa to travel to the EU. Anyone living in the remote provinces of the vast country would have to take an overnight train to one of the few consulates and then stand in line for hours from the crack of dawn. If any of their documents were missing or not accepted, the whole process would start again (Turks have faced the same problem since 1980 whenever they want to visit Germany). In this way, Western countries squandered an opportunity for social rapprochement. Furthermore, the preferential treatment they gave to thieves seemed to confirm communist propaganda about predatory capitalism.

On account of his country's internal weakness, President Yeltsin was restrained in his foreign policy and even passed up chances to expand Russia's sphere of influence again. In 1994, pro-Russian separatists in Crimea won a two-thirds majority in the regional parliamentary election. They wanted to integrate with Russia at the time but encountered closed doors in Moscow, so the pro-Russian movement soon fizzled out.[17] During the Bosnian War of 1992–5, Russia went along with Western policy even though it was directed against Serbia, traditionally a Russian ally. In principle, this could have been the time to consider having Russia join NATO to form a true North Atlantic alliance. But Russia was too unstable for this in the 1990s, and the USA was too fond of its role as the only superpower to share its leading position in the defensive alliance.

This phase of rapprochement ended in 1999, but not because of the imminent election and transfer of power to Vladimir Putin. The West was the driving force behind the deterioration of the relationship this time around. The spring of 1999 saw the first eastern expansion of NATO to include Poland, the Czech Republic and Hungary. This expansion was also a way for the USA to signal that it was leading a more dynamic and open Western alliance than the EU. Moscow grudgingly accepted this first round of expansion because it had no other choice. The new member countries were joining of their own free will in an effort to rapidly (re-)integrate with the West, and also because of their negative experiences under Russian occupation after 1956 and 1968.

Just two weeks later, NATO intervened in the Kosovo conflict and began a bombing campaign against Serbia. This intervention, too, was based on historical experiences in Bosnia-Herzegovina and the crimes committed there by Serbian paramilitary forces and army units during the war of 1991–5. NATO's simultaneous expansion and military intervention were just a coincidence, but the war against Milošević's Serbia led to a rupture with Russia nonetheless, even before Putin was appointed prime minister in August 1999 and then became president in May 2000.

As was so often the case after 1989, the USA and its allies justified their policies by claiming to defend human rights. The civilian population of Kosovo was, in fact, seriously threatened by war crimes and ethnic cleansing. But is it productive or right to use massive military force to prevent other forms of violence? Western double standards, a common trope in Russian propaganda, and yet something that cannot be denied to exist, were the problem here. Albanian refugees were able to return to their homes after the war, but NATO was unable to protect the Serbian minority in Kosovo. Approximately 200,000 Serbs (and Roma) fled from the region in 1999, but even that was not enough for the Albanian nationalists. Shortly before the fifth anniversary of NATO's intervention, these nationalists incited nationwide pogroms which led to the deaths of nineteen people. Most of the remaining minority groups in Kosovo fled in 2004. The USA was busy with the Iraq War at the time, and the European units of the Kosovo Force (KFOR) were taken by surprise. But NATO's insufficient preventive measures and inadequate response in Kosovo, and the USA's illegal invasion of Iraq, discredited the principle of humanitarian intervention (often referred to at the time as a 'responsibility to protect').

In another unfortunate case of synchronicity, NATO decided in 2004 to incorporate seven more countries in East Central and South East Europe, including traditional Russian allies like Bulgaria as well as the three former Soviet republics in the Baltic region. Once again, competition between the two big Western alliances played a role here. By ensuring that NATO expanded before the EU, Washington strengthened Eastern Europe's allegiance to the USA and reminded Brussels who was pulling the strings there.

Political scientists have debated ever since whether the expansion of the military alliance (Croatia and Albania joined in 2009, Montenegro in 2017 and North Macedonia in 2020) was an unnecessary provocation of the Russian Federation. The political scientist John Mearsheimer takes this view, arguing that the world is divided into different spheres of influence.[18] According to this thinking, the successor states of the Soviet Union are in a Russian area of interest which the West would be better off leaving alone. This neo-realist – and, it must be said, neo-imperialist – view might apply to the nineteenth century and the Cold War, but it ignores the fact that when Europe's empires collapsed in 1918 and 1991, what emerged were sovereign nation-states.

The historian Mary Elise Sarotte also takes a critical view of NATO's ongoing expansion. She claims that the alliance should have been enlarged only once.[19] But when was this enlargement supposed to take place? The newly sovereign and independent states in Eastern Europe were wary of Putin's growing aggression, which drove them into NATO's arms. Russia's needling grew worse in the early 2000s; Poland and Lithuania were repeatedly subjected to arbitrary economic boycotts, while a trade war plunged parts of Georgia into famine. This revealed the imperialist leanings of the Russian elites, who apparently did not understand that using a cudgel is not a constructive form of foreign policy. And Putin's background as a former KGB official increased the distrust in countries already inclined to be wary on account of their past experiences with Russia.

Putin began to revise history in his second term in office. In 2005 he declared National Unity Day (*den narodnogo edinstva*) to be a public holiday, replacing the annual celebration of the anniversary of the Russian Revolution. In doing so, he revived the memory of the invasion of Russia by the Polish-Lithuanian Commonwealth in the early seventeenth century. Poland-Lithuania was a great power at the time, and it exploited the succession crisis in Russia. Unlike Napoleon, the Polish-Lithuanian army was able to hold Moscow for more than three years before a Russian counter-offensive forced it to retreat. Most Russians know about this Time of Troubles either from school or the operas of Glinka and Mussorgsky.[20] The holiday was celebrated under the tsars, and Putin rescued it from historical obscurity to impress upon the public consciousness that nothing good comes from the West. This anti-Western and especially anti-Polish stance undergirded Russia's attacks on Ukraine in 2014 and 2022. These attacks were further bolstered by Stalinist and old imperialist notions of history in which Ukrainians are depicted as traitors to the great Russian nation, while Poles are depicted as agitators.

This view of history was the basis for Russia's two genocides in the 1930s, one against the Poles who had remained behind in the Soviet Union and became the first minority to fall victim to Stalin's Great Terror, and one against Ukrainians in the Holodomor during collectivization (though this was first and foremost a sociocide directed against the land-owning peasants known as kulaks). The West took little notice of Putin's introduction of this new holiday and its political ramifications. Only recently have Western experts on Russia more carefully read Putin's tracts on history, in which he announced the war on Ukraine back in the summer of 2021. Like Alexander II and Stalin, Putin views Ukraine as an invention he wants to erase from the map.

Foreign policy alone did not spoil Russia's relations with its Western neighbours, however; there were also too many ugly scenes on the ground. During a partnership with the university in Kaliningrad from 2004 to 2007 (I was working for the European University Viadrina in Frankfurt an der Oder at the time, which had a large proportion of Polish students), I saw first hand how Russian officials and members of the military dealt with the citizens of the new EU states. From the Russian perspective, there was an obvious hierarchy here. Russian officials would bark at German citizens and subject us to pointless bureaucracy at the embassy and border, but all in all we were dealt with correctly. I put up with the poor treatment because I knew how Russians (and Ukrainians, Belarusians, Georgians, etc.) were treated inside and outside of Western embassies. They had to queue for hours for visas, and their applications could be rejected at any time for trivial reasons (I once invited a colleague to give a lecture, but he was sent home by a German consular department because he had to prove he was a professor – apparently the invitation from my university was not proof enough). These bureaucratic procedures were humiliating, and they were tolerated largely without complaint by Russians and the citizens of other post-Soviet states, probably only because these people had been subject to even more arbitrary red tape before 1991. The way visa applicants and incoming visitors were dealt with was like a kind of retributive injustice, with Russia and Germany each treating the citizens of the other country poorly, or at least more poorly than necessary.

But the German students and professors stopped complaining as soon as they found out what was happening to their Polish counterparts. Polish truckers, bus drivers, lecturers and students all faced intolerable harassment when they applied for visas, crossed the border and spent time in Russia. The authorities delayed their visas until the applicants were forced to accept the most expensive option, they penalized Poles in Russia for supposedly having the wrong visas (even though the visas had been issued by the Russian consulate), and they communicated with them solely by shouting and ordering them around.

Was this because of Russia's old imperialist mindset, was it compensation for Russia's own complexes or was it a product of the general brutalization described in the essays and elegies of Nobel Prize winner Svetlana Alexievich? This hierarchical conception of Europe and its nations after 1991 could almost be described as postcolonial, but the social relations between Russians themselves speak against this. Unfortunately, the habit of punching down and mistreating fellow citizens as if they are subordinates shapes everyday life in Russia.

Russia's hierarchical treatment of its European neighbours corresponded to the geopolitical model which Putin has preached ever since taking office. This dialectical and social-Darwinist perspective, which is ultimately based on Soviet 'vulgar Marxism', conceives of world history as a permanent power struggle. In the fight for resources and spheres of influence, only one side can win. Violence is considered legitimate if it serves one's own interests, and suspicion ranks above trust.

When another two former Soviet republics – Georgia and Ukraine – moved closer to NATO after the 'colour revolutions' of 2003 and 2004, it was obvious that Russia would suspect it was being encircled. Did NATO go too far in the subsequent years, as critics often claim? In the case of Ukraine, no. After Russia invaded Georgia in 2008 – a military conflict which began with a poorly planned intervention in the breakaway region of South Ossetia – requests by Georgia and Ukraine for NATO membership were put on hold at the urging of Germany and France. But the USA and the new eastern member states did not want to entirely rule out the possibility of accession. This compromise, for which Angela Merkel bears the main responsibility, was the worst of all worlds, because it left Ukraine and Georgia in limbo. With the invasion of South Ossetia, Putin established military precedents in Georgia. The Russian army has stood at the gates of Tbilisi ever since and could intervene at any time if Georgia decided to insist on full national sovereignty.

Putin also did not trust Ukraine to remain neutral in the long term. He took advantage of the country's uncertain position between East and West and its internal conflicts during the revolution of 2014 and used this opportunity to occupy Crimea and intervene in the Donbas region. This makes it tremendously difficult to end the war now. Putin has destroyed the option of Ukrainian neutrality – because why would Ukraine agree to such a thing, seeing as neutrality has brought nothing but grief? What security guarantees would be needed to prevent the kind of near-daily shelling from Russian-controlled regions that Ukraine experienced in the Donbas after 2014?

Russia's aggression against Ukraine in 2014 and the full-scale war eight years later have inadvertently confirmed the decision of NATO's new members to join the alliance. These military actions have also triggered a new wave of accessions; even Sweden and Finland, which have been neutral for more than a century, have now joined NATO. With his aggressive foreign policy and wars against Ukraine, Putin has achieved the exact opposite of what he actually wanted. NATO now borders the Russian Federation from a distance of more than 2,000 kilometres.

Nonetheless, it is worth asking why the West was unable to more closely integrate Russia into its alliances and security systems after the country gained independence. There were half-hearted attempts at inclusion, like the Permanent Joint Council established in 1997 and the NATO-Russia Council which replaced it in 2002. But NATO's continued expansion and George W. Bush's decision to station missile systems in Central Europe after the invasion of Iraq destroyed the fragile trust. These missile plans were primarily about Iran and the threat to the USA from the Middle East, but the location of the planned defence facilities in Poland and Romania for intercepting enemy nuclear missiles in space (an idea going back to Ronald Reagan and his Strategic Defense Initiative, which was picked up again by Clinton in 1999) spoke for itself: the sites surrounded Russia, not Iran. Technically speaking, national missile defence is a utopian idea, and such a system would probably offer little protection against missiles with multiple warheads or faster intercontinental ballistic missiles. The supposed security gains do not outweigh the loss of trust and the cost. But the arms race during the Cold War was not rational either – so in this sense, American policy is also following a long-established pattern.

The EU also needs to ask itself why it did not provide more assistance to Russia during the disastrous 1990s or Putin's first term, when the Russian president was still relatively liberal and reform-minded. France and Germany were too self-centred at the time, with all attention focused on the expansion of the EU. But even then, they knew the expansion would change the relationship between Russia and the EU. Missed opportunities do not come around again, but it is important to bear them in mind when it comes to rebuilding Ukraine.

NATO as a military alliance is often contrasted with the EU as an economic alliance. This contrast is used especially by critics of the USA and anti-Americans (of whom there are more than enough in Western Europe) to differentiate the two most important Western alliances and portray the EU primarily as peacemaker. But this view is too naïve and does not align with how the EU is perceived externally, something Brussels has taken little interest in for a long time. Putin considers both NATO and the EU to be 'geopolitical' opponents. The relationship between the EU and Russia is inevitably tense, not least because the largest territorial state in the world cannot join the union – at least not in its current structure. In principle, Russia might have been able to join NATO in the mid-1990s, but the alliance would have had to define a new mission and develop new structures.

Brussels responded to this dilemma by developing an EU 'neighbourhood policy' after its major eastern enlargement.[21] The first concept paper on this policy from 2003 lists all the neighbours of the expanded union, including Russia, Ukraine, the Caucasus states, Turkey, Israel, Egypt and the Maghreb. Russia was granted a special form of cooperation in the context of a fuzzily formulated policy known as the Northern Dimension, though exactly what this entailed was never explained in detail. Russia brusquely rejected this offer, which was not really an offer at all. By the time the concept was reformulated in 2006, Brussels had at least learned that Russia did not want to be lumped together with small and medium-sized countries. But all the other neighbouring states in Eastern Europe, the Middle East and North Africa continued to be lumped together, which only makes sense if you consider yourself the centre of the universe and think everyone else revolves around you.

Sweden and Poland subsequently initiated the EU's Eastern Partnership in 2008, a joint initiative including Ukraine, Belarus, Moldova and the Caucasus states which was designed to limit Russian influence. Bypassing Russia was one understandable reaction to Putin's increasingly open, neo-imperialist claims to power in the post-Soviet sphere. But the Eastern Partnership unintentionally strengthened Russian fears of encirclement. It included no security guarantees for the partner states, because the EU is not a defence alliance.

The annexation of Crimea and intervention in the Donbas were a historical turning point. The transformation that was envisioned after 1989 was based on the premise that the post-communist countries could develop within their internationally recognized borders. This principle also applied to the states that emerged from the Soviet Union and Yugoslavia. A war was waged for four years in the former Yugoslavia to enforce this principle and ensure that the country's constituent republics could continue to exist as independent states.

Putin ended this two-decade period of peace with his first attack on Ukraine in 2014. While Russia managed to occupy and annex Crimea in a flash, the Russian-backed 'separatists' employed massive military force against Ukraine in the Donbas region. Despite this, the West consistently referred to the war as the 'Ukraine conflict', suggesting that it was an internal problem brought on by Ukraine itself. Another notorious claim was that eastern and western Ukraine were deeply divided. This view, which was held even by some Ukrainian intellectuals,[22] is not entirely wide of the mark, as tensions did rise between regions and their respective strongest parties during elections and the Orange Revolution. However, regional voting behaviour was no more varied than in any other large European country; in Germany, too, people in the north, south, east and west vote for very different parties. Viktor Yanukovych, who was ousted as Ukraine's president in 2014, had his power base in Donetsk, but the separatist movement in the Donbas was never as strong as it was in Crimea.

Focusing on the so-called separatists – whose leadership and military forces were riddled with Russian citizens and Federal Security Service (FSB) agents – blinded the rest of the world to the larger dimensions of the conflict. On one side is the Russian Federation, which has evolved from an authoritarian system into a hard dictatorship since Putin's second term. On the other side is Ukraine, which has continually moved in the direction of liberal democracy ever since the Orange Revolution, and especially since 2014. For all of this democracy's flaws, it is important to remember that Ukraine has held two free and fair parliamentary and presidential elections since the Revolution of Dignity. This makes Ukraine more democratic than Hungary, an EU member where power over the media, judiciary and state resources is distributed in such a lopsided way that the opposition has no chance against Orbán and Fidesz. Power was also transferred quite smoothly from each outgoing to incoming president and government in Kyiv, something that unfortunately cannot be said for the USA since the storming of the Capitol.

The attack on Ukraine is therefore also a war on democracy which is evidence of a fundamental systemic rivalry. Political and cultural elites in the West (especially Germany) were too slow to realize and still do not fully understand that Russia's two wars against Ukraine are also a declaration of war against the EU and a free Europe.

After the annexation of Crimea and the war in the Donbas, Germany in particular acted as though relations with Russia could largely continue in the same vein as before. Former German chancellor Gerhard Schröder defended Russia and demonstratively cultivated a friendship with Vladimir Putin. Schröder's activities for the Russian state-owned Rosneft, and similarly well-paid positions for a whole raft of other Western politicians (including former Austrian chancellors Wolfgang Schüssel, Alfred Gusenbauer and Christian Kern) and lobbyists like Paul Manafort (Trump's former campaign manager who also worked for Viktor Yanukovych), confirm Putin's impression that Western elites can be bought. When Malaysia Airlines flight MH17, a passenger airliner mostly carrying Dutch citizens, was downed by a Russian missile over the 'separatist'-controlled Donbas in the summer of 2014, it briefly caused outrage. But the world grew accustomed to the fact that military forces equipped by Russia in the breakaway republics of Donetsk and Luhansk were continuing to shell Ukrainian territory. The 15,000 casualties of this eight-year war died largely disregarded.

Sanctions against Russia remained half-hearted and impacted only a few individuals and companies. From Putin's geopolitical perspective, therefore, the first military attack on Ukraine in 2014 paid off. The attack severely weakened Ukraine's strategic position, allowing the Russian army to subsequently attack from the south as well, which is exactly what it did in 2022. Furthermore, the annexation of Crimea was a very popular move in Russia and gave Putin a big boost in the polls. And the Donbas gave Putin a security against the further expansion of NATO, because the alliance cannot accept new members involved in a territorial conflict with a neighbouring state since this would trigger Article 5 of its treaty, which calls for collective defence.

Despite these conflicts – as well as the Western sanctions and continued shelling of Ukrainian territory from the Russian-occupied Donbas – the German government pressed ahead with the construction of the Nord Stream 2 pipeline. This came at the strategic and financial expense of Ukraine, and it was also vehemently protested by Poland and other new EU member states. The USA even threatened to impose sanctions on German companies involved in building the pipeline. But on account of the fractured relationship between Trump's government and the German government – not least thanks to the impertinent US ambassador in Berlin – these threats wound up achieving the opposite of what was intended. The transatlantic confrontation also drew attention away from the actual relevant argument, which was that the second Baltic Sea pipeline was a strategic mistake for Germany because it would make the country even more dependent on Russian gas.

The pipeline deal cannot be blamed on the German government alone, much less on Angela Merkel. A coalition of interests was behind it, one which included current and former SPD politicians (Putin corrupted Gerhard Schröder not only by securing a board member's salary for him, but also by pulling strings which enabled the former chancellor to adopt two very young Russian children, something that would have been impossible under German adoption law considering Schröder's age). The coalition also comprised big corporations that made money off of the pipeline's construction and wanted to continue getting cheap gas, as well as the government of Mecklenburg-Western Pomerania, which hoped the pipeline would offer economic prospects to this relatively poor federal state. Local elites in Mecklenburg had previously opened their doors to criminal Russian investors in the 2000s, and Russian money was even used to establish a 'climate foundation' – a case of state corruption, since the entire endowment capital came from Moscow.[23] The politicians in Mecklenburg and Berlin who were involved in the project presumably dreamed of turning the pipeline's end point near Greifswald into a gas hub on the scale of the oil port of Rotterdam.

For Putin and the investors close to him, all of this seemed to confirm their suspicion that the West was ultimately interested only in economic advantages, not in values or preserving the post-1989 order. The Russian president also managed to play off different EU countries against one another, as well as Republicans against Democrats in the USA, and Trumpian conservatives against the 'hawks' left over from the Cold War. The realization that Russia could break every principle of international law and still do good business with the West, and then the lightning-fast capture of Crimea, were like an invitation for Putin to attack Ukraine again, this time on a broad front.

It is also important to not underestimate the self-radicalization of Russia's right-wing nationalist regime. At some point, Putin himself apparently started to believe the lies he was telling about Ukraine. The myth Moscow began spreading in 2014 that the Ukrainian revolution was actually a fascist coup is patently absurd, but it has found a remarkably receptive audience in the West. The European Left in particular fell prey to the old fallacy that the enemy of my enemy must somehow be my friend. For many anti-Americans in Europe, the enemy was the USA, and all of their prejudices were confirmed first by the illegal invasion of Iraq and then by Trump.

Putin has squandered these Western sympathies with his second attack on Ukraine and the massive war crimes being committed by Russian forces. A few right-wing populists and neo-fascists still admire him, but they are not quite as open about it as they used to be. The bigger threat to Ukraine is the world's growing indifference. The general public in the West was appalled by the mass graves filled with executed Ukrainian civilians in Bucha, Borodianka and Motyzhyn, just as it was shocked thirty years earlier by the images that came out of the Bosnian cities of Višegrad, Prijedor and Foča. But the condemnation of Russia's crimes was not nearly as universal outside of Europe (see India, for example – apparently the increasingly authoritarian Indian prime minister and the Russian president get along quite well). The almost total annihilation of Mariupol, which certainly cost more lives than the genocide of Srebrenica, was witnessed with dismay, but it had no further military consequences. By contrast, Srebrenica was one of NATO's main justifications for finally intervening in Bosnia in 1995 after dithering for a long time.

Like Serbia in the 1990s, Russia has an advantage in that there has not yet been any combat in its own territory. Putin can therefore continue to sell the war as a 'special operation'. Only the growing number of zinc coffins holding fallen Russian soldiers might change Russian attitudes towards the war – which is not allowed to be referred to as such. Even when Putin announced the 'partial mobilization' of reservists in September 2022, he avoided the term war. At the same time, however, if most Russians remain largely unaffected by the war and never see the damage being done, Russian society could go along with Putin's warfare for a long time (regarding the Russian war against Ukraine, also see the last chapter). This is what happened in Serbia, and unfortunately the same thing occurred along the front lines in the eastern Donbas between 2014 and 2022, where the shelling never stopped. As the violence continues externally, it becomes easier for Russia to justify the use of violence internally, not least in the form of random arrests and heavier censorship. Russia is ultimately at war with itself, and the war will only end when the country casts off its imperial legacy.

A window of opportunity to do so opened up in the 1990s, but it closed again as a result of Russia's crisis of democracy and failed economic reforms. The key moments here were the 1993 shelling of the Russian White House, the seat of the Russian parliament at the time, where opponents of the reforms had holed up (in 1991, Boris Yeltsin had courageously defended the seat of what was then the Supreme Soviet against the putschists), and the rouble crisis of 1998, when most of the Russian middle class sank into poverty again.

Neither of these traumatic moments had anything to do with the expansion of NATO or the EU; they were domestic problems first and foremost. Although the collapse of the rouble, along with many Russian banks, was a result of the Asia crisis (the first serious, de facto already global financial crisis after 1989), it was also a homegrown problem. Estrangement is always a two-way process, and in this case it was a tragedy which started in the 1990s and continues with no end in sight.

Someday there will be a debate about who was responsible for the new confrontation between East and West after the turn of the millennium, just as there was after the Cold War.[24] There were three different views in Cold War scholarship: a dogmatically anti-communist one which placed the blame on the Soviet Union and Stalin; a revisionist one in the 1960s which subjected Western policy to long-overdue self-critique; and a post-revisionist one in the shadow of the failure of détente, which emphasized the internal momentum of conflicts and fears, as well as the problem of mutual perceptions and all the associated misunderstandings. In this sense, this essay is post-revisionist.

While there is no chance that Putin's reign will end peacefully in Russia, it is conceivable that President Erdoğan will one day be voted out of office in Turkey. The economic crisis, which has been exacerbated by Covid-19 and the war against Ukraine, and Turkey's skyrocketing inflation speak in favour of this. Paradoxically, Erdoğan's hunger for power could be his undoing. Because he controls vast swathes of Turkey's politics, economy and, most recently, its central bank, there is no doubt about who is responsible for the country's misery. Corruption has also been on the rise, and it is now literally carved in stone in the form of the ostentatious presidential palace in Ankara.

Despite distancing itself from the West, Turkey is still a member of NATO and connected to the EU by a free trade agreement. Measured against this, Turkey's estrangement from its partners is dismaying. Erdoğan's evolution from a proponent of democracy (at least outwardly) to an autocrat and its deeper social and cultural roots will have to be picked apart by Turkish historians someday.

But as with Russia, Turkey's growing economic and domestic policy tensions do not bode well for the country's relations with the West and its neighbouring states. On the contrary, we can expect Erdoğan to continue peddling his nationalist rhetoric and foreign policy as a distraction from internal problems. Authoritarian-capitalistic systems have always had a tendency to engage in foreign policy escapades and imperialist expansion.

One difference between the two countries is that, as a major military power and supplier of commodities, Russia is actually capable of pursuing a neo-imperialist policy and waging a major war – as it is currently doing in Ukraine. Turkish neo-Ottomanism, by contrast, is a fantasy which fails to resonate in Turkey's neighbouring countries (with the exception, perhaps, of Turkic-speaking Azerbaijan). Nonetheless, this fantasy briefly took solid form during the short war between Armenia and Azerbaijan in the summer of 2020, when Turkish-made drones destroyed numerous Armenian tanks and tipped the scales in Azerbaijan's favour. But Turkey's soft power remains modest. Meanwhile, Russia has once again grown into a feared major power under Putin, spooking even the country's closest allies in the post-Soviet space. Russia will be hated in Ukraine for a very long time now – two generations at least. This is especially true for the largely Russian-speaking population in eastern and southern Ukraine, the very people Putin wanted to claim for his 'Russian world', the people he has ruthlessly gunned down and bombed instead.

Despite all of this, I will continue to read Tolstoy, see Chekhov plays and listen to Tchaikovsky. Putin can no more destroy this cultural heritage than Erdoğan can destroy the Republic of Turkey.

6

Eastern Europe as a Pioneer
Polanyi's Pendulum Swings to the Right

Karl Polanyi's great transformation was open-ended and left room for optimism. Polanyi's lack of pessimism was not a foregone conclusion considering what he had lived through: the counter-revolutionary White Terror in Hungary with its violent anti-communism and antisemitism, the demise of the republic in his adopted Austrian home, the rise of Hitler, the Second World War and the industrial mass extermination of Europe's Jews, which he certainly knew about while living in exile in England. Like his contemporaries Joseph Roth and Stefan Zweig, Polanyi could have fallen into despair in the face of the events around him. But he did not, and the last chapter of his book is full of the hope that modern industrialized society could bring about greater freedom and justice provided that capitalism was tamed and 'embedded' in it.

The opposite was obviously true from the 1980s onward, when capitalism was disembedded. This was not a natural process emerging from economic dynamics; like the laissez-faire capitalism described by Polanyi, it was a product of political will. The USA forged ahead here, affirming its role as the leading political and economic power in the West. The strategy behind Reaganomics was to generate new capital flows, investments and growth by deregulating and liberalizing the financial sector. In keeping with this, the USA passed a law in 1982 which allowed American savings and loan associations to lend to companies and massively expand their business with consumer and property loans. A real estate bubble developed in the space of just a few years – a harbinger of the global financial crisis of 2008–9, though it only affected the USA at the time. This bubble burst in the Savings and Loan (S&L) crisis of 1985, resulting in the insolvency of more than 1,000 S&L institutions. The losses amounted to over 400 billion dollars and had to be covered by the Federal Deposit Insurance Corporation, a state institution. All in all, the S&L crisis cost American taxpayers 124 billion dollars, and the much-maligned state had to intervene for the first time to prevent a chain reaction and the collapse of the financial industry. The stock market boom ended on 19 October 1987 – Black Monday – when the Dow Jones Industrial Average dropped 22 per cent, Wall Street's biggest one-day loss in its history to that point. But these financial and stock market crises, along with growing government debt, did not change the course of America's economic policy. George H.W. Bush, Reagan's long-standing vice president, defeated his Democratic challengers with ease in the 1988 elections to become president himself.

British conservatives also won two elections back to back in the 1980s, even though Margaret Thatcher's actions against trade unions and privatization of the railway, postal service and other state-owned companies were highly controversial. But the Iron Lady also got lucky. During her first term, her insistence on a resolute military operation in the Falklands decided the war for the UK, and she was later helped by the Labour Party's left turn, which no more appealed to Britons than Walter Mondale's Keynesian election platform did to Americans in 1984.[1] The UK additionally profited from the development of the North Sea oil and gas fields. Without this income, the UK would have been deep in the red in its balance of payments, just at it had been in the 1970s when it was eventually forced to apply for an emergency loan from the International Monetary Fund. Economists and economic historians have tended to overlook this special factor when evaluating Thatcherism, however. The UK's radical deindustrialization was an indirect consequence of the North Sea oil boom, because without this new energy source it would have been difficult to sustain Thatcher's fight against the miners' union and the loss of production through strikes and pit closures. Neoliberalism thus became firmly established in both the USA and UK in the 1980s, despite all the crises and conflicts.

A 'market society' cannot remain stable in the long term; according to Polanyi, only democratic socialism can. But there is a broad spectrum between these two poles. In the post-war period, it ranged from social market economies to the 'third way' of Yugoslavia and other non-aligned states. When Polanyi published his magnum opus in 1944, other options included Stalinism and so-called people's democracies (which Stalin brought into line in 1947–8), while the Labour Party in the UK advocated a democratic version of socialism. Polanyi did not comment on these options in *The Great Transformation* but instead looked far back into the past. In the final pages of his dense book, he made a case for a Christian-Jewish ethics and the early socialism of Robert Owen. Polanyi can therefore be interpreted in any number of ways, which may explain why he remains so popular amongst left-leaning intellectuals today, and why prominent social scientists have always foreseen yet another 'Polanyian moment'.

This was the case in the early 1990s, when the recession of 1992 seemed to bring an end to Reaganomics and Thatcherism. It occurred again during neoliberalism's first global crisis around the turn of the millennium. The crisis in Asia plunged East and South Asia into their worst recession of the post-war period, and it also ended the boom in Chile and brought Russia to the brink of insolvency. The crash of the rouble, collapse of numerous Russian banks and new wave of mass impoverishment triggered a pivot towards authoritarianism. But looking at the 1990s, one could also conclude that the form of the political system followed that of the economy; in the later years of Boris Yeltsin's presidency, the hegemony of the oligarchs developed into a political oligarchy with Vladimir Putin at its head. The far-reaching Asia crisis was followed by the dot-com crisis and the stock market crash of 2001, which probably would have happened even without the terrorist attacks of September 11. And then came the global financial crisis, the full force of which also hit the EU and Eastern Europe.

On each occasion, academics and political observers expected the pendulum to swing left, at least towards more heavily regulated capitalism. And the Polanyian pendulum did initially move slightly to the left after these three socio-economic turning points at the start of the 1990s, in the early 2000s and in 2009. In the USA and UK, Bill Clinton and Tony Blair took over from conservative governments; in Germany, Gerhard Schröder defeated Helmut Kohl in 1998; the post-communists won elections a second time in Hungary and soon afterwards in Poland; and at the end of the decade, Barack Obama was elected president in the USA. Each event was connected to prior recessions and global crises of capitalism.

But none of these (social-)democratic politicians fundamentally changed their countries' economic and social policy. They all tried to move their centre-left parties even more to the centre. Their strategic aim was to represent a broad spectrum of opinions, secure a political majority and present themselves as forward-looking reformers. This, too, was very much in keeping with the logic of contemporary neoliberalism and the marketization of politics, which was always geared towards opinion polls and public relations. The social democrats also moved to the centre and away from their traditional voter base, because the unions had less reach than they once did. They had failed to adapt to the increasingly post-industrial labour market and embrace precariously employed workers and the new service proletariat. As a result of the weaker bond between unions and social democrats, the Left forgot how to talk to its former voter base. The new generation of left-wing politicians was recruited largely from universities and thus the middle class. The electoral victories of Barack Obama, François Hollande in France and Matteo Renzi in Italy after the global financial crisis only masked these problems. These politicians also won elections by moving to the centre and further changing the balance between left and right. This strategy on the part of American Democrats and European social democrats shifted the entire political coordinate system to the right.

No counterweight could be established further to the left because socialism – even in its Western variants – was delegitimized by the collapse of the Soviet Union and the Eastern Bloc. Now that so much time has passed, it might be easier to acknowledge that the failure of communism was a deep cut and even a loss for the West. I concede this reluctantly, because I met too many people prior to 1989 who had suffered under the communist dictatorship in every respect –professionally, physically and psychologically. But communism as an ideology (black books not withstanding) is still the intellectual child of the European Enlightenment.

The political coordinate system of liberal democracies shifted again in 2016, as if the weight of Polanyi's pendulum had ripped it right out of the ceiling, taking the entire political tableau with it. Now even centrists like Hillary Clinton, liberals like George Soros and seasoned Christian democrats like Angela Merkel and Jean-Claude Juncker were painted as nasty lefties – at least in the deeply partisan election campaigns conducted by the Right in the USA, UK, Italy, Austria, Poland and Hungary.

The right-wing populist victories came as a shock; neither pollsters nor political scientists had reckoned with a win for the Brexiteers or the Republicans hijacked by Trump. In historical hindsight, however, this lurch to the right was apparent much earlier. The rise of right-wing populists and nationalists started back in the mid-1990s – we need look no further than the political careers of Pat Buchanan, Jean-Marie Le Pen, Jörg Haider or Umberto Bossi (regarding Bossi, see the essay on Italy). In Germany, the right-wing fringe of the the Christian Democratic Union of Germany (CDU)/the Christian Social Union in Bavaria (CSU) was still integrated in the party, though the tenor of its migration policy differed only slightly from that of today's AfD. But if we want to understand this drift to the right, it is not enough to focus on the early right-wing populists and nationalists. Democracies are based on the competition of ideas, and not even dictators can entirely get around this. In this respect, the growing appeal of extreme right-wingers cannot be explained without looking at their political competitors.

This essay has focused on the Left so far, but it is important not to overlook the role of conservatives. Right-wing populists in Europe were able to take office for the first time thanks to the conservatives who entered into coalitions with them. Berlusconi appointed Lega Nord members as ministers in his four cabinets even though the Lega was under investigation by the Italian state security agency at times, and the Austrian People's Party (ÖVP) twice paved the way for the Austrian Freedom Party (FPÖ) to enter the Austrian government. Viktor Orbán could never have amassed so much power in the EU had his Fidesz party not been a member of the EPP (an alliance of Christian democratic parties). Even when Orbán ridiculed European Commission President Jean-Claude Juncker on campaign posters and forced the Central European University out of Hungary (an unprecedented action – not even the communists dared to close an entire university after 1945), this was not enough to get him thrown out of the EPP. Conservatives in Germany and Austria paid court to him for a long time because he positioned himself as an opponent of Angela Merkel's refugee policy. At least there has been a consensus amongst all German democratic parties to shut the AfD out of the government. The contribution of conservatives to the rise of right-wing populists is even more apparent in democracies with majority representation and a two-party system. In the UK and USA, Boris Johnson and Donald Trump managed to subvert and dominate their respective conservative parties. The number of prominent conservatives who resisted this could be counted on the fingers of two hands.

The spectre of fascism

Have Europe and the USA been sliding back in the direction of fascism since the *annus horribilis* of 2016? Following Polanyi's arguments, this would be one likely consequence of global laissez-faire capitalism. Though the elder stateswoman Madeleine Albright warned against fascism, and historians like Timothy Snyder have published handbooks on how to resist tyranny,[2] I am not sure whether history will end this way. Is Trump a fascist? If so, he would have mobilized a mass movement and paramilitary units during his presidency and led them into Washington himself in January 2021. This is obviously not how the storming of the Capitol played out, so any parallels with Mussolini's march on Rome almost exactly a hundred years ago do not amount to much.

We find yet more differences if we go back to the classic definition of fascism.[3] Trump did not establish a youth movement or develop a cult of masculinity (like Putin has with his infamous bare-chested photos), and besides, he is simply too old to embody the dawn of a new post-democratic age. But some core elements of fascism – namely, a cult of personality and violence – are present in a weakened form, including the idolatry of Trump by his followers. One of these devotees is presumably Tommy Zegan, who unveiled a gilded statue of the outgoing president at the Conservative Political Action

Conference in Orlando on 28 February 2021 (though the artist may simply be an enterprising businessman).

A hard core of Trump fans are also prepared to commit violence, as evidenced by the clashes and shootings against Black Lives Matter demonstrations. And Trump obviously has a certain charisma, otherwise the hijacked Republican party would not have remained so loyal to him after his defeat. This loyalty is astonishing at first glance because the two main parties have always turned away from their losing presidential candidates in the past. But Trump seems to still have his party firmly in his grasp, which puts him a position to install a candidate he has anointed – or to run again himself.

All the same, the institutions of American democracy withstood Trump, and even the US Army positioned itself against him in January 2021. And despite some flaws – including the politically polarizing majority vote system, making voting rights subject to the laws of individual states, and the overrepresentation of small rural states – the Constitution has one key strength: it limits the president's term in office and thus the amount of damage a single president can do. This has not prevented Trump from running again, however. Trumpism – a term admired by its namesake because it feeds his narcissism, and a concept which, unlike fascism, is only minimally about ideology – will therefore continue to exist in the USA, at least as long as the former president is still around.

For all the differences between the interwar period and today, the spectre of fascism is currently more present in Eastern Europe than in the USA. This has to do with the relatively short time in which (neo-)liberal democracy could become established and the long tradition of right-wing radicalism. But it is important to differentiate here, too, because while the authoritarian rulers in Poland and Hungary in the 1920s and 1930s were reactionary and conservative, they were not fascist leaders like Hitler and Mussolini. True fascists, such as the

Polish Falangists under Bolesław Piasecki or the Hungarian Arrow Cross Party under Ferenc Szálasi, were either unable to prevail or could only do so under certain circumstances. But Piasecki's breathtaking career in communist Poland (where he rose to become leader of the pro-regime Catholic PAX movement) demonstrates that this tradition lived on after 1945, and that national communism and fascism were not far removed from one another.

Viktor Orbán is a charismatic speaker, but he is also too old and lumbering to be the leader of a classic fascist movement. He does not use violence, and while he muzzles his critics, he does not throw them in jail.

When political scientists and historians are not quite sure how to categorize a phenomenon, they like to use the term 'hybrid', and the recent transitions to authoritarianism in various countries have indeed been fluid. Viktor Orbán has governed Hungary since 2010, and he has employed various tricks to ensure that he does not have to relinquish power for the foreseeable future.[4] He apparently learned a lesson from his own defeat after his first term of office from 1998 to 2002, and the voting system has been manipulated so that his Fidesz party would have to fall well below 40 per cent to lose the majority of seats in the national assembly. The national assembly has also lost some of its budgetary rights, there is no longer any separation of powers, and the media has been brought into line with the government. The only hope for the opposition lies in the critical websites and portals that continue to appear online.

The sociologist Bálint Magyar refers to this as a 'mafia state' in which nothing happens without the patronage of Fidesz.[5] Orbán has institutionalized and cemented his party's dominance through a system of councils which subverts the state at every level and ensures well-paid jobs for his supporters. One example of this is the parliament's budget committee, to which the government can delegate three members with a term of between six and twelve years. Another example are the privatized universities that have been transformed into foundations whose governing bodies are also populated with Orbán supporters serving very long terms in office. A new government would therefore have to annul the current constitution to re-establish a pluralist democracy and restore the rule of law. But a majority large enough to amend the constitution is out of reach even in the next elections (which are due to take place in 2026). Essentially, the constitution would have to be breached in order to restore the division of powers and rule of law. Such an approach could quickly lead to violent clashes, however – and Orbán, like Trump, has followers who are prepared to take up arms.

Hungary's governing party is not as omnipresent as the communists were before 1989, but nothing gets done in public administration, the media or state-affiliated organizations unless you have close ties to Fidesz. This excessive power leads to rampant corruption which extends far into the private sector. To mention just one famous example: Lőrinc Mészáros, a plumber and childhood friend of Orbán, has become the richest man in Hungary, and the government funded the construction of a football stadium with a completely excessive capacity in his hometown. But the EU has also played a part in his phenomenal rise 'from plumber to billionaire', since Mészáros has enriched himself mainly through construction contracts funded by the EU. And Fidesz was only able to finance its expensive 2022 election campaign (and all of its previous election sweeteners) thanks to the copious flow of EU funds.

The ubiquitous corruption and patronage in Hungary pose a dilemma for young people looking to enter the job market after graduating. They either have to reconcile themselves with the system and find a patron, or live with the prospect of severely diminished career opportunities. Because of this and the low salaries in Hungary, young people are leaving the country in droves.

But the low wages are attractive to international investors, particularly Germans. Orbán gave Hungary an additional competitive advantage with the labour reform law passed at the end of 2018, which allows Hungarian employers to demand up to 400 hours of overtime from their workers each year and then take three years to compensate them for it.[6] For the German automotive industry, these location advantages – to use the language of investors and business consultants – apparently outweigh the dismantling of democracy and the constitutional state.

BMW has been building a factory in Debrecen since 2020. Audi and Mercedes have been in Hungary for a longer time, but they have also not proven themselves to be defenders of Hungarian democracy or the rule of law. Will the alliance between German industry and an authoritarian regime pay off in the long run? BMW cannot have failed to notice how the Hungarian government dealt with foreign investors after the financial crisis of 2008–9; the country clearly aims to nationalize corporate profits.[7] The government's treatment of the Central European University – both an academic institution and a mid-sized company with more than 1,000 employees – shows that the rule of law now exists only on paper. The exodus of young people has further exacerbated the shortage of skilled workers. BMW's major shareholders, who like to present themselves to the German public as philanthropists, are now responsible for strengthening right-wing populism twice over: in Hungary by validating Orbán's government, and in Germany by contributing to the loss of well-paid jobs, which can lead to fears of social decline that prompt voters to turn to protest parties.

If a German firm wants to move its production to Hungary, it can seek advice from the German-Hungarian Chamber of Commerce and Industry, which represents approximately 900 companies and institutions. German investors are clearly interested in close relations with Viktor Orbán and the Fidesz party. In 2017, the German Business Club presented its German-Hungarian Friendship Award to Mária Schmidt, one of the ideologues behind Fidesz who takes the view that the EU is a new version of the Soviet Union, Merkel ruined Germany and the Jews were not only victims but also perpetrators.[8]

The increasingly crude nationalism from the ranks of Fidesz points to a mechanism I mentioned in the second essay, namely, that by spreading hate propaganda about external and internal enemies, right-wing populists wind up radicalizing themselves. This stems in part from the constant repetition of the propaganda; Orbán and Schmidt, two former Soros scholarship beneficiaries, have probably come to believe that the billionaire in his nineties is actually the leader of a Jewish-liberal world conspiracy, and that the EU is a union of left-wing republics. And this hate propaganda crosses borders, directed as it is against Germany and Austria, particularly social democratic Vienna. In 2018, János Lázár, the Hungarian Minister of the Prime Minister's Office at the time, shot a short film which depicted Vienna as a hotbed of multiculturalism where 'real' Austrians no longer felt safe, nearly all the women wore headscarves and the 'native' population was being replaced by Muslims.[9]

This could be dismissed as a fleeting incident, but while I was on a lecture tour in Ukraine in the fall of 2019, I met a group of cheerful insurance agents who were enjoying some drinks in the expensive hotel that their boss had booked for them in Kyiv.[10] After the first round of beverages, they asked me if you could still go out onto the streets in Vienna at night and how dangerous the situation was. Their boss was from the part of Ukraine bordering Hungary and had apparently seen the film, or something similar to it, on Hungarian state television.

Poland is often mentioned in the same breath as Hungary, and PiS likes it that way. The head of the party, Jarosław Kaczyński, has repeatedly referred to Orbán as a role model. When it comes to analysing right-wing populism, Poland is fundamentally interesting because it thwarts the temptation to take an all-too-deterministic view of contemporary history as a direct line from neoliberalism to antiliberalism. Seemingly omnipresent phenomena like the crisis of parliamentary democracy and rise of right-wing populism can have very different origins depending on the country.[11] Circumstance – or contingency, as historians say – played a role in Poland, though this does not mean that structural factors should be ignored.

PiS won the 2015 parliamentary elections with 37.6 per cent of the votes because the previous liberal-conservative government was washed out after eight years in power. At the same time, the election result was an expression of protest against severe regional and social inequality and the short-term, poorly paid employment contracts that were frequently being offered even by state institutions (referred to in Poland as *śmieciówki*, or 'garbage contracts'). However, voter turn-out was also very low, meaning that not even 19 per cent of Poles eligible to vote actually opted for PiS. The fact that the party gained an absolute majority in parliament anyway can be attributed to the fragmentation of the left-wing parties (all of which just missed out on seats in parliament) and the weakness of the liberals.

After its first victory, PiS acted as if it had a two-thirds majority which would enable it to change the constitution. This kind of power grab has also been seen in other countries as soon as right-wing populist parties come to power. Despite brutal and sometimes unconstitutional power politics, PiS is popular thanks to its generous social welfare policies, and it won the parliamentary elections again in 2019. The child benefit of 500 złotys (approximately 120 euros), which almost all experts had previously dismissed as being unaffordable, has been a great success and actually even economical thanks to increased domestic demand. The child benefit is popular not only because it helps poor families, but also because it strikes a chord with the middle class. Though Poland has become wealthier since 1989 than at any other time in its history, this alone is not enough to make people feel truly secure.

Polanyi wrote about the memory of past misery, of social decline and unemployment, and such a memory is still very present in Poland.[12] The population's insecurity during the post-communist transformation goes some way towards explaining the popularity of the caring – but also, under the aegis of PiS, authoritarian – state. The feeling that the government is concerned even with local matters is clearly more appealing to Poland's rural and small-town populations than the promises of freedom from 1989.

Furthermore, anyone over the age of fifty in Poland grew up under an authoritarian regime. If it were up to Kaczyński, they would get a new version of the people's republic, only this time it would not be socialist but rather nationalist-conservative – a kind of Catholic Polish People's Republic. Like Orbán, PiS is trying to bring the media under its control. This happened quickly with Polish public television because the government had direct access to it. The news on TVP1, still the most important source of information for much of the population, only spreads government propaganda and rarely gives a voice to the opposition. The government's second step in 2020 was to buy most of the regional newspapers, which had previously been acquired by a German publishing group when they were privatized in the 1990s. They were purchased by Poland's largest energy company, Orlen, which is run by a former village mayor and member of PiS. The third step was taken in the autumn of 2021 when the licence for the private broadcaster TVN was suspended despite international protests. The licence was eventually extended again following protests from the USA, since the broadcaster is owned by an American corporation. In the end, Polish President Andrzej Duda vetoed the bill known as Lex TVN, thus heading off another attack on the freedom of the press in Poland. But pressure from the Biden administration played a part as well; Donald Trump would never have taken a stand for press freedom and an independent television station in Poland.

Growing corruption is another problem facing PiS and all right-wing populist and nationalist ruling parties. Though Kaczyński himself lives a modest lifestyle, scandals piled up around PiS during the party's second period of governance. They have not done much damage to the ruling party, however; even the scandal surrounding the Pegasus software used to spy on leading members of the opposition and campaign managers went nowhere (though the actual wrongdoing was much worse than Watergate). The war against Ukraine began not long after the Pegasus revelations and attracted the full attention of politicians and the media. The party's approval ratings have risen since then, not least on account of the gutsy journey to Kyiv undertaken by Prime Minister Mateusz Morawiecki and the *'Prezes'* (Kaczyński's almighty-sounding nickname). The two travelled to Kyiv with the Czech and Slovenian prime ministers at a time when the Russian army was still shelling the capital from the city's suburbs. This gesture of solidarity was emulated by many other politicians in the spring of 2022, with one notable exception: Viktor Orbán.

The most significant differences between Hungary and Poland lie in their respective policies towards Russia, and in Poland's size and the internal fractures that result from it. PiS has multiple centres of power with different regional bases which have often clashed. The party's Achilles' heel is its economic and social welfare policy, because Poland can no longer afford the spending policy it pursued prior to the Covid-19 pandemic. Sooner or later, the high budget deficit will force the government to limit or cut social benefits. Inflation is another big problem, and it has only grown worse since the start of the war against Ukraine.

Additionally, Poland (like Hungary) is dependent on transfer payments from the EU, without which it would run into serious problems with its national budget and balance of payments. Despite this, the government continually rails against Brussels and has escalated its conflicts with the EU on various occasions. Warsaw became embroiled in a number of legal conflicts and declared that it no longer wanted to be bound by the judgments of the European Court of Justice, and the right wing of PiS under justice minister Ziobro agitated fairly openly for Poland's withdrawal from the EU. But PiS would be overreaching with a 'Polexit' because the EU remains popular even in rural Poland, where farmers would be hard pressed to cope without the subsidies from Brussels. On top of this, Russia's attack on Ukraine demonstrated the importance of allies and the much-maligned EU. PiS subsequently toned down its polemic against Brussels in 2022 and agreed to a compromise in the dispute about the rule of law. The question remains, however, whether Russia's aggression has merely papered over the cracks in this relationship, or whether it will lead to a more constructive policy towards the EU in the long term.

Moving away from right-wing populism

Slovakia's development since 2019 shows that populists can lose their backing just as quickly as they gain it. The Smer party, which was originally social democratic, ruled in Bratislava from 2006 to 2020 (apart from a brief liberal intermezzo in 2010–12). The election of a left-wing party was a counter-reaction to the neoliberal reform policies of the early 2000s, when Slovakia introduced a flat tax while vigorously cutting social benefits at the same time. These policies attracted international investors and drove economic growth, but they also created deep social and regional divides, just as they did in other new EU member states. During the 'refugee crisis' of 2015, Smer and its leader Robert Fico pivoted to the right and subsequently followed a line similar to that of Fidesz and PiS.

But the mood turned against the ruling party in the 2019 presidential election. This shift was triggered by the contract killing of an investigative journalist and his fiancée, which led to mass demonstrations as well as Fico's resignation and a general aversion to Smer. The politically untainted environmental lawyer Zuzana Čaputová joined the presidential race, took a stand against the nationalist rabble-rousing and growing corruption, promised more decency in politics and won the election decisively.

The example of Slovakia – and, more recently, the Czech Republic, where Andrej Babiš and his coalition partners lost the parliamentary election in 2021 – also refutes the idea prevalent in Western Europe that there is a deep East–West divide in Europe (right from the start, Babiš was the odd one out in some respects amongst East Central European right-wing populists; the former prime minister, who calmly accepted his electoral defeat, is Slovakian by birth and thus comes across as much less of an ardent nationalist than Orbán or Kaczyński). Čaputová's electoral victory and the change of government in the Czech Republic in 2021 and Slovenia in 2022, along with Hungary's pro-Russian tack after the invasion of Ukraine, have left Orbán completely isolated in Eastern Europe.

It may also eventually dawn on Hungary that right-wing populism does not pay off economically. After the global financial crisis, Hungary and Slovakia (which are structurally similar in many ways) both experienced economic growth of about 3 per cent. But rampant corruption meant that only a sliver of Hungary's population benefited from this after 2009.[13] This is especially noticeable on the Slovakian side of the border, which is home to a Hungarian minority of about 450,000 people. Southern Slovakia has grown wealthier than northern Hungary, which delegitimizes the politics of Fidesz and its attempt to claim the minorities in neighbouring countries for itself. The bigger this gap grows, the more the Hungarian population might come to realize that a pluralistic democracy leads to greater prosperity than Orbán's illiberal democracy. But Orbán still won the elections in April 2022 with a record result because he skilfully portrayed himself as the guardian of the nation – though this involved taking a stance which was anti-Ukrainian and subservient to Putin.

Why did Hungary and Slovakia take such different political and social paths after the Eastern European bubble burst? The Velvet Revolution of 1989 was a pivotal moment in the development of democracy, and it remains an important touchstone for many people in Slovakia despite the disappointments that followed.[14] Large demonstrations took place in Hungary, too, in the spring and summer of 1989, but the country never made such a clean break with its socialist past. Furthermore, Slovakia was ruled between 1992 and 1998 by Vladimír Mečiar, a nationalist left-wing populist who steered his country away from the EU and NATO. During his time in office, there was an increase in corruption, criminality and the prosperity gap between Slovakia and the Czech Republic. Slovakian voters never forgot this and wanted to prevent the country from turning down another dead end like it had in the 1990s. At the same time, the history of Mečiar's HZDS party (Movement for a Democratic Slovakia) and Smer reveals that the boundaries between left-wing and right-wing populism in Eastern Europe are blurry, and that socio-political populism can easily be combined with a nationalist agenda.

Wherever left-wing and right-wing populists have competed, the right has eventually won. This happened in Poland between 2005 and 2007, when PiS outmanoeuvred its coalition partner Samoobrona, a left-wing populist party which had been founded as a rural protest movement. In eastern Germany, the PDS (Party of Democratic Socialism, which was subsumed by The Left party in 2007) initially garnered the most protest votes, but it has been largely crowded out by the AfD since 2015–16. Developments have been similar in Italy, where the Five Star Movement (M5S) was originally much stronger than the Lega Nord. The tables turned in the European parliamentary elections of 2019, when the Lega and Matteo Salvini received twice as many votes as the M5S (see the essay about Italy). Completing the picture is Spain, where the right-wing populist Vox party overtook the left-wing populist Podemos for the first time in the parliamentary elections of November 2019. Greece is the only exception here, but it carries little weight in the EU.

It is hard to draw clear political lessons from the outcomes of these elections. One option for left-wing populists would be to adopt more nationalist, anti-EU positions, though this would certainly lead to fierce infighting, further weakening the respective parties. A fundamental problem shared by the populist Left, social democrats and the US Democratic party is that their parties are closely tied to academic and metropolitan milieus. This limited social basis has accelerated the parties' shift from a corporatist to culturalist orientation. While the corporatist Left mobilized industrial workers and sought alliances with trade unions until the 1980s, the culturalist Left now focuses on the rights of minorities and migrants, and it places a strong emphasis on the LGBT community. As a historian, I feel it is important to remember that the hard-won rise of social democracy in the nineteenth century started with grassroots work and the establishment of cooperatives, workers' councils and trade unions. This mobilization from below is much weaker today, even though the new service proletariat could be a potential target group here. But some of this proletariat consists of shift workers, many of whom are labour migrants who are often not eligible to vote. Time constraints and linguistic barriers also make it difficult to reach the members of this group, many of whom are, in any case, probably relatively satisfied with their wages and working conditions, which are better than they would be in their countries of origin. And while the internet and social media are theoretically ideal channels for mobilizing new supporters, even they are of little help here, because while websites can be published in multiple languages, people tend to communicate in a single language in social media forums.

Considering the weakness of left-wing populist parties, are there other political competitors who could take up the fight against right-wing populists? All over Europe but especially in Italy, the erosion of conservative centre-right parties has motivated them to adopt the positions of right-wing populists and thus become almost indistinguishable from them. Austria is another good (or bad) example of this. In his appearance and speech, Austria's smart young chancellor Sebastian Kurz (who was forced to resign in 2021 after a corruption scandal) came across like a bourgeois-conservative politician. But the substance of his policies scarcely differed from those of the far-right Austrian Freedom Party (FPÖ) – which had lurched further to the right to enhance its profile after losing government power. The Austrian People's Party (ÖVP) maintained its rightward trajectory even after entering a coalition with the Greens in 2020. Conservative parties have moved to the right in recent years in France and Sweden, too, distancing themselves from migrants, minorities and Islam.

In light of this, it is the centre-left parties which currently have the most potential to halt the further rise of right-wing populists and nationalists – a rise which was probably only temporarily interrupted by the Covid-19 pandemic. But even as I write these lines, I realize what a defensive position this is. Defending liberal democracy is a hard and thankless task because it forces the Democrats in the USA and social democrats in Europe to adopt the position of constitutional conservatives.

This implicitly contradicts the former distinguishing characteristic of leftists and liberals, namely, their ambition to develop social and political utopias. In the nineteenth-century society of Polanyi's magnum opus, the term 'social democratic' had utopian overtones. Following the economic and social transformation after 1989, the promise of social democracy receded into the distance again, even in countries with a strong social welfare system. The principles of social democracy have therefore almost become a utopian ideal once more, though not one that is focused on tackling the greatest challenge of our time: global warming.

The question for all democratic parties is how to deal with right-wing populists once they have been voted out of office. Hungary and Turkey should serve as a warning here. Politicians like Orbán and Erdoğan will probably only relinquish power once after losing an election, not twice. Poland is an instructive example of how not to deal with a defeated antiliberal party. As mentioned, PiS came to power in Poland in 2005 and governed for two years with the support of a nationalist-Catholic party and the left-wing populist Samoobrona. Even at the time, PiS tried to restrict judicial independence and sometimes used unlawful means to attack its political opponents. The main culprit in this was a close confidante of PiS chairman Jarosław Kaczyński: Zbigniew Ziobro, the minister of justice who was simultaneously appointed chief public prosecutor (the fusion of these two offices says a great deal about how PiS interprets the rule of law). When the government fell apart in 2007 due to internal disputes and was replaced by the liberal-conservative Civic Platform party under Donald Tusk, the new coalition could have brought Ziobro before a state court for his legal violations, which included abuse of office, issuing unlawful orders to anti-corruption authorities and breaching the constitution. This never happened, however, so after PiS won the election in 2015, Ziobro could become minister of justice and chief public prosecutor again – with predictable consequences for the rule of law and democracy in Poland.

Will former president Donald Trump face legal consequences now that he has been denied absolute or sovereign immunity by a US district court? His impeachment proceedings were sobering in this regard. Trump batted away the accusations with a mixture of denial, rejection of responsibility and chutzpah. Two months *after* the Mueller report was published, Trump gave a disarmingly straightforward answer to the question of how he would react in the future if a foreign power presented him with damaging material about a political opponent. Would he indicate that he was interested in a meeting, or would he inform the police and FBI? With apparently no remorse for his previous dealings with Russia, Trump said, 'They have information – I think I'd take it.'[15] This was not an actionable comment, as Trump used the subjunctive case in his response. Investigators looking into Trump's potential tax fraud need to move fast, however, because the next presidential elections are not far off.

Maybe a lesson can be learned here from the Italian judicial system – which, admittedly, is not known for its speed. The investigations into Silvio Berlusconi and his corporate empire stretched back into the 1990s, when he became prime minister for the first time. Berlusconi was unscathed by the many scandals during his subsequent terms of office because they drew public attention to him as a person and away from issues of substance – and, as prime minister, he had immunity anyway. But after he resigned in the wake of the euro crisis, Berlusconi found himself in court once again, and he was convicted in two separate trials in 2013 for dealings with underage prostitutes, abuse of office and tax evasion. Berlusconi managed to get an appeals court to overturn the conviction relating to his sex parties, because he supposedly did not know how old the prostitutes were. His tax fraud conviction was upheld, however, bringing a temporary end to the long political career of *Il Cavaliere*.[16] Over the years, Berlusconi made no secret of his disdain for the rule of law. He repeatedly railed against 'communist judges' and the partisan judiciary[17] – though he had no problem with the appeals court that acquitted him. It will be interesting to see how Donald Trump reacts to the charges to come, and whether he will get away with it like he did in his impeachment and earlier investigations.

The Democrats' narrow victory in the 2020 congressional and presidential elections produced no cheers of relief in the USA or anywhere else. And there is no cause for cheer, because we have moved a step closer to a political scenario familiar from Eastern Europe, in which power is passed back and forth between a moderate left or liberal, constitutionally conservative party and antiliberal right-wing populists and nationalists. This scenario is a grave threat to liberal democracy because, by their second electoral victory at the latest, antiliberals everywhere have managed to push through systematic changes including the partial or complete political coordination of the judiciary and media, and the manipulation of voting rights. Such actions clear the way for a 'tyranny of the minority', to put a spin on Alexis de Tocqueville's famous dictum about democracy in America. After the midterm elections in 2022, though the Republicans won only the House, such a scenario has moved closer in the USA.

In light of these threats, liberal democracies and constitutional states must take a firmer stand. The lack of assertiveness seen in Poland after 2007 and the foreign complicity seen in Hungary can have dangerous consequences. But there is a dilemma here, because if constitutional states respond in kind to the agitation of right-wing nationalists, they might quickly find themselves violating the foundations of liberal democracy and their own laws. In general, it is very hard to determine how a constitutional state should deal with politicians and parties that are fundamentally anti-legalistic but continually invoke their basic rights and the constitution.

Maybe we can take a lesson from the right-wing populists. Regarding Hungary specifically, if there is the slightest doubt about the country's proper use of EU funds, the European Commission should employ methods similar to those used by Orbán to hound the Central European University and NGOs:

random tax audits, reclaiming previously approved funds and other bureaucratic harassment. These conflicts touch on a fundamental question for the EU, namely, whether it can exist as a mixed political system which brings together liberal constitutional states and increasingly authoritarian regimes. Can the EU maintain its competence to make decisions if democratically elected politicians are sitting at the same table as autocrats?

Hungary's attempt to blackmail the EU over the coronavirus recovery fund does not bode well for the prospect of a functioning European Union. Orbán ultimately managed to have investigations into Hungary's violations of the rule of law postponed until 2023. Angela Merkel's compliance during Germany's EU Council presidency meant that Orbán was able to start the 2022 election campaign with well-filled coffers. Immediately after winning the election, Orbán dealt another serious blow to the EU's joint foreign policy. In his victory speech, he lambasted Ukraine and its president Volodymyr Zelensky and announced that Hungary was willing to pay for Russian gas in roubles. In doing so, Orbán unnecessarily met one of Putin's key demands and broke ranks with Western countries united in their sanctions against Russia. Economic interests explain Orbán's pro-Russian stance even after the attack on Ukraine, as do the similarities between the political systems of Hungary and Russia. The autocrat Orbán (who has thus far refrained from the use of violence – the most important difference between him and Putin) would apparently rather cooperate with a dictator than with the democratically elected president of Ukraine.

The EU – and especially Germany, its leading economic power – has to defend liberal democracy not just with words, but with deeds. And it has to understand that rotten compromises like the one for the coronavirus recovery fund can have far-reaching consequences. Their repercussions will impact the children of today and tomorrow, just like climate change.

I do not want my children to grow up in a country where patriarchal relationships and dependencies determine their career prospects, and where even in school they have to think carefully about what they should say and what they should keep quiet. This is the case today in Hungary, in Turkey and of course in Putin's Russia.

Polanyi's magnum opus can encourage us to think about how liberal democracies and the EU wound up in this predicament in the first place. Until 2016, the EU could still claim that the rightward lurch was an Eastern European problem. But the *annus horribilis* and the storming of the US Capitol revealed just how vulnerable the old Western democracies have become. This was apparent even before the Covid-19 pandemic, and now the social consequences of the health crisis and the new war in Europe could intensify the erosion of liberal democracy. The next chapter in this book will therefore look at the pandemic, its social repercussions and the potential political fallout.

7

Systemic Competition during the Covid-19 Pandemic

Contemporary history might be divided into two ages someday: one before the Covid-19 pandemic and one after. This deep rupture has been felt most acutely by children, adolescents and students. Though they did not face the same threat to life as older generations, they will surely never forget the time when schools and universities were closed and they were confined to their family home, away from all of their friends. We are talking about more than 1.5 billion young people globally who will never be able to make up for the year of school or training that they missed.

The lockdowns felt endless, and time slowed down after having seemingly accelerated since 1989 in the eyes of those who lived through the period, like Václav Havel.[1] Fear permeated everyday life, and social contact suddenly appeared to be dangerous instead of enriching. That said, cancelled gatherings, conferences and birthday parties seem like a minor loss compared with the trauma of people who lost close relatives, their jobs or their entire livelihood.

Poor countries and 'emerging markets' (as they are known in neoliberal parlance), and the lower classes in wealthy countries, have been most profoundly affected by Covid-19 and its economic repercussions. Poverty and social inequality negatively influenced the course of the pandemic and must be tackled head-on to bring the health crisis under control again, but the gulf between rich and poor has widened on a global level and in Western industrialized countries. The pandemic thus reinforced developments that were characteristic of the entire era of neoliberal transformation. It is impossible to say when the social crisis will end, because while the economy has recovered since 2021, key indicators such as economic growth, national debt and inflation have worsened everywhere, reaching levels not seen since the global financial crisis of 2008–9.

Russia's attack on Ukraine has been like a second knockout. The war has disrupted the post-pandemic economic recovery and driven up energy and food prices around the world. Disposable income and standards of living will decline for the foreseeable future, and the Middle East and Africa face potential famines. In the space of just two years, Covid-19 undid two decades' worth of progress in the global fight against poverty, and the war in Ukraine will only make this worse. This raises the question of whether the increase in prosperity that was held up as an argument for 'neoliberal globalization' after 1989 was at all sustainable.[2] Middle-income countries in Southeast Asia, South Asia, Latin America and Eastern Europe were particularly affected by Covid, as was the USA.

At the time of writing in mid-2022, approximately 6.3 million people worldwide had died 'of and with' Covid-19.[3] As shocking as it is, this number is actually too low because it is based on reports sent from UN member states to the World Health Organization (WHO). It is easy to manipulate the number of reported infections by carrying out less testing, and many countries are not even in a position to determine the exact cause for every person who dies. Excess mortality is a more telling statistic, but this can only be determined after the fact by comparing the number of deaths annually before and after the outbreak of the pandemic. According to the latest estimates from the WHO, at least 15 million people died of the direct and indirect consequences of Covid-19 in 2020 and 2021, while the medical journal *The Lancet* estimates that this figure is actually about 20 per cent higher.[4]

These numbers are devastating, as was the worldwide approach to the pandemic. The United Nations and WHO have repeatedly stressed that emergency situations can only be handled with a concerted global effort. But Covid-19 instead mutated into a competition between political systems and power blocs. This became apparent even in the first phase of the pandemic in the spring of 2020, when the focus was on sourcing basic medical supplies like masks and disposable gloves and initiating the first measures to prevent the virus from spreading. Even the process of developing and distributing vaccines turned into a kind of competition between Russia, China and the West. And it was not a given that 'the West' would be viewed as a single entity again after all the conflicts between the EU and USA under Donald Trump. The cooperation between German research and American entrepreneurship – in the form of BioNTech and Pfizer – is emblematic of the renaissance of transatlantic cooperation.

Rivalry between countries and power blocs is not new, and it is very much in keeping with the logic of neoliberal competitive thinking. The global indices that were developed in the mid-1990s (see chapter 1) to compare, evaluate and rank countries and their economies based on quantitative indicators have been consistently applied to the pandemic since March 2020. The respective figures for infections, deaths and (since the end of 2020) vaccination rates have been treated like a sports competition.

Some countries were at the top of the list for a long time and felt like winners, while others embarrassed themselves by plummeting in the rankings. On the upside, these indices can be taken as an incentive to learn from other countries and adopt their 'best practices'. Learning effects were shown to have improved preventive measures and vaccination campaigns in many small and medium-sized countries during the pandemic. It is important to mention this to avoid painting an entirely negative picture of how the pandemic was dealt with. It is generally remarkable – and a positive side effect of globalization – that so many countries were capable of developing vaccines almost simultaneously. This would have been impossible during the global vaccination campaigns for smallpox and polio in the 1960s and 1970s, when the whole world relied on the research and pharmaceutical industries of a handful of Western industrialized states.

But these positive developments have been overshadowed by hyperactive 'Covid nationalism' and 'Covid imperialism', in the form of attempts to use health care policy to create a national identity and acquire international power. Too many countries and their citizens think only about themselves instead of the common good and the global community. This claim may sound moralizing, but it is unfortunately justified when we compare the competition and conflicts surrounding Covid-19 with the communal fight against lethal diseases half a century ago. Vaccines against Covid-19 were developed faster than vaccines back then, but this scientific progress is of little benefit to the wider world as it currently stands.

Most countries in the Global South, along with poor European countries like Bosnia and Ukraine, received vaccines far too late and in quantities that were far too small because they were unable to produce them domestically. Some middle-income countries which benefited from the accelerated globalization after 1989 (at least in some respects) were able to create their own vaccines, but these are apparently not as effective and they inspire little confidence amongst the countries' own citizens. These states include China and Russia, which has seen the world's second-highest excess mortality rate in proportion to its population size (at least one million people have died of Covid-19 in Russia; I will go into the reasons for this in more detail below).⁵ Sputnik, Sinovac, IndoVac, Turkovac – the names alone are evidence of the Covid nationalism I mentioned earlier.

In light of the new health crisis triggered by the Omicron variant, it would have made sense for China, especially, to import the innovative messenger ribonucleic acid (mRNA) vaccines from the USA or EU. Financially this would not have been a problem thanks to China's export surplus, but apparently there were political hurdles that virologists and other medical experts were unable to overcome.

The virus therefore continues to run rampant, increasing the risk of more new variants. As a result, it is no easier for us to foresee where the pandemic will go from here than it was at the start. This is something no one reckoned with in the spring of 2020. This essay will therefore follow the other threads running through this book and look back on the past two years of the pandemic with an eye to systemic competition (even between Western countries) and, as always, old and new inequalities and their political consequences, which will only become fully apparent in the coming years.

Covid-19 was the first big test for right-wing populist and nationalist leaders who suddenly found themselves facing a problem they had not created themselves and could not easily 'frame' (unlike the 'migration crisis' or threat of terrorism). The political fallout varied drastically, ranging from Trump's loss of office to Viktor Orbán's big win in April 2022. The EU's longest-serving prime minister was not harmed by the fact that Hungary's excess mortality rate was amongst the highest in the EU.⁶ What do these differences tell us about each country and, above all, how they were shaped during the age of transformation?

The 'Chinese virus' and an 'American failure'

Thanks to the pandemic, recent history has reached an end I could not have imagined when I submitted the original German manuscript of this book three years ago. When the first reports appeared of a previously unknown coronavirus in the Chinese province of Hubei in December 2019, the epidemic still seemed very far away from Europe and North America, both temporally and geographically. The Chinese government's initial response was reminiscent of the Soviet Union's approach to the Chernobyl nuclear disaster: news about the epidemic was first suppressed, then trivialized. When it was no longer possible to deny the gravity of the situation, the Chinese government locked down entire metropolises and provinces. Beijing enforced curfews by employing the Orwellian surveillance system it had developed over the years using mobile apps and artificial intelligence tools such as facial recognition. These mechanisms were originally based on American technologies, which shows once again that increased economic exchange and growing wealth do not necessarily lead to democratization.

The information blockade and lockdowns made it hard for outsiders to figure out what was really happening in Hubei and the rest of the People's Republic of China (PRC). The communist government of Vietnam seemed to have the best insight into the local situation and China's approach to communication. Vietnam banned flights from Wuhan as early as the end of January, and soon afterwards the country closed its border with the PRC, stopping passenger traffic and preventing a serious health crisis. Meanwhile, global air traffic to and from China continued even after the WHO warned of a worldwide pandemic at the end of February. The Chinese government took on a double role here, protesting when the USA and Italy closed their borders at the end of January to foreign nationals who had recently been in the PRC, but also refusing to tell the world what it knew about the rapid proliferation of the disease in China itself.[7] And so Covid-19 began to spread.

China's close trading partners were especially hard hit – including Italy, continental Europe's second-largest export economy and home to more than 300,000 Chinese nationals, most of whom work under miserable conditions in the textile and food service industries.[8] The exploitation of Chinese workers and outsourcing of industrial production are two of the building blocks of global capitalism, which relies on open borders for capital, goods and people. But increased labour migration was the political weak point of neoliberal globalization. Migrants – at least, those who come from far-off countries and continents – are identifiable and vulnerable, unlike capital flows or the imported goods whose foreign origins are betrayed only by the ubiquitous 'made in China' label.

The border closures during the pandemic could have a paradoxical effect, because they at least temporarily eliminated the stumbling block of mass labour migration. During the pandemic, countries like Germany and Austria realized just how dependent they are on this influx of labourers, especially in agriculture and geriatric care. But right-wing populists and nationalists still blame migrants for all manner of social ills, particularly in the USA. Migrants also continue to be used as an argument against globalization as a whole, which admittedly could have taken a different path than it did in the decades after 1989 (during the first phase of globalization in the late nineteenth century, for example, global and especially transatlantic migration was far higher, while capital flows were lower).

The virus spread from East Asia to North America and Europe along the connecting lines and nodes of the 'network society' described by sociologist Manuel Castells. His 1996 book of the same name was the first volume in a trilogy entitled *The Information Age*, which can now be read as a historical source text on the third major wave of globalization (following the 'discovery' of America in the early modern period and then the long nineteenth century).[9] But it was a lack of information that posed a problem in the case of Covid-19. The infected businesspeople who flew from China to the global centres of trade and industry in New York, London, Paris and Milan did not know they were carrying dangerous pathogens with them. The virus was just as invisible as the global flow of capital.

On top of this, in early 2020, right-wing populists and nationalists like Donald Trump and Boris Johnson ignored the information that *was* available and woefully underestimated the spread of the virus for a long time.[10] Castells had no way of knowing that the internet, which held the promise of universal education and democratization in the 'information age' of the 1990s, would primarily become a source of disinformation two decades later. Social media platforms are now a resource for authoritarian rulers and the Western politicians who would like to emulate them, and the deliberate circulation of false information has become a structural problem for democracy. This had deadly consequences in many countries during the Covid-19 pandemic because people were too slow to protect themselves by wearing face masks, and many subsequently refused to get vaccinated. This put further strain on hospitals, which then had little capacity to treat 'ordinary' patients. For this reason, too, excess mortality rates are a better reflection of the true scale of the pandemic than the officially reported Covid deaths.

The pandemic 'de-networked' the world with breathtaking speed. Historians such as Tara Zahra refer to this as a 'de-globalization' comparable to the period between the two world wars.[11] In February and March 2020, airports around the world closed, borders were sealed and tens of thousands of tourists and expats were evacuated or flew home on their own, as if being in their home countries would make them safer from the virus. The border closures were especially troubling for Europeans working in different countries or with partners of a different nationality. Militarized inner-European border controls were lifted again after the first wave of the pandemic, but they will no longer be taboo in the future.

Communist China was the first major power to recognize the element of global competition in Covid-19. By enforcing strict lockdowns, isolating infected individuals and conducting effective contact tracing, the country managed to get the pandemic under control again by April 2020. At home and abroad, China's state and party leadership touted the declining infection rate and small number of Covid deaths relative to population size as a national success, chalking it up to their wise leader Xi Jinping. But the seemingly unstoppable spread of the Omicron variant fundamentally called into question the zero-Covid strategy that the PRC continued to pursue even in 2022, unlike the situation in New Zealand, Australia and Singapore (more about this in the sub-section about Omicron).

Such experiences have already become part of the contemporary history of the pandemic. In keeping with the Bible quote that 'the first will be last and the last will be first', the countries that were ahead of the curve in earlier Covid waves faced even greater problems later on and vice versa. But modesty and humility were also in short supply during the pandemic and would have been at odds with the sense of international rivalry and, above all, the PR strategies of right-wing populists and nationalists. Even the populist leaders of smaller countries like Austria and Serbia insisted on announcing that they had made great strides in the fight against Covid and extolling their own nations as international role models.

In March 2020, foreign and domestic policy considerations drove US president Donald Trump to throw himself into controversy with China. Trump referred to Covid-19 as the 'Chinese virus', first to distract Americans from the danger facing the USA and from his own failures, and ultimately to place the blame on his geopolitical rival. But by claiming that the virus had been deliberately created in a lab in Wuhan,

Trump went too far yet again and lost credibility in this area, too.

The 'America First' slogan took on a new and tragic meaning as the USA recorded the world's highest Covid-19 infection and mortality rates during the first and second waves of the pandemic. But this outcome was not the fault of the president alone, though he was clearly incompetent and out of his depth.[12] The huge gap between rich and poor was reflected in Covid mortality rates that were 70 per cent higher amongst Black Americans than whites.[13] A toll was also taken by the profit-oriented health care system, the privatization of which had been promoted by Reagan in the 1980s, in keeping with the neoliberal order, and then continued by the Democrats under Clinton. As a result, there was a dearth of hospitals and intensive care unit (ICU) beds in poor regions. Well-developed welfare states like Germany, Austria and the Scandinavian countries had an advantage in this regard, while countries in Southern Europe were at a disadvantage, partially because of the austerity measures introduced after the euro crisis.

In the USA, many of the approximately 45 million people without health insurance (about 15 per cent of the population) did not seek out a doctor or hospital until their Covid symptoms were severe and they had already infected a number of other people. Some people with Covid continued to go to work because they were not entitled to sick pay. Trump cannot be blamed for these structural deficits, however, which can be traced back to older social, regional and racial dividing lines. Barack Obama was the only president in the last half century with the will and necessary powers of persuasion to reform the overly expensive and socially selective health care system. But 'Obamacare' was only a partial success and did nothing to increase the number of hospitals and intensive care beds in the country.

Another problem with the American approach to the pandemic was that the country ricocheted back and forth between lockdowns and openings, with public health interests often pitted against economic ones. Incidentally, this was also the Swedish argument against tougher restrictions and lockdowns.[14] The zigzagging in the USA, and the different tactics from state to state, were motivated by a fixation on opinion polls and social media. However, even smaller countries like Germany and Austria changed their preventive measures and rules for opening and closing so often that many people eventually lost track of which regulations applied.

The consequences of the wide-scale lifting of restrictions were not felt until the autumn after the first wave. Then the scenario repeated itself in 2021. Governments seemed to think it would be asking too much of the public to accept ongoing preventive measures, like wearing masks, because the trajectory of the virus was massively uncertain. Another dire failure was the delay in acquiring and enforcing the use of FFP2 masks in the summer of 2020 when it had long been clear that they provided far more protection than simple surgical masks.

The two oldest democracies in the world did an especially poor job of protecting their citizens. The UK experienced the most Covid fatalities relative to population size in Western Europe, despite having a more well-developed public health care system than the USA. This is yet more evidence of the failure of right-wing populist governance, and it confirms the rule of thumb that everything turns out much worse than expected once its proponents have come to power.

The new EU member states and Austria initially seemed to refute this rule in the spring of 2020. These countries were also governed by right-wing populists: Viktor Orbán in Hungary, Jarosław Kaczyński in Poland and Andrej Babiš in the Czech Republic, a successful entrepreneur and multi-millionaire who had promised voters that he would manage the state as well as he managed his companies. Like Austria, these three countries fared relatively well in the first Covid wave; Austrian chancellor Sebastian Kurz even proclaimed his nation to be a role model. But the relatively low number of infections and deaths ultimately came down to a coincidence here, as it did in Germany: countries north of the Alps had seen the catastrophe unfold in Italy in March of 2020 and were able to implement counter-measures in time. The next section will go into more detail on how the lockdowns affected children and young people in particular.

The new EU member states had an additional advantage in that, although they were increasingly integrated into the European and global economy after 1989, they are still on the periphery (though this does not apply to the strong Czech industrial sector). They had less direct contact with China than the USA and major trade hubs in Europe, so fewer infected businesspeople crossed their borders. Furthermore, their radical lockdowns in the spring of 2020 were motivated by the realization that the poorly developed health care systems in these countries (the Czech Republic being an exception once again) would be even less able to cope with a wave of infections than Italy or Spain. Doctors and nurses lacked access to protective gear, so the strict approach to containing the virus was partially a product of necessity.

The governing parties in Hungary and Poland did not want to admit this, of course, so they associated their border closures with their agitation against foreigners and migrants (a tactic familiar from the 'refugee crisis'), and with the smear campaign against George Soros in the case of Fidesz. There were parallels to Trump's rhetoric here in that the virus was portrayed as 'a foreigner'. Educated people saw right through this nationalistic propaganda, but surveys revealed an astonishingly high level of support for closing the borders and 'protecting' society against allegedly external threats.

Right from the start, the democracies in East Asia were most successful in combatting the pandemic. This was due in part to cultural and religious influences that should not be underestimated, even in China. Thanks to Confucianism and its national variants, values such as serving the community, protecting the elderly and respecting authority have a different weight than they do in the West, where individualism became an absolute value in the age of neoliberalism, one often confused with ruthless egoism. For this reason, too, appeals to protect others by wearing a mask or getting vaccinated failed to resonate in the West.

An affinity for digital technology was another advantage for the democracies in East Asia. Like China, South Korea used mobile apps in its fight against the pandemic, which made it possible to carry out contact tracing more quickly and effectively than in Western nations. Although the citizens of the old EU countries and the USA have now lived in democracies and constitutional states for three generations or more, they apparently had little trust in their own governments. Covid apps were criticized as an invasion of privacy and breach of data protection laws in the West, and only a small proportion of the population wanted to download them. Even in the Northern European societies that generally have more confidence in their governments, contact-tracing apps never really took off.

Sweden and the Netherlands in particular – predominantly Protestant Europe, in other words – counted on their citizens to take responsibility for themselves. This high degree of top-down trust meant that residents faced fewer restrictions and were instead expected to make their own choices about social interaction and protection against the virus. Most people in these countries did, in fact, modify their behaviour voluntarily, which wound up thwarting the other goals of Sweden's libertarian coronavirus policy. The social democrats in Sweden had hoped a libertarian approach would prevent the economy from collapsing. But even Sweden eventually fell into a deep recession because, of their own accord, Swedes reduced their social contacts, went shopping less and stayed home more. The concept of herd immunity, which was based both on epidemiological calculations and an economic rationale, also proved to be illusory as the virus mutated. Comparing these various approaches to dealing with the pandemic reveals that countries fell back on established structures, attitudes and patterns of behaviour which were influenced by their culture and religion.

The USA is also a predominantly Protestant country, but it has always been more self-centred. This comes down to its sheer size and geographic position, as it is nearly a continent unto itself. The country struggled to learn lessons during the pandemic, in part due to formative psychological influences which developed over the course of the twentieth century and intensified after 1989. A nation that won two world wars and considered itself the victor in the Cold War, and that was long viewed as a model for many states and societies around the world, was apparently less open to external impulses than the EU countries which were willing to learn from one another. Trump's 'America First' nationalism closed off the nation even further. Many Republicans now view the EU as an alliance of decadent welfare states, and China tends to be reflexively rejected on emotional grounds rather than approached with real interest.

Systemic competition can lead researchers and, above all, the media to underestimate internal differences, just as thinking in terms of blocs and spheres of influence did during the Cold War. Within the EU, individual countries are muddling through the crisis in very different ways, but so are individual regions within countries. In Italy, for example, the Veneto region had far fewer Covid cases and deaths than neighbouring Lombardy. This apparently had to do with the different regional health care systems, which are organized federally in Italy. Lombardy relied on medical centres and hospitals, which proved to be hotbeds of incubation. Veneto, by contrast, has a solid network of general practitioners who responded quickly by treating suspected Covid patients and isolating them at home instead of having them come into the practice. Viewed on a more abstract level, a decentralized system with a focus on local resources worked better. The high number of deaths in heavily centralized France backs this up. In Spain and the UK, the austerity measures introduced after the 2008–9 financial crisis played a role as well. However, it is difficult to precisely gauge their long-term effects and square them with other factors, such as the intensity of global tourist travel up until March 2020. Despite these varying approaches to the pandemic, two distinct poles are clear here, with a country decisively positioned at each end: the PRC and the USA.

China was able to expand its status as a major global power by exporting critical supplies to more highly developed but struggling EU countries such as Italy. Beijing's influence grew especially in the Global South – where Chinese latex gloves and masks prevented conditions in hospitals from deteriorating even further – but also in poorer Eastern European countries such as Serbia. The USA under Trump, by contrast, devolved into chaos,[15] and the president made a laughing stock of himself by recommending that people take daily doses of hydroxychloroquine (an anti-malarial and anti-rheumatic drug) to prevent Covid.

Russia played a negligible role internationally in the first phase of the pandemic and was overshadowed by China. But Moscow worked frantically to develop its own vaccine, because it was clear that this would be an important trophy in the global competition against the coronavirus. The USA invested in Operation Warp Speed, which was launched in May 2020 and pumped more than 12 billion dollars into vaccine research and development. In characteristic neoliberal style, this funding was officially presented as a public–private partnership, but it was actually a massive intervention on the part of the previously maligned state.[16] Operation Warp Speed was the only smart decision Donald Trump made in his coronavirus policy. However, the spending programme was the product of a bipartisan consensus in Congress which the president had previously torpedoed.

Pride comes before a fall

A lack of strict counter-measures caused the first wave of Covid-19 infections to merge almost seamlessly with the second in the USA. Meanwhile, the right-wing populists and nationalists in Central and Eastern Europe imagined they were on the right track and prided themselves on their seemingly successful leadership, pointing to their low case numbers in the spring of 2020. The same self-reinforcing government propaganda mechanisms which they had previously deployed against migrants (see chapter 6) and in other ideologically loaded policy areas were on display again here. The governing right-wing populists apparently believed in the myth of their own success, which made them careless. They were also hesitant to introduce unpopular measures, though this reluctance was certainly not restricted to a specific political spectrum. In general, it remains an open question as to whether a distinction can still be made between conservative or centre-right parties and right-wing populist or extremist parties and just how strong traditional conservatism still is.

I want to briefly shine a light on Austria here, which is where I had the most direct experience with Covid-19 and policies to fight the pandemic. The answer to the question above is quite clear in Austria, and it is relevant even beyond the borders of this small country. From the spring of 2020, Austrian chancellor Sebastian Kurz – who had captured the conservative parties much like Boris Johnson did in the UK – boasted that the measures he introduced to fight the pandemic were necessary, successful and internationally exemplary. He had, in fact, quickly imposed a strict lockdown relatively early, at the start of the pandemic in March. But this proved to be the only good decision he made for dealing with Covid-19. Angela Merkel was less resolute (in keeping with her usual style), which indirectly enhanced Kurz's reputation in Germany as a man of action and beacon of hope for traditional conservatives.

In the summer of 2020, Austria did away with all Covid restrictions, even the wearing of masks (with a few exceptions). The government wavered only when it came to schools, which remained closed or only partially open even longer than DIY shops and other temples of mass consumption. When the number of cases rose sharply in August and a second wave loomed, Kurz remarked that 'the virus is coming into Austria by car', and he warned against worrying developments in the Balkans.[17] Austria subsequently became the first EU country to reinstate border controls, which once again implied that the virus was coming from abroad.

It would have been more effective for Austria to coordinate its border controls with neighbouring countries so that people returning from their summer holidays could test themselves at home. Slovenia and Hungary are mainly transit countries for tourist traffic from South East Europe. They are also Schengen member states, so they were obligated in any case to control the external borders of the Schengen Area. Instead, Austria's unilateral policy led to hours-long traffic jams at its own borders, so the strict controls were abandoned again after a few days. This lack of coordination with neighbouring countries is equivalent to what social scientists refer to as methodological nationalism, where countries are so focused on themselves that they are unable to recognize urgent problems, much less solve them. As a result, even the smallest nations will first introduce measures which are primarily intended to demonstrate the state's own capacity to act.

Shortly before Christmas, Kurz said again that people from the Balkans and Turkey were 'bringing in' the virus.[18] This policy was a kind of 'Orbán light', as the Hungarian prime minister had scapegoated foreign students in the spring of 2020. The similarity between Kurz and Orbán is not a coincidence; Kurz had previously supported his Hungarian colleague multiple times in his conflicts with the EU and EPP (the conservative party alliance which Fidesz left in 2021 after long squabbling).

Kurz was fast to point fingers at migrants, but he hesitated to impose new restrictions in the autumn (by contrast, the more cautious German government never lifted the requirement to wear masks in supermarkets, for example). As a result, while Austria made it through the first wave relatively well, in November 2020 it raced to the top of the list of EU countries with the most Covid-19 infections.

Hungary might have challenged Austria for this dubious distinction, but it was carrying out less testing. Furthermore, Orbán had introduced a kind of censorship in the spring; this emergency legislation made it a punishable offence to spread false information about the pandemic, and it imposed a gag order on hospitals. Only Hungary's extremely high excess mortality rate eventually revealed the full scope of the country's disastrous health care policy.

The Czech Republic followed a path similar to that of Austria. In the summer of 2020, prime minister Andrej Babiš probably believed his own propaganda that the government was doing everything right and had the pandemic under control. At the end of August, Babiš even dismissed his health minister, who wanted to reintroduce some restrictions. Unlike Austria, however, the Czech government continued to reject almost all restrictions even into late autumn and the pre-Christmas period. As a consequence, the Czech Republic overtook Austria in December 2020 in the number of Covid infections. But there were still critical voices in the media in the Czech Republic, just as there were in Slovakia. This destroyed Babiš's reputation as a man of action and cost him his office in the October 2021 election. Sebastian Kurz, whose image had taken a blow during the long lockdowns in the winter of 2020 and spring of 2021, ultimately lost his own post due to a corruption scandal.

If Donald Trump's public health policies had not been such a failure, would he still have lost the election? Like any counterfactual claim, it is impossible to prove after the fact. But

Trump's chaotic approach to fighting Covid-19 and the high number of deaths in the USA certainly contributed to the close election results in the 'swing states' in the 2020 presidential election. Absurdity is not a trait suited to the stereotypical charismatic male leader of right-wing populist and nationalist politics – and Trump made himself look thoroughly absurd in the course of the pandemic. (Another of Trump's strategic errors – one which cannot be addressed in detail here – was his smear campaign against postal voting and his claim that these votes had been faked. This demobilized many of his voters, especially those who would have preferred to vote by post for various reasons.)

Putin and Orbán, by contrast, were untouched by their mismanagement of the pandemic and high number of Covid deaths. The Polish government, too, was unharmed by the high Covid casualty rate in Poland, and the war against Ukraine subsequently distracted the population from the more than 200,000 Covid victims (the number of deaths in Poland was at least twice as high as in neighbouring Germany, relative to population size). This indicates that right-wing populist governments were able to hold their ground and consolidate their position even when they clearly failed to deal well with the pandemic. The most important prerequisite for retaining power is maintaining control of the media, and especially television, which is still the main source of information for elderly people and rural populations.

The USA did not cross this Rubicon under Trump, but the Republicans' strident defence of freedom of speech hints at their future line of attack. Furthermore, defeat is often more instructive than victory, so it is not out of the question that Trump or a similar candidate could use tax legislation or other tricks to try to reduce media pluralism after winning the next election. Elon Musk's takeover of Twitter is an example of what a charismatic figure with huge financial leverage can do. Musk's announcement that he would restore Trump's Twitter account also suggests there might be a political consensus between the two autocrats. Jeff Bezos previously extended his reach into a key political sector by acquiring *The Washington Post*. Considering the power and structure of these two corporate empires, we can say there are already two American oligarchs in the Russian mould. We know where this development led in Russia, where first an economic oligarchy formed in the 1990s, then a political one.

In late 2020 and in 2021, China continued to pursue the course it had taken during the first wave of the pandemic. This consolidated its position in the international systemic competition surrounding Covid-19. In absolute numbers and measured against its size, the country had almost no new infections. At the National Congresses of the Chinese Communist Party, Xi Jinping portrayed himself as an international pioneer in the fight against the pandemic. Trump responded with furious attacks on China and then the World Health Organization. The US president even accused the WHO of covering up disinformation from Beijing about the supposed origins of the virus in a lab. But this just served as a diversionary tactic in the middle of the pandemic's second wave and during the US election campaign.

Vaccines as a supply-side offer

The unprecedented investments in pharmaceutical research bore fruit in the autumn of 2020. The German-American corporate alliance between BioNTech and Pfizer was the first to announce the development of a vaccine, one based on new technology which worked in an innovative way. This cooperation was interesting in that the economic policy roles were reversed. Germany invested large amounts in Covid-19 research, but not nearly as much as the USA.[19] Viewed somewhat more abstractly, we could say that a private capitalist model led to success in Germany, while the USA banked on a more interventionist model in which the state absorbed most of the risk for pharmaceutical companies. This especially benefited Moderna, which was the second company to announce an innovative mRNA vaccine.

But even earlier, in August 2020, Russian president Putin (and not a private company) announced that a Russian vaccine had been developed.[20] The vaccine's name – Sputnik V – attested to its propaganda value, bringing to mind the Cold War and the Sputnik shock, when the Soviet Union became the first superpower to launch a satellite into orbit. But Russia's vaccine had not yet completed its final clinical trials, so mass testing was going to be carried out on 'volunteer' subjects in the army. In essence, Putin had taken an interim stage of vaccine development and inflated it into a huge success.

The tepid response from Russian society reflects a weakness evident in every authoritarian regime (though this term is now just as outdated as 'hybrid regime', thanks to the war in Ukraine: since 24 February 2022, Russia has been a hard dictatorship which tolerates absolutely no dissent). Russia's citizens did not trust their own government, and most of them refused the Sputnik V vaccine. In any case, the majority of doses were exported, another way for Russia to stake its claim as a global superpower.

Russia's vaccination strategy differed from that of the West mainly in how the vaccine was allotted to different age groups. The first people to be vaccinated in Russia were those with a high number of social contacts, such as teachers and bus drivers. The idea behind this was to prevent the virus from spreading. Meanwhile, older people who were most at risk from the virus had to wait. Functional arguments thus outweighed the principle of protecting the highest-risk groups, which was the most important criterion for Western countries. But it is difficult for elderly people to isolate, so Russia's strategy backfired and had dire consequences. As mentioned, excess mortality statistics show that at least one million Russians died of Covid-19. This was despite the fact that, because of Russia's low life expectancy, older people make up a relatively small proportion of the total population.[21] As the war against Ukraine has shown, human life does not have the same value in Russia as in the West or China, where the act of respecting and protecting older people is enshrined in the culture.

Russia's biggest problem was its low vaccine acceptance rate. Despite all the propaganda around Sputnik V, not even half the Russian population had been fully vaccinated by the start of 2022.[22] There are parallels here to Serbia, which took advantage of the competition between the superpowers and managed to acquire doses of the Russian, Chinese and EU vaccines. Serbia became a vaccine forerunner in South East Europe in early 2021, proudly announcing that it was vaccinating its population even faster than many EU states. But this newly found prestige was short-lived, since even fewer people took the jab in Serbia than in Russia. This lack of demand enabled president Aleksandar Vučić to make a show of regional supremacy by offering vaccinations to citizens of Bosnia and Herzegovina, amongst others, who were having to wait on account of the (scandalously) slow delivery of vaccines from the EU. In this regional rivalry in South East Europe, the EU was the clear loser in vaccine diplomacy. Both Russia and the PRC supplied vaccines faster to the Western Balkans, and Serbia thanked its 'friend' Xi Jinping with pictures of him and words of gratitude on oversized billboards.

China and Russia were also very active in the Global South, where they either directly supplied vaccines or licensed the production of Sputnik V and Sinovac. In terms of vaccine diplomacy, these countries with state capitalist systems had an advantage over the West because their companies export goods by order of the government, which can then claim the credit for supplying the goods itself. Private companies like BioNTech and Pfizer, by contrast, work on the basis of demand

and do not sign contracts in the presence of presidents, foreign ministers or high-ranking diplomats. Furthermore, demand for the most popular vaccines from BioNTech/Pfizer and Moderna rose in the West during the booster campaigns in the third and fourth waves of the pandemic, leaving fewer of these vaccines available for poor countries and the Global South.

The EU therefore missed its chance to emerge as the secret winner in the competition between the superpowers, which is what the EC did in the last phase of the Cold War. Though it was a German laboratory that developed the world's first mRNA vaccine – a technological breakthrough with relevance far beyond Covid-19 – Germany itself was unable to convert this success into a higher vaccination rate or greater international prestige.

While Germany's Covid infection rate was relatively low during the first wave, Angela Merkel's government was hesitant to act in the second and third waves, which ultimately forced the population and economy into a second long lockdown. In terms of vaccination rates, too, Germany lags well behind the southern and western EU states which had been scolded during the euro crisis for their supposedly free-spending, undisciplined, hedonistic ways. As a result, Germany has a high excess mortality rate; in addition to the 138,000 official Covid-19 deaths, there were approximately 90,000 more deaths than in the years prior to 2020 (according to the data available in June 2022). One of the main reasons for this was that patients with other illnesses were unable to get adequate treatment.

It is hard to measure the indirect consequences of the pandemic, but they were certainly significant, and they are a big question mark hanging over the oft-invoked notion of solidarity. Even in social and representative democracies – political systems and societies ostensibly oriented on consensus – too many people thought first and foremost about themselves. Maybe this is not so surprising on closer examination, but a key source of legitimacy for social democracies and thus the

'European model' is that they are more stable and solidarity-minded than countries based purely on a market economy. We therefore could have expected more, especially from Germany, the leading economic power in Europe.

The pandemic as an EU problem

In the spring of 2020, the pandemic drove the global economy into the sharpest recession since the Second World War. The economic shock was even worse than it had been during the global financial crisis.[23] As Adam Tooze explains in his book about Covid-19, the US Federal Reserve and central banks in other countries responded using tools similar to the ones employed in 2008–9.[24] They supplied the financial markets with liquidity and propped up the national budgets of their respective states, thus preventing another financial crisis and even stronger decline in demand. Considering the starting point, this was no mean feat on the part of a radically anti-cyclical and thus fundamentally Keynesian policy.

Economic recovery – or how a country emerges from a crisis – is another element of global systemic competition. In the case of the pandemic, China portrayed itself as a stable anchor of the global economy and thus the winner of this competition. And, indeed, the People's Republic experienced only a brief recession in the spring of 2020, from which it recovered quickly because it was able to get Covid-19 under control in April.[25] Even beyond public health policy, one of the advantages of a hybrid system is that the state plays a much more significant role than it does in a free market economy. In China, the state (not necessarily Beijing, but rather the regions and provinces) still offers a helping hand when large enterprises falter. It is also probably easier to redirect global exports to the domestic market in a state-directed system than in a market-oriented export economy like Germany.

In the USA and other Western countries, it was left mainly to the central banks to play the role of white knight. This emergency monetarism fulfilled its purpose, just as it did during the financial crisis, but it has now reached its limits in the third year of the pandemic. After the global financial crisis, the additional liquidity and low interest rate policy (though interest rates had effectively been negative for a while) triggered sectoral inflation which primarily affected property prices and stock exchanges. Thanks to the collapse of global supply chains, rising energy prices and a shortage of computer chips and many other products, this has now become general inflation.

Russia's invasion of Ukraine has driven up gas and oil prices even further. Vladimir Putin will undoubtedly have taken this into account, as it now enables him to finance his war. It remains to be seen whether this inflation can be brought under control without stifling growth, which is already weak. A sharp rise in interest rates would put too much strain on the debt-ridden euro countries in Southern Europe and probably endanger the very existence of the euro. It would also increase the likelihood of Donald Trump being re-elected in the USA.

The EU responded to the first Covid wave with a recovery package that cushioned the effects of the pandemic for all EU members, especially hard-hit countries like Italy and Spain. This vaguely named Next Generation EU (NGEU) programme was adopted in 2020 and funded with an unprecedented sum of 750 billion euros. For the first time in EU history, financial aid is being provided not only in the form of loans, but largely as direct grants to member states. Federico Fabbrini, an expert in European law, views this as 'an unprecedented leap forwards' for European integration,[26] particularly compared to the EU's policy during the euro crisis of 2011–13, which focused on budget deficits, debt and safeguarding banks. This is because NGEU (we need a dictionary for all the abbreviations invented in Brussels) was the product of a learning process on the part of the EU's member states, which did not want to repeat the mistakes of the euro crisis. As a result, they banked on a spending programme instead of austerity policies. Furthermore, the EU is now allowed to take on debt for the first time and has the right to levy its own taxes. At first glance, this seems to confirm the old saying that every crisis is an opportunity.

The problem is that the recovery plan has raised expectations massively. Will the spending programme work as hoped, leading to an economic upswing and the modernization of Europe's economy, which has fallen behind the USA and East Asia in new sectors like digitalization? The answer to this question lies not in the hands of the EU, but rather in those of its member states, which are responsible for implementing the recovery plan. It would be impossible for the EU itself and its 35,000 civil servants to put the individual measures of the plan into practice, so a decentralized allocation of funds is the right choice here. But the state capacity and competencies necessary for this were continually eroded during the age of neoliberalism. Even member states with relatively efficient public administration systems have struggled to carry out large-scale projects over the past years (examples in Germany include the new airport in Berlin, the much-discussed backlog in investments for roads and bridges and, most recently, the German army's lack of readiness in the face of Russian aggression).

There are a variety of factors behind these deficiencies, a key one being the neoliberal doctrine that the state should keep its hands off the economy and not act as a business itself. A number of major projects have also been delayed because of competition law, which requires contracting authorities to always choose the cheapest but not necessarily most reliable provider. A one-sided focus on monetary policy can help prevent the collapse of the global financial system, as it did in 2008–9, but it can never be more than a framework for the 'recovery' under discussion now. It will take a long time for the liquid assets from the EU recovery plan to reach companies. Additionally, the low level of digitalization in the EU (especially

Germany) seems to show that it is hard to initiate sustainable modernization with a policy of cheap money. The attempts to carry out Covid-19 contact tracing via email and sometimes even telephone revealed just how big this challenge is. And the transition to a green economy is also still up in the air.

The EU's usual structural problems were very much apparent in the six months of discussion preceding the final ratification of the recovery plan. Viktor Orbán blackmailed the other member states by threatening to veto the plan until they finally weakened the EU's rule-of-law regulations and postponed their implementation (until after the 2022 parliamentary election in Hungary, which Orbán handily won in part because he was able to transparently divert transfer payments from the EU to finance his own party, the election campaign and expensive election sweeteners).

The German EU Council presidency under Angela Merkel was responsible for this compromise, which once again did a disservice to liberal democracy in Central and Eastern Europe. This policy, along with the billions of euros invested in Hungary by German corporations (see chapter 6), has essentially sabotaged democracy in Europe. The consolidation of Orbán's regime (in contrast to the consolidation of democracy which was the focus of study in the noughties) has already severely impeded the functionality of the EU and poses a very fundamental challenge – because no one knows how a system comprising both liberal democracies and authoritarian regimes is supposed to work.

Hungary's subversion of EU sanctions after Russia's attack on Ukraine indicates that an increasingly authoritarian ruler like Orbán – who can probably never be voted out now on account of unfair political competition and no separation of powers – will instinctively side with politicians of a similar stripe, be it Trump, Salvini, Kaczyński or Morawiecki.

The time frame for the NGEU programme is another problem. When the plan was developed, no one could know the pandemic would drag on for more than two years as more new variants of the virus emerged. It is not clear now whether the 750 billion euros will be enough to get the European economy going again for the long term. Furthermore, the programme is limited to the years 2021–6, and all large expenditures have to be agreed by the end of 2023.[27] But will Europe's deep economic crisis, which has only been worsened by Russia's war of aggression, be over by then? And how well do state spending programmes even work, especially when every state decides for itself where the money will go?

The EU Commission had the last word in approving each nation's spending plans, and it used this authority to initially reject Hungary's plan (Orbán wanted to use some of the money as endowments to privatize universities in which Fidesz members and supporters would then have the say – something which has nothing to do with either digitalization or a green deal). However, experience has shown that Brussels has very limited influence over what really happens with its money after the fact.

On the one hand, the principle of subsidiarity (i.e., implementation by the member states) makes sense. On the other hand, projects such as the transition to alternative energies depend on the construction of cross-border power lines from south to north for solar energy, for example. Digitalization is another patchwork which varies massively from member state to member state. Anyone who has tried to buy a train ticket to get from Germany to France will probably be somewhat doubtful about whether the recovery plan will deliver on its promises. If things go badly, EU sceptics could someday say that NGEU stands for 'no governance for the EU'.

If the EU wanted to approve another crisis programme in a few years, it would face the same problem it did in 2020 due to its outdated unanimity principle for important resolutions. Although Orbán is now isolated in the Visegrád Group on account of his closeness with Russia, his friends from PiS could come to his aid again if necessary.

Additionally, the recovery plan has widened the gap between the expectations placed on the EU and the EU's ability to take action.[28] This problem was already apparent during the first wave of Covid, when everyone looked to Brussels to help organize – or at least coordinate – preventative measures and the distribution of medical supplies. But the EU is hardly qualified to implement health care policies, and it also had to grin and bear it when borders were closed during the pandemic and inner-European export bans were imposed on medical equipment. The EU Commission largely had to stand aside as the Schengen treaties were violated by multiple member states (especially the Visegrád countries and Austria) because the agreement's emergency clauses permitted such measures.

Brussels partially seized the initiative again with its recovery plan and joint vaccine purchasing scheme, but this has increased the risk of inflated expectations. Furthermore, the EU Commission has little hope of ever being thanked for any of its achievements. A striking example of such ingratitude occurred in May 2022, when the Polish government announced that it would not pay for unused vaccines, which the EU Commission had ordered for all member states at a relatively low price. First Poland reached out to the EU for help – because the country is not producing any vaccines itself – and then it made Brussels the bogeyman once again. It is hard to establish common policies on such shaky grounds.

The problems are different when it comes to the recovery plan. It was developed in the summer of 2020 and approved in the autumn, but it had already partially become obsolete by the winter on account of the new lockdowns. These lockdowns caused a further economic slump, rising government debt and both social and generational upheaval. The EU might have gotten lucky because these restrictions were imposed by national governments, so the shortcomings of NGEU were pushed into the background. In Italy, where Mario Draghi once again distinguished himself as a rational manager in an emergency (just as he had done during the euro crisis), the recovery plan demonstrably helped companies and individuals,[29] but more credit for this was given to the Italian government than to Brussels.

Things did not go quite as well for the EU when it came to ordering and distributing vaccines. The EU Commission initially banked heavily on the cheaper AstraZeneca vaccine for its joint purchasing strategy, not least due to pressure from poorer member states. But the vaccine soon lost its reputation on account of its side effects and lesser efficacy compared to the two mRNA vaccines. Whether this was justified is another question, but if competition between vaccines is going to be allowed, then there will always be winners and losers (doctors and public health institutions have never offered patients competing vaccines for polio, tick-borne encephalitis (TBE), flu or many other diseases). Furthermore, the EU Commission was slower to order vaccines than the USA and UK, leading to much gloating on the part of Donald Trump and Boris Johnson. The delay was caused by tough negotiations regarding liability in the event of unexpected side effects, as well as frugality.

The aversion to risk was irrational inasmuch as it was clear to everyone involved that the vaccines were completely new. They had been sufficiently tested, however, and public demand for them was overwhelming. Refusing to take any risks can have its own side effects, as the long lockdowns in late 2020 and early 2021 showed.[30] It also would have been a political risk to make vaccination mandatory once there were finally enough vaccines for everyone in June 2021. This would have been a logical choice at least for people in certain professions with many social contacts, and for vulnerable older people. But instead, the governments of Austria, Germany and many other countries 'offered' the vaccines to their populations. This term fit well with the neoliberal age, but it resulted in a sense of optionality instead of responsibility when it came to vaccination. An offer can be refused – this is in the nature of both the concept and the market economy.

The coronavirus measures – from the nationwide lockdowns to the vaccination campaigns – led to a considerable loss of trust, not just amongst Covid deniers and anti-vaxxers, but even amongst the (much larger) part of the population which would have liked to see stricter measures. Protests and demonstrations attracted most of the attention in the media. I live in Austria where, on several weekends in the autumn of 2021, more than 40,000 anti-vaxxers marched through Vienna on unapproved routes while not wearing masks. Meanwhile, strict rules were in place in schools and universities, on public transport and in many other areas. The freedom demanded by a minority was very much at the expense of the vast majority.

The social and economic consequences of the pandemic are an equally explosive long-term problem. The lockdowns particularly impacted small companies, self-employed workers and people in labour-intensive and high-contact jobs such as in hotels, bars or restaurants, where much of the service proletariat is employed. People with lower incomes were affected far more often by the rapid rise in unemployment than well-paid, highly-qualified employees who could easily work from home. The latter also benefited more from the state support and rescue programmes for big companies. This triggered a redistribution from bottom to top, just as we saw during the global financial crisis of 2009. Rising inflation exacerbated the problem, as this also has a much greater effect on low earners. It is not clear whether this development can be reversed.

Does the return to state interventionism herald the end of the neoliberal withdrawal of the state from the economy? Adam Tooze is justifiably doubtful. He believes the legacy of neoliberalism lives on in 'hyperglobalization, fragile and attenuated welfare states, profound social and economic inequality, and the overweening size and influence of private finance'.[31]

Vulnerable youth

Since a politically loud minority which was hyperactive on social media first denied the danger of Covid-19 and then refused to get vaccinated, the risks were passed on to children, who could not get vaccinated for a long time in 2021. While young people rarely fell seriously ill (though it happened frequently enough), they could still spread the virus. More rigorous testing was therefore carried out in schools than in adult workplaces (Italy was an exception here, where unvaccinated employees had to test regularly and even pay for the tests themselves). The youngest generation was further stigmatized by lengthy debates amongst virologists about the extent to which children could transmit Covid-19 (someone should have asked a sociologist about the effect of this framing). Meanwhile, many coronavirus measures and the hierarchies of vaccination eligibility were justified as attempts to protect the older population, as if they were the only ones who were vulnerable. I have yet to hear any pensioners' association or government thank my children or any others for missing a total of nearly three quarters of a year of school in order to protect the older generations and general public.

As a social historian, I sometimes feel the urge to make calculations when I suspect that a quantitative approach to an issue might reveal new insights, or at least raise new questions. When the number of infections rose sharply in the autumn of 2021 because so many people had refused to get vaccinated, the Austrian government toyed with the idea of closing schools again or returning to a 'shift system' (which was even less effective and less popular amongst children than pure online teaching). This finally triggered a broader public debate about the mental and physical toll these measures were taking on children. Regional studies on the impact of Covid revealed a large increase in psychological problems and weight gain amongst children and adolescents. These studies showed that the proportion of overweight and obese primary school children jumped from about one fifth to more than one quarter during the pandemic.[32] According to the Organisation for Economic Co-operation and Development (OECD), complications associated with moderate overweight reduce a child's life expectancy by an average of three years, while severe overweight or obesity reduces it by approximately seven years – more than smoking tobacco. Even if we take the lower figure and conservatively estimate that 350,000 of the good 1.5 million minors in Austria were affected, this means that at least one million years of life have been lost.

This calculation can be challenged inasmuch as there were already far too many overweight children before 2020. Of course, families and parents can take action to prevent their children becoming overweight or suffering other health problems. But children are constantly bombarded with advertisements for unhealthy food containing too much fat, sugar and other harmful ingredients. The capitalist food economy is geared towards profiting off of children, even if it makes them ill and results in huge costs later on for both individuals and health care systems. A lack of exercise has also become a growing challenge since the invention of the motor car. The lure of cable TV and then computer games has added to the problem since the 1980s, as has the constant distraction of smartphones over the past decade. In this respect, the pandemic only exacerbated the existing defects of the neoliberal supply-side economy; it did not create them. But the statistics about overweight show that Covid-19 made things much worse.

Diseases of civilization, unlike premature death, are not irreversible. Nonetheless, the number of lost years of life – which was nearly ten times higher in Germany than in Austria on account of the larger population, amounting to about ten million years – should prompt us to think about whether children and adolescents, the biggest 'vulnerable population group' on Earth, are being given enough consideration and protection. The World Bank, United Nations Educational, Scientific and Cultural Organization (UNESCO) and United Nations

International Children's Emergency Fund (UNICEF) have calculated that the current generation of schoolchildren and university students will experience losses in lifetime earnings amounting to 17 trillion dollars because of missed schooling and thus fewer professional qualifications.[33]

The pandemic additionally solidified the traditional distribution of family roles, which meant that women, and mothers in particular, suffered most from the closure of schools and kindergartens. They were also disproportionately affected by job losses. The pandemic and 'shecession'[34] thus ultimately worsened inequality between social classes, countries and, ultimately, the sexes.

When historians look back on the pandemic someday and rank the performance of different countries, the nations at the top of the list may well be those which did the most to protect not only their elderly but also their children and thus, indirectly, working mothers. In the first wave of the pandemic, every country was overrun by Covid-19 and they all closed their primary schools for between seven weeks and fourth months; secondary schools were closed even longer. Sweden was the exception in that its schools remained open, and schools in the other Scandinavian countries along with Switzerland, Germany and France closed for only a relatively short time.

In the second and third waves in the winter of 2020 and spring of 2021, national Covid policies began to diverge sharply. Scandinavia and countries in the west of Europe made it a priority to open their schools, while children in Germany, Austria (where the restrictions were especially tight even during the first wave) and the new EU member states had to stay home once again for many weeks or even months.[35]

The number of days in which children were not allowed to enter primary schools in 2020 and 2021 (for simplicity's sake, I am only taking primary schools into account here) ranged from 34 days in Switzerland, 39 days in France and 45 days in Spain, to 87 days in Germany, 89 days in Austria, 94 days in the

Czech Republic and up to 98 days in Poland. Mexico and Brazil lead the pack in terms of the number of days their primary schools were closed in 2020 and 2021. The discrepancy was even greater when it came to partial or 'shift' openings, and while it was not as pronounced at universities, it was still high.[36]

This divergence cannot be explained by the course of the pandemic or number of new infections. Instead, it seems that the welfare of children and adolescents is prioritized differently in different societies. China would also have been ranked amongst the states with the fewest number of lost schooldays in the OECD tables, as schools were only closed there during the strict lockdowns in early 2020 (however, the situation for children was much worse in the spring of 2022 – see the section on Omicron below).

One systemic deficit – which does not explain the discrepancy between different European countries, however – is that the citizens of Western democracies cannot vote until they are 18 years old (there are a few exceptions, like Austria, where the voting age was reduced to 16). Children and adolescents have no say in the outcome of elections and thus play a negligible role in the calculations of political parties. By contrast, no political party can afford to ignore the interests of pensioners, especially in an ageing society. The proportion of finances spent on each group reflects this. It is especially clear in Germany, where pensions increased 5.35 per cent in 2022, resulting in additional costs of at least 16 billion euros financed largely by state contributions to pension funds.[37] Meanwhile, the special programme for 'Recovery after the coronavirus pandemic for children and adolescents' received just two billion euros for 2021 and 2022 together.[38]

Consumer societies live very much in the here and now because customer needs have to be met promptly and most offers are designed around this. Very few consumer goods are long-lived and can be passed from one generation to the next. The motto before the Second World War was 'our children should have it better than we did', but growing wealth has caused societies to lose sight of this. On account of the multiple crises of capitalism and the one–two punch of the pandemic and the war in Ukraine, most young people in the West would now be happy simply to maintain the same standard of living as their parents. The number of children living in poverty has been far too high for many years, even in well-organized welfare states like Germany. The problem is worse in 'emerging markets' and the post-communist states, where universities have expanded since the 1990s but schools are underfunded and teachers can barely make a living to support a family. The situation has improved in parts of the Czech Republic and Poland since 2004, but teachers are still badly paid compared to other professions. The Programme for International Student Assessment (PISA) studies conducted by the OECD drew more attention to schools in general, but only in the sense of international competition. Covid-19 has made many children even poorer and limited their life opportunities. Dealing with these consequences of the pandemic someday will be just as important as tackling the macroeconomic challenges.

Omicron as a game changer

After the first wave of Covid-19 abated in the summer of 2020 and the vaccination campaigns progressed in the spring of 2021, everyone started talking about the time *after* Covid. Even the EU recovery fund and the rhetoric of war that was bandied about during the pandemic were semantically based on the premise that, at some point, the pandemic would be over – which indirectly suggested that life could continue as before. But now that we have experienced five major waves of infection and dozens of new virus variants, it is clear that we will always have to live *with* Covid.

Just as rising vaccination rates and declining case numbers led the majority of humanity to hope the pandemic was subsiding at the end of 2021, a new variant emerged: Omicron. Due to its even higher transmissibility and correspondingly rapid spread, Omicron created a panic which resulted in new border closures. However, it soon became clear that Omicron generally caused less severe illness than earlier variants of the virus. Hospitalizations therefore fell even while the number of infections worldwide broke new records. But the Omicron variant managed to evade the immunity provided by the existing vaccines, which now have to be modified or developed anew. The Russian and Chinese vaccines in particular, which were developed conventionally, seem to offer only minimal protection. The protection offered by mRNA vaccines is higher, at least for people who have recently had a booster injection. My own booster unfortunately did not protect me from catching Covid, but after three vaccinations, the illness was no worse than a seasonal cold.

The milder course of the new variant influenced the debates about Covid-19. Anti-vaxxers felt justified in their claim that Covid was no worse than flu, and that vaccination was an unacceptable coercive measure. Here, too, there is a crossover with the age of neoliberal transformation. Since the 1980s, the state has not only withdrawn from the economy, it has also increasingly left health care, nutrition, recreational activities and raising children to the forces of the market and the individual. This self-regulation could be viewed as a gain in freedom, but it has also led to new pressures, self-optimization through sport, a healthy diet and morally loaded forms of consumption. Against this backdrop, it felt unusual and anachronistic in 2021 when the state suddenly wanted to make vaccination compulsory, like in the age of polio and diphtheria.

Omicron thwarted this ultimate measure in the fight against the pandemic, a measure that had essentially already been decided in some countries (including Austria and Germany) on account of the new Covid waves with the Delta variant in the autumn and winter. Universal compulsory vaccination is a hard sell when the available vaccines are only partially effective. The governments interested in collectively protecting public health would have had to take action in the summer of 2021, when it became apparent that fewer people than expected were getting vaccinated. They could not bring themselves to do this, however, and by the time Omicron arrived half a year later, it was too late.

In terms of systemic competition, the latest virus variant was a game changer. Until early 2022, the People's Republic of China presented itself as a pioneer in the fight against Covid, pointing to its relatively low number of infections and deaths. The regime had an advantage in that censorship prevented the population from hearing any critique of the government's inhumane approach at the start of the pandemic (which was documented by Ai Weiwei in his film *Coronation*).[39] But this kind of official Covid nationalism can be counterproductive if a country's preventative measures no longer work.

Even though Omicron was far more contagious, the PRC held firm to its zero-Covid strategy. This led to lockdowns lasting weeks and even months, especially in the coastal region around Shanghai, which makes a disproportionately large contribution to the country's GDP. Despite all counter-measures, the new variant spread; lockdowns could only slow the course of the pandemic, not stop it altogether.

It is currently impossible to predict how this situation will develop and what the political fallout will be. Xi Jinping's government has built up trust thanks to its achievements after the outbreak of the pandemic and in the first two years of Covid. The party can also bank on its country's culturally founded conscientiousness and respect for authority. But respect and trust can quickly turn into hatred and rejection if the power of the state continues to employ ever more repressive measures. Eventually the party leadership gave in and abandoned its zero-Covid policy at the very end of 2022. Nature turned out to be stronger than ideology.

The uncontrolled spread of the virus will cost many people their lives and further damage the Chinese economy, which has already suffered from the lockdowns in 2022. The growing wealth in the past four decades was the basis of the social contract that was violently enforced in 1989, which coupled growing wealth to political silence. But if public dissatisfaction and protests should grow, there are three potential scenarios here, just as there are in nearly every dictatorship. The first involves softening or liberalization, though the impetus for this would have to come from the Communist Party itself. The second scenario involves a hardening of the regime and increased use of police force, not least in response to larger protests. And then there is always the possibility that growing domestic tension will lead to foreign policy escapades and military interventions, as they did in Russia.

Afterword: A Bad End
The War against Ukraine

The Russian attack on Ukraine shocked the world, but it happened in stages. Vladimir Putin first intervened massively in Ukrainian politics in 2004, though without the use of force. He openly supported the candidacy of the eastern Ukrainian Viktor Yanukovych, the head of an oligarchic clan, and even travelled to Ukraine to promote his campaign. To Putin's dismay, Yanukovych's supposed victory was declared invalid because of massive election fraud, leading to the street protests of the Orange Revolution (see chapter 5). As Ukraine increasingly developed into a pluralistic democracy, Yanukovych got a second chance. He won the elections in 2010, in part due to the havoc in Ukraine caused by the bursting of the Eastern European bubble and the global financial crisis.

Yanukovych had no economic policy concept other than self-enrichment and installing himself as the single most powerful oligarch. The attempt to convert his regional economic clout into national political domination ultimately failed, however. Unlike Putin, he was unable to reign in the oligarchs and establish a clear vertical hierarchy of power. In his foreign policy, Yanukovych tried to maintain balance between the West and Russia – a reasonable strategy, since NATO had rejected Ukrainian membership in 2008, and the EU was also hesitant to establish a deeper cooperation. One of the reasons for this was the blatant and systemic corruption which made Yanukovych ever more unpopular in Ukraine.

Meanwhile, trouble was also brewing for Putin in Russia. Protests erupted when he took over the presidency in 2012 for the third time after switching office with Dmitry Medvedev (his former prime minister and successor as president) in a barely concealed breach of the constitution. Young urbanites in particular demonstrated against the prospect of Putin's perennial rule, but the police and Federal Security Service (FSB) quashed the resistance (see chapter 5).

At the same time, Russia became more aggressive in its foreign policy, especially in the region it considers to be the 'near abroad'. The EU finally offered Ukraine a free trade agreement in 2013, though this came too late and was extended to the wrong man, Yanukovych. Putin had always viewed the EU as a competitor for power, so he tried to weaken and divide it. He urged Yanukovych to reject the free trade agreement in 2013, and was able to use financial leverage because Ukraine was heavily in debt to Russia as well. Yanukovych's badly communicated decision to end the rapprochement with the EU triggered the Euromaidan protests that ultimately led to the Revolution of Dignity.

Putin subsequently took advantage of the revolution's turmoil to invade Crimea and intervene in the Donbas region. The Russian president was aware of a post-imperial longing for Crimea, where many Russians – especially former party members and KGB officials – had gone on holiday and attended youth camps. After Russia annexed the Crimean Peninsula, Putin's approval ratings soared despite stagnating incomes (Russia was seriously afflicted by falling energy prices after the global financial crisis). Putin seemed to follow the playbook of imperialism and fascism, whereby external aggression distracts from interior problems and conflicts and thus pays off politically. Even the military intervention in the eastern Donbas met with approval thanks to the state's control of the media and cleverly placed propaganda about the threat of Ukrainian fascists.

Western sanctions against the annexation of Crimea and the invasion of eastern Ukraine remained weak and half-hearted, and Germany was largely at fault for this. By jointly building the infamous Nord Stream 2 pipeline, Angela Merkel's government offered Russia even more business opportunities and deepened Germany's dependence on Russian gas. Historical research will someday reveal precisely how this ill-fated decision came about, but it is already obvious that big business interests (especially those of the German oil and chemical industry) prevailed over basic political instincts and strategic thinking. Russia also succeeded in corrupting part of the German political elite, with the Social Democrats bearing more of the blame here than Merkel's Christian Democrats.

Ukrainian politicians and academics often argue that their country was first attacked not in 2022, but in 2014.[1] This is true, but the different scale of the current war is a good justification for distinguishing between the first Russian war against Ukraine beginning in 2014 (which never entirely ended) and the second war starting in February 2022.

There are three dimensions to the current war: the 'classic' military warfare, which has received the most media attention so far; the economic war, where the West is directly involved; and the war on the home fronts, which has decided major conflicts in the past, including the First World War. There is an interesting parallel between the first and second dimensions of the war. While Putin's regime has avoided and even banned the use of the word 'war', insisting on the term 'special operation' (*specialnaya operaciya*), the West has never declared an economic war, but instead speaks of sanctions. It was naïve to expect that these sanctions would not lead to Russian retribution on various levels. At the time of writing, it is impossible (at

Afterword: A Bad End

least for a historian) to predict how and when this war might end. The uncertainty is connected to the contradictory goals of the war, which need to be discussed first.

Russian soldiers encountered no resistance when they invaded Crimea in 2014. Unfortunately, Putin took this to mean that a large-scale attack on Ukraine would quickly succeed in 2022, allowing him to install a puppet regime. In this scenario, Russia would have been able to leave the dirty work of supressing resistance and partisan activities to a pro-Russian Ukrainian regime (Russia is facing partisan attacks in some of the occupied areas in southern Ukraine, a reminder that giving up Ukraine or reaching a quick compromise with Putin, as demanded by some anti-war German and European intellectuals, would certainly not bring about peace). However, the blitzkrieg on Kyiv and Kharkiv in February and March 2022 obviously did not force Ukraine to its knees.

Ukraine's army, territorial defence and civilian population resisted ferociously and effectively, fighting off Russian attacks on Kyiv, Kharkiv in the north, Mykolaiv in the south and then, in spring and summer, in the Donbas in the east. Ukraine also withstood these attacks because of the courage of President Zelensky, who decided to remain in Kyiv despite the immediate danger to his life.

The second objective of the war – one which Russian propaganda does not mention as often in 2022 as in 2014 – is the occupation of what is referred to as 'Novorossiya' (New Russia), meaning eastern Ukraine on the left bank of the Dnipro River and southern Ukraine. It is one of the paradoxes of the war that the Russian army is bombing and shooting the very Ukrainians who mostly speak Russian and who had been claimed by Putin as part of his 'Russian world'.

The third and minimum objective is to establish a land bridge between the territories occupied in the eastern Donbas in 2014 and the Crimean Peninsula. This goal was largely achieved in the first weeks of the war and after the conquest of Mariupol.

Russia later suffered humiliating defeats on the eastern front and lost almost a third of the territory conquered in the spring of 2022. Ukraine liberated the entire oblast of Kharkiv, destroying dozens of tanks and Russian elite troops. In the autumn, Russia was forced to retreat from the left bank of the Dnipro in the south and give up the regional capital Kherson.

However, this retreat was certainly tactical, and towards the end of the first year of the war the Russian army started to dig in. This might eventually enable a repetition of the scenario in the Donbas after 2014, where the military stalemate was followed by a de facto territorial partition as well as a ceasefire that was never kept in order to weaken Ukraine and deter investors. Low-level protracted warfare would certainly be an option for Russia, one which was tested after the first invasion and worked well enough.

Although Russia now seems to be resorting to this third option, it is critical to remember that it started the war with much wider ambitions, including the withdrawal of all NATO troops from the countries that joined the military alliance after 1997. This would neutralize all of the new NATO and EU member states, allowing the partial restoration of the outer Soviet empire. Russian officials have also mentioned another goal, namely, the creation of a corridor across Lithuanian territory from Belarus to Kaliningrad. Moreover, Putin's older propaganda about the *russkiy mir* directly threatens all three Baltic states with their large Russian minorities. Russia's ambiguous objectives will make it difficult to reach a peace agreement, especially one that lasts longer and is more reliable than the ceasefire agreements in the Donbas.

Are the military goals of Ukraine and its Western supporters more realistic and unequivocal? In March 2022, Ukrainian president Zelensky hinted that Ukraine might relinquish Crimea and the eastern Donbas. This would be a return to the status quo before the second Russian invasion. Zelensky added that he would want to hold a referendum on any cession of territory. This pledge to democracy left the door open for a retreat from any unfavourable peace settlement, but it would also be a difficult test of Ukrainian democracy considering the many military and civilian victims of the war.

After the failure of the Russian offensives in the north and east, Ukraine called for the liberation of all territories occupied or annexed by Russia. This would be a return to the internationally recognized borders which were intact until 2014. Such an ambitious solution would only be possible through a comprehensive military offensive which would require a much more massive rearmament of the Ukrainian army. Ukraine lacks the financial means for this, so it would mostly have to be financed by the West, along with Ukrainian debt relief at the IMF. Is this feasible considering the rising inflation, government debt and other burdens that have already been brought on by Covid-19 and the war?

The second dimension of the conflict is the economic war launched by the West in direct response to the invasion of Ukraine in February 2022. So far, Russia has fared better than expected on the economic front. Western sanctions will have a long-term effect on the Russian economy, of course, but this is mitigated by the fact that China and India, the two most populous nations on the globe, do not support the measures. Even NATO countries like Turkey and Hungary have not fallen in line, but are instead trying to make a profit by partially subverting the sanctions.

When the West declared economic war on Russia (without labelling it as such), it naïvely assumed that Russia would continue with business as usual by supplying gas and other raw materials as it did before the war. The interruption of the gas supply has hit Central Europe especially hard. Germany, which voluntarily made itself dependent on Russia, has been particularly affected, but it is worth mentioning Austria and other smaller countries here as well. Austria played a part in building the Nord Stream 2 pipeline after the annexation of Crimea and the first invasion of eastern Ukraine, and its business association greeted Vladimir Putin in Vienna with standing ovations in 2015. The medium-term effect of Russian retaliation on the economic front might be a real energy crisis, not just an energy price crisis which has been in the making since 2021, and which partially motivated Putin to start the war. The energy crisis is likely to be averted in the winter of 2022–3, but it might only be postponed until the following winter. For Russia, it was completely rational to cut off the gas, because Ukraine is also supplied with gas channelled through the EU.

The medium- and long-term effect of Russia's economic warfare might be Europe's loss of industries with high energy consumption, such as the chemical and steel sectors. If these industries relocate, it will probably benefit the USA and Canada, which are self-sufficient in their gas and oil supply and can offer much lower energy prices to their producers. This intra-Western competition was also a major component of the Cold War, when Germany and the EC were able to overcome the two oil crises by replacing Middle Eastern oil and gas with Soviet deliveries. There does not seem to be a similar way out this time around, so it is all the more important to develop alternative energies.

Though the negative consequences of Russia's counter-sanctions are clear, there is no way back from the economic war. Putin will certainly not supply gas as he did before 2022, even if the EU (or some EU countries, such as Hungary) decides to lift or weaken the sanctions. The Russian dictator would then demand much more in return for a regular gas supply: the end of weapons deliveries to Ukraine. The economic and the military dimensions of the war are therefore intertwined. Nevertheless, 'stop the sanctions' is a rallying cry with strong allure. It has given right-wing populists and nationalists, some of whom were supported or even paid by Russia, a new topic to mobilize and enlarge their electorate.

This pro-Russian stance can only be countered by explaining

to the public why the economic war is necessary. Unfortunately, there is a communication problem here. When the West talks about 'sanctions', it functions as an equivalent to Russia's 'special operation', i.e., the strategy of not calling a war by that name. The sanctions have been justified mainly through moral arguments, which are correct but insufficient. Governments must help the public understand why the sanctions will benefit the West, and in particular the EU, in the long run. One key argument here is reducing dependency on imported fossil fuels, a problem that has haunted Europe since the oil crisis in 1974. Accelerating the switch to renewables will also contribute to the modernization of the economy. Last but not least, it will help the West become a leader in the technologies needed to slow down global warming.

The basic message needs to be an optimistic one, namely, that every political and economic crisis offers an opportunity. This forward-looking communication was missing in the spring of 2022 when the debate about boycotting Russian oil and gas altogether was halted. Such a move would have destroyed Putin's potential for blackmailing the EU, and Germany in particular. Instead, Putin regained the initiative in the economic warfare by stopping and starting the gas supply, which contributed to steep price hikes. He can now export much less gas and still get three times the revenue he did before the invasion of Ukraine. Because of its defensive stance in the economic war, the EU is now financing Russia's war through higher gas bills. The Russian army has lost some battles and territory, but so far Putin does not look like a loser in the economic war.

The limited impact and reach of the sanctions also strengthens Putin's grip on his home front, the third element of the war. The situation is more complicated for Ukraine and its Western supporters because we are dealing with multiple home fronts. If any European country flounders under Russia's economic warfare and rising inflation – experiencing street protests, for example – it would have an impact on other countries and their home fronts. This is especially true if a big EU country called for weakening or lifting the sanctions, or if several small countries followed Viktor Orbán's path of collaboration (something that could happen after a change of government in Slovakia, which has a long tradition of Russophilia).

Home fronts are not only impacted by the supply of materials, but also by social structures and cultural habits. Russia might have an advantage here as well, and this should not be underestimated. When Western luxury firms and restaurant chains like McDonald's withdrew from Russia, Western media and governments expected the Russian populace to grow angry and blame Putin for the lack of Mercedes and Big Macs. This expectation was driven by Western consumerism, and it was apparently forgotten that the vast majority of Russians always had to live without these goods. Moreover, the middle generation and the elderly (at least those who survived Putin's mishandling of the Covid-19 pandemic) still vividly remember the late Soviet Union and the economic depression in the 1990s, and they know how to deal with a scarcity of almost everything. Two thirds of the urban Russian population own a dacha and can grow fruit and vegetables to sustain them in hard times. How strong would such resilience be in the West, where people have been used to a much higher standard of living for many decades?

The goal of these arguments is not to paint a bleak picture but to point to the fact that, in every major war, it is pivotal to know the weaknesses and, above all, the strengths of your enemy. A major disadvantage for the Ukrainian home front is that the war is being fought almost entirely on Ukrainian territory. In response to its military defeats, Russia has increasingly destroyed Ukraine's civilian infrastructure since the autumn of 2022. While Ukrainians are freezing and sitting in the dark, daily life in Russia continues much as it did before. The growing number of fallen soldiers and compulsory conscription disturb the picture, but the Russian government is smart enough to present the casualties as a contribution to another great patriotic war, and to limit conscriptions whenever protests have mounted.

If we believe that history can teach us a lesson – unfortunately, the amateur historian Vladimir Vladimirovich Putin learned all the wrong lessons – then the war in the former Yugoslavia can act as a point of reference. The Serbian president Slobodan Milošević was the mastermind behind the ethnic warfare in Croatia and Bosnia. He wanted to replace the republic's borders with ethnic borders in order to create a greater Serbia. In 1995 he lost the military war in Croatia, and the Serbian army was on the retreat in Bosnia as well. Living standards in Serbia decreased dramatically over the 1990s, in part due to Western sanctions. Nonetheless, Milošević remained safely in power because Serbia's territory was not directly affected by the war. This changed when NATO bombed Serbia in 1999 to prevent another major ethnic cleansing in Kosovo. Even then, Milošević continued to be the president for more than a year, and his strongest argument for stabilizing the home front was to present Serbia as a victim of evil Western aggression, as Putin does today. The NATO bombing closed the ranks in Serbia and reinforced a defensive and simultaneously very aggressive nationalism. This is where the historical analogy ends, however, because Russia is a nuclear power and cannot be bombed like Serbia.

So far, there is no sign that the Russian home front is crumbling. The protests against the compulsory army draft in October were short-lived even in regions where Russia rules like a colonial power, such as the North Caucasian Dagestan. Russia's fallen soldiers are being killed by Ukrainians, so the many casualties might have the effect of consolidating Russian support for the war. Though the Russian army's disregard for its own soldiers and their chances of survival in the field is appalling, government propaganda and censorship mean that the Russian populace rarely hears about the incompetence of the military leadership, friendly fire, the privileges of the privatized Wagner army or the lack of even the most basic goods for its own soldiers. Ukraine is in a more difficult position since any failures on the part of its own military, which are inevitable in every major war, will be much more openly discussed and criticized.

The same is true for the economic and financial situation, which is rapidly deteriorating. While Russia can finance its war with its growing gas and oil revenue, and it still has huge foreign currency reserves, Ukraine is massively in debt to the IMF and other Western creditors. Financing the war will be a huge strain on the state budget and the economy, which has already been hit hard by the Russian invasion and deliberate destruction of civilian infrastructure. At the time of writing, Ukraine's GDP was projected to fall by about a third in 2022 – a logical outcome, seeing as a third of the country is either occupied or being heavily shelled by the Russian army. Compared to Ukraine, Russia is in a favourable economic situation, though its dependence on China will increase.

The respective home fronts in this war are also influenced by systemic differences between the West and Russia (as well as its ally Belarus, which does not seem to be moving towards a regime change either). Dictators have an advantage in that they can assume they will rule indefinitely, while democratic elections often lead to foreign policy changes. If Trump or another politician of his ilk wins the next US presidential election, it is not out of the question that the USA could return to isolationism and reduce or even stop its military and economic support for Ukraine. There is also an imbalance in the reach of war propaganda. While Russia can still broadcast fake news via social media and divide Western public opinion on various contested issues, very few Western messages or disturbing information about the war are reaching Russia. To sum up, Russia has certain advantages on the home front as well, and the West should develop a clever strategy to counter its structural disadvantages in this area.

Afterword: A Bad End

Since it is hard to imagine a dictated peace with a nuclear power, calls for a compromise with Russia will grow louder the longer the war drags on. However, it is equally hard to envision negotiations with a president who is responsible for heinous war crimes, and who is already pursuing a scorched earth policy and bombarding all the parts of Ukraine his army was unable to conquer. The history of the past ten years does not speak in favour of a compromise with Putin. Russian-backed units repeatedly broke the ceasefire after 2014 and kept Ukraine in a permanent state of war. Russia has now invaded Ukraine a second time, so what would prevent Russia from attacking yet again, this time from a more favourable military position since Ukraine is encircled in the north, the east and now also the south? Hence, there will be very little trust in future ceasefire lines. Ukrainian neutrality is also no longer an option, because after the country's derailed attempt to join NATO, it was not a member of any military alliance but was attacked twice by Russia nonetheless. These conditions make it tremendously difficult to contemplate, much less negotiate, a lasting peace. And perhaps such a thing is impossible anyway as long as Putin and his inner circle rule in Moscow.

* * *

What will future historians see when they look back on the three decades after 1989? The West lost much of its political, economic and social cohesion in this period – the basis of the metaphorical assertion in the title of this book. The new Russian war against Ukraine has brought much of the West closer together and reinforced the support for Ukraine. But the economic war and the war on the home fronts will be more difficult to win than military battles in the field. In the end, both sides of the 'classic' military conflict – Russia and Ukraine – are going to suffer losses in this war and come out of it very much weakened, just as Great Britain, France and Germany did after the First World War. The war is also an additional strain on Western democracies, as the loss of the external peace will increase the internal pressure on them, and the EU might be an economic loser in the war as well.

It is the global climate, however, that is suffering the most. Global warming has been a proven fact since the end of the 1980s and a topic of discussion in powerful political bodies like the US Senate. But for all the alarming research findings, declarations and global agreements, not nearly enough has been done. The pandemic and Russian war against Ukraine have further clouded the prospects for the world's climate because they are swallowing up attention and resources. This is what the world looks like three decades after the Cold War. It is not the ending I would have wanted for this book, but luckily it is also not the end of history.

Postscript and Acknowledgements

For a long time I contemplated whether I should publish these essays in English. Essays, especially fairly long ones, have somewhat fallen out of fashion in the Anglophone world. Smartphones are the younger generation's information channel of choice, but who wants to read a thousand-word essay on their phone? Would this book just be preaching to the choir? What good does it do for academics to analyse the strategies of right-wing populists and nationalists and lament the downfall of the Left, all of which is just a distraction from the decline of liberalism and conservatism? Does this content and form of writing belong somewhere else, perhaps – in the public sphere of social media?

My concerns and self-doubts were assuaged by a friendly email from my colleague Joachim Whaley at the University of Cambridge, who had read the German version of my book and recounted his students' enthusiastic response to it. This feedback encouraged me to submit the manuscript to an excellent publisher like Polity. The long journey to publication also involved two constructive expert reviews, for which I would like to express my thanks. My experience with Polity Press was very good indeed, and I would especially like to thank John

Thompson and Elise Heslinga, as well as my translator, Jessica Spengler. Over time she became much more than a translator, and I thank her for all the great suggestions about the content of this book.

Most of the essays in this book stem from my time at the Remarque Institute at New York University (NYU), where I was personally and professionally inspired by Larry Wolff. I also want to thank my wife, Martina Steer, who brightened my dark mood when I was struggling to prepare the manuscript for translation after a total of nine months of school closures during the pandemic ('home schooling' is one of the biggest euphemisms of recent times) as well as various lockdowns. Some of the essays here are new, particularly the introduction and the text about the pandemic. The texts on Polanyi and the estrangement of Russia and Turkey have been expanded significantly. Finally, I was encouraged to take on the elegant but challenging format of the analytical essay in 2018–19 by my editor at Suhrkamp, Heinrich Geiselberger, whom I would also like to thank once again.

Notes

Preface: The Great Transformation after 1989

1 Francis Fukuyama, 'The End of History?' in: *The National Interest* 16 (1989), pp. 3–18. In his 1992 book of the same name, Fukuyama was already somewhat more sceptical, so it is unfair to reduce his thinking to this essay alone. The shift from an optimistic to sceptical world view was even more apparent in the case of Samuel Huntington and his two books from the 1990s, *The Third Wave of Democracy* and *The Clash of Civilizations*.
2 Tony Judt, *Postwar: A History of Europe Since 1945*, New York: Penguin, 2005.
3 David Stark has published a large number of works; see, e.g., 'From System Identity to Organizational Diversity: Analyzing Social Change in Eastern Europe' in: *Contemporary Sociology* 21/3 (1992), pp. 299–304.
4 Social and cultural anthropologists were the exception here; see, e.g., Michał Buchowski, *Rethinking Transformation: An Anthropological Perspective on Postsocialism*, Poznań: Humaniora, 2001; Christopher Hann (ed.), *Postsocialism: Ideals, Ideologies and Practices in Eurasia*, London: Routledge, 2002; Elizabeth Dunn, *Privatizing Poland: Baby Food, Big Business, and the Remaking of Labor*, Ithaca, NY: Cornell University Press,

2004; David Kideckel, *Getting by in Postsocialist Romania: Labor, the Body, and Working-Class Culture*, Bloomington: University of Indiana Press, 2008; and the exciting new book in Polish by Aleksandra Leyk and Joanna Wawrzyniak, *Cięcia: Mówiona historia transformacji*, Warsaw: Krytyka Polityczna, 2021.

5 See Quinn Slobodian, *Globalists: The End of Empire and the Birth of Neoliberalism*, Cambridge, MA: Harvard University Press, 2018.

6 This definition is based on Claus Offe, 'Das Dilemma der Gleichzeitigkeit: Demokratisierung und Marktwirtschaft in Osteuropa' in: *Merkur* 4/505 (1991), pp. 279–92.

7 This was one of the main theories in my chronicle of contemporary Europe, which dealt with neoliberal reforms and was published in German in 2014. The German title was *Die neue Ordnung auf dem alten Kontinent: Eine Geschichte des neoliberalen Europe* (The New Order on the Old Continent: A History of Neoliberal Europe). The English version, *Europe Since 1989: A History*, was translated by Charlotte Hughes-Kreutzmüller and published by Princeton University Press in 2016.

8 The original quote is on p. 17 of his article 'The End of History?' in: *The National Interest* 16 (1989), pp. 3–18.

9 This theory is proposed by, e.g., Steven Levitsky and Daniel Ziblatt, *How Democracies Die*, New York: Crown, 2018.

10 Thank you again, Stefan Troebst.

11 I have never visited Chile, however, so I have had to make do with secondary literature and sources from the World Bank archives.

12 See Branko Milanović, *Global Inequality: A New Approach for the Age of Globalization*, Cambridge, MA: Harvard University Press, 2016.

13 See Adam Tooze, *Crashed: How a Decade of Financial Crises Changed the World*, New York: Viking, 2018, pp. 419–61.

14 The exact title of the book is *Civilization: The Six Ways the West Beat the Rest*, London: Allen Lane, 2011. In the wake of the global financial crisis, Niall Ferguson himself apparently began to have

doubts about the supremacy of the West, which he expressed in the last chapter of the book (see pp. 295–325).
15 References and citations can be found in the third essay.
16 See Andrei Shleifer and Daniel Treisman, 'Normal Countries: The East 25 Years After Communism' in: *Foreign Affairs* 93 (2014), available online at http://www.foreignaffairs.com/articles/142200/andrei-shleifer-and-daniel-treisman/normal-countries.
17 See Colin Crouch, *Post-Democracy: A Sociological Introduction*, Cambridge: Polity, 2004; Cas Mudde, *The Ideology of the Extreme Right*, Manchester: Manchester University Press, 2002.
18 The difference between taking risks and banking on safety is a main theme in the first contemporary historical account of the pandemic; see Peter Baldwin, *Fighting the First Wave: Why the Coronavirus Was Tackled So Differently Across the Globe*, Cambridge: Cambridge University Press, 2021.

1. From Neoliberalism to Antiliberalism: The Enduring Relevance of Karl Polanyi

1 The Swiss magazine *Geschichte der Gegenwart* is published online at https://geschichtedergegenwart.ch by editor Philipp Sarasin and his colleagues. It is worth noting that the title of the site's main section does not use the word *Geschichte* in the singular, meaning history, but rather *Geschichten* in the plural, meaning stories.

The German author is Andreas Rödder, *21.0: Eine kurze Geschichte der Gegenwart*, Munich: C.H. Beck, 2017; he promises a 'crash course in the problems of the present'. The textbook by Peter Schade and Hans-Joachim Stark, *Geschichte in der Gegenwart: Lehr- und Arbeitsbuch Geschichte und Gemeinschaftskunde/Sozialkunde*, Cologne: Bildungsverlag EINS, 2005, is already in its tenth edition.

2 There is ample secondary literature about Polanyi. Political scientist Gareth Dale has especially distinguished himself in this field, and my interpretations build on his. Dale's study of the history of Polanyi's ideas (*Karl Polanyi: The Limits of the Market*,

Malden, MA: Polity Press, 2010) is especially important, as is *Karl Polanyi: A Life on the Left*, New York: Columbia University Press, 2016.

3 See, e.g., Friedman's affirmative essay 'Neo-liberalism and its Prospects' in: *Farmand* (17 February 1951), pp. 89–93, available online at https://miltonfriedman.hoover.org/internal/media/dispatcher/214957/full; see also Angus Burgin, *The Great Persuasion: Reinventing Free Markets Since the Depression*, Cambridge, MA: Harvard University Press, 2012, p. 170. Regarding the history of the idea of neoliberalism, see Slobodian, *Globalists*; Daniel Stedman Jones, *Masters of the Universe: Hayek, Friedman, and the Birth of Neoliberal Politics*, Princeton, NJ: Princeton University Press, 2012; Philip Mirowski and Dieter Plehwe (eds), *The Road from Mont Pèlerin: The Making of the Neoliberal Thought Collective*, Cambridge, MA: Harvard University Press, 2009.

4 A German version of Polanyi's book was first published in 1973 with the title *The Great Transformation: Politische und ökonomische Ursprünge von Gesellschaften und Wirtschaftssystemen* (Political and Economic Origins of Societies and Economic Systems), translated from English by Heinrich Jelinek, Frankfurt am Main: Suhrkamp, 1973. For this English edition of my book, I am using the second paperback edition published by Beacon Press in 2001.

5 Historians to date have often fuzzily defined globalization as increased exchange. A more convincing definition and chronology can be found in Stefan Link, 'How Might 21st-Century De-Globalization Unfold? Some Historical Reflections' in: *New Global Studies* 12/3 (2018), pp. 343–65.

6 Regarding these radical leftists, see Dale, *A Life on the Left*, pp. 11–40.

7 This is not to say that Polanyi was *only* a Marxist; regarding his ideas about Christian socialism, see Dale, *The Limits of the Market*, pp. 6–8.

8 See the second chapter of *The Great Transformation* entitled

'Conservative Twenties, Revolutionary Thirties'; Polanyi returns to this point again in chapter 18.

9 Regarding the reception of Polanyi in the 1990s, see Dale, *The Limits of the Market*. Dale refers to a four-stage model here consisting of 'marketization, countermovement, disruptive strains, socialist resolution/fascist irruption' (p. 227).

10 For a global perspective, see also the intelligent work by Kiran Klaus Patel, *The New Deal: A Global History*, Princeton, NJ: Princeton University Press, 2016. Polanyi pays remarkably little attention to the New Deal. Regarding heavier regulation and the subsequent financialization of capitalism, see Jürgen Kocka, *Capitalism: A Short History*, translated by Jeremiah Riemer, Princeton, NJ: Princeton University Press, 2016, pp. 114–24.

11 See Karin Fischer, 'The Influence of Neoliberals in Chile before, during and after Pinochet' in: Philip Mirowski and Dieter Plehwe (eds), *The Road from Mont Pèlerin: The Making of the Neoliberal Thought Collective*, Cambridge, MA: Harvard University Press, 2009, pp. 305–46.

12 Regarding these reform concepts, see the files on Chile in the World Bank Archives, particularly an eleven-page manifesto from 1988. The records of discussions during a visit to the World Bank in 1989 are also stored in the archives. See World Bank File 16435 (Chile – Lending, Economy and Program (LEAP) – General – Volume 2), the annex to the World Bank report of 18 October 1988, as well as World Bank File 16436 (Chile – Lending, Economy and Program (LEAP) – General – Volume 3), the report dated 30 October 1989 (all World Bank files cited here are unpaginated). Regarding Chile's economic policy and the historical changes of 1989, see also Ricardo Ffrench-Davis, *Economic Reforms in Chile: From Dictatorship to Democracy*, London: Palgrave Macmillan, 2010.

13 See John Williamson, 'A Short History of the Washington Consensus', available online at https://www.piie.com/publications/papers/williamson0904-2.pdf.

14 Regarding his justifications for the reforms at the time, see

Leszek Balcerowicz, *800 Dni Szok Kontrolowany. Zapisał: Jerzy Baczyński*, Warsaw: BGW, 1992. Balcerowicz also used the term 'shock' in this book, a word he had wisely avoided in 1989. Regarding the concept behind the radical reforms from the perspective of the American economic advisors to the Polish government, see David Lipton and Jeffrey D. Sachs, 'Poland's Economic Reform' in: *Foreign Affairs* 69/3 (1990), pp. 47–66.

15 See the figures in the *wiiw Handbook of Statistics 2012*, 'Structural Indicators', Table II/1.7, pp. 74f.; regarding Balcerowicz's predictions, see 'Albo szybko, albo wcale' in: *Polityka* 33/48 (2 December 1989), pp. 1 and 5 (particularly column 2 on p. 1). Kołodko also had the prestige of being published in English; see Grzegorz Kołodko, *From Shock to Therapy: The Political Economy of Postsocialist Transformation*, Oxford: Oxford University Press, 2000.

16 Regarding the international debates about the reforms in Poland, see the IMF Staff Report dated 8 June 1992, which is available in the World Bank Archive: World Bank Archive, World Bank File 30029780 (Poland – Privatization – Volume 2). Experts from the World Bank criticized the downward spiral that had been triggered by austerity measures, while representatives of the IMF called for even more radical reforms; regarding the 'liberal myth of the "collectivist" conspiracy' which crops up again and again, ensuring that the beneficial effects of a liberal programme can never really flourish, see Polanyi, *The Great Transformation: The Political and Economic Origins of Our Time*, Boston, MA: Beacon Press, pp. 156–62.

17 Andrei Shleifer and Daniel Treisman, 'Normal Countries: The East 25 Years After Communism' in: *Foreign Affairs* (November/December 2014). Jeffrey Sachs subsequently turned his attention to economic development and the fight against poverty, and he is now to the left of the mainstream Democratic party in the USA.

18 Ivan Krastev and Stephen Holmes, *The Light that Failed: A Reckoning*, New York: Allen Lane, 2019.

19 See Hilary Appel and Mitchell Orenstein, *From Triumph to Crisis: Neoliberal Economic Reform in Postcommunist Countries*, Cambridge: Cambridge University Press, 2018, pp. 116–41.
20 See Philipp Ther, *Europe since 1989: A History*, translated by Charlotte Hughes-Kreutzmüller, Princeton, NJ: Princeton University Press, 2016, p. 113.
21 See Kevin M. Kruse and Julian E. Zelizer, *Fault Lines: A History of the United States Since 1974*, New York: Norton, 2019, p. 210 (more on this in the following essay about the USA).
22 See the statistics in Zenonus Norkus, *On Baltic Slovenia and Adriatic Lithuania: A Qualitative Comparative Analysis of Patterns in Post-Communist Transformation*, Budapest: CEU Press, 2012.
23 See Branko Milanović and Lire Ersado, 'Reform and Inequality during the Transition: An Analysis Using Panel Household Survey Data, 1990–2005' in: Gérard Roland (ed.), *Economies in Transition: The Long-Run View*, London: Palgrave, 2013, pp. 84–108, p. 101.
24 Regarding the data cited here and elsewhere, see Robert H. Frank, *Falling Behind: How Rising Inequality Harms the Middle Class*, Berkeley: University of California Press, 2013, pp. 6–15 (and chapter 2 on income and wealth inequality).
25 See the submissions to the competition 'Rok 1989: koniec, przełom, początek . . .?' (The Year 1989: End, Turning Point, Beginning . . .?). The winning texts are no longer available on the KARTA website, but the jury's comments, which provide a brief overview of the content, can still be found at http://uczycsiezhi storii.pl/konkurs/rok-1989-koniec-przelom-poczatek. A total of 144 texts can be viewed in the archives of the KARTA Center.
26 See Dorothee Bohle and Béla Greskovits, *Capitalist Diversity on Europe's Periphery*, Ithaca, NY: Cornell University Press, 2012, p. 225.
27 See Paul Collier, *The Future of Capitalism: Facing the New Anxieties*, New York: HarperCollins, 2018, pp. 31–56.
28 Polanyi, *The Great Transformation*, p. 145.

29 Ibid., p. 160.
30 Polish linguists take pains to point out that this is a Russian loanword. It was first mentioned in a dictionary in 1992 and was used increasingly frequently from the mid-1990s; see Michał Sarnowski, '"Nieudacznik" – pożyczka leksykalna czy wyraz obcy?' in: *Acta Polono-Ruthenica* 13 (2008), pp. 521–30, available online at http://bazhum.muzhp.pl/media//files/Acta_Polono_Ruthenica/Acta_Polono_Ruthenica-r2008-t13/Acta_Polono_Ruthenica-r2008-t13-s521-530/Acta_Polono_Ruthenica-r2008-t13-s521-530.pdf.
31 See Pierre Bourdieu, *Distinction: A Social Critique of the Judgement of Taste*, translated by Richard Nice, Cambridge, MA: Harvard University Press, 1984.
32 For reasons of space, it is not possible to list all of the specialist literature on this subject. However, for a very critical analysis of Hartz IV, see, e.g., Christoph Butterwegge, *Hartz IV und die Folgen: Auf dem Weg in eine andere Republik?*, Weinheim/Basel: Beltz Juventa, 2015.
33 Several sections in *The Great Transformation* are dedicated to examining the creation of markets for what Polanyi refers to as the 'fictitious commodity' of labour, especially chapter 14, 'Market and Man', pp. 171–86.
34 Polanyi grapples in detail with the deliberate use of fear and the 'scourge of hunger' by looking at statements from conservative English authors such as Joseph Townsend (1739–1816) about the Elizabethan Poor Law, which would have offered at least some degree of protection until it was repealed in 1834; see Polanyi, *The Great Transformation*, chapter 10.
35 A recent master's degree thesis on Slovakia shows just how much the IMF and World Bank pushed for cuts to the social welfare system; see Lukas Schweighofer, *Vom Aschenputtel zum Tatra-Tiger: Die slowakische Wirtschaftspolitik im Lichte des IWF und der Weltbank 1993–2006*, Vienna: Master's thesis in the Faculty of Historical and Cultural Studies, 2018.
36 This is one of the conclusions reached in the astute book (and

earlier publications) by Philip Manow, *Die politische Ökonomie des Populismus*, Berlin: Suhrkamp, 2018.
37 See Tooze, *Crashed*, pp. 419–61.
38 See Krastev and Holmes, *The Light that Failed*. However, their book can also be interpreted as an indictment of Western arrogance and a plea to listen more to Eastern Europeans.
39 These verbal escalation mechanisms have been analysed in depth and in international comparison by the linguist Ruth Wodak. See Ruth Wodak, *The Politics of Fear: The Shameless Normalization of Far-Right Discourse*, 2nd edition, London: Sage, 2021.

2. Lost Social and Political Equilibrium: The USA after the Cold War

1 See Kruse and Zelizer, *Fault Lines*. Prominent political scientists and scholars of democracy similarly argue that political polarization is the biggest problem facing the United States. See, e.g., Steven Levitsky and Daniel Ziblatt, *How Democracies Die*, New York: Crown Publishers, 2018. In the case of Russia, which is discussed as a point of comparison, I would instead argue that the economic form of the oligarchy ultimately produced its political equivalent.
2 See the lucid account in Svetlana Boym, *The Future of Nostalgia*, New York: Basic Books, 2001.
3 Specifically, Clinton said: 'Our hopes, our hearts, our hands, are with those on every continent who are building democracy and freedom. Their cause is America's cause'; William Jefferson Clinton, 'First inaugural address' (20 January 1993), available online at https://avalon.law.yale.edu/20th_century/clinton1.asp.
4 See Didier Eribon, *Return to Reims*, translated by Michael Lucey, Los Angeles: Semiotexte, 2013. Strangely enough, this book mostly attracted attention for its author's open description of his coming out, not for his social and political analysis. Steffen Mau's book has not yet been translated into English, perhaps because international publishers think wrongly that it is too specific to Germany. The German title is *Lütten Klein: Leben in*

der ostdeutschen Transformationsgesellschaft, Berlin: Suhrkamp, 2019.

5 This term comes from the book of the same name by C. Wright Mills, *The Sociological Imagination*, Oxford: Oxford University Press, 1959.

6 Health care costs tripled under Ronald Reagan and George Bush, in part due to the neoliberal privatization of health care; regarding this rise in costs, see Kruse and Zelizer, *Fault Lines*, p. 211.

7 See his book *Identity: The Demand for Dignity and the Politics of Resentment*, New York: Farrar, Straus and Giroux, 2018. On pages 113–16, Fukuyama is quick to identify his culprit for the turn to identity politics: the Left. For more on this bold claim, see below.

8 The social stigma surrounding homosexuality at the time makes it difficult to precisely estimate the proportion of gay men and lesbians in the overall population. The proportion of people identifying as LGBT has risen steadily since the 1990s. According to a Gallup poll, 5.6 per cent of the adult population in the USA identified as LGBT in 2020, which is nearly twice as high as in the early 1990s. However, more than half of these LGBT adults identified as bisexual. See https://news.gallup.com/poll/329708/lgbt-identification-rises-latest-estimate.aspx.

9 This should not be taken as a criticism of my alma mater, because in other seminars we learned all the more about social history and African-American emancipation.

10 Regarding the shutdown, see Kruse and Zelizer, *Fault Lines*, p. 222. Regarding Gingrich, see also the more recent political biography by Julian Zelizer, *Burning Down the House: Newt Gingrich, the Fall of a Speaker, and the Rise of the New Republican Party*, New York: Penguin, 2020.

11 Mudde and Kaltwasser define populism as '*a thin-centered ideology that considers society to be ultimately separated into two homogeneous and antagonistic camps, "the pure people" versus "the corrupt elite," and which argues that politics should be an expression of the* volonté générale *(general will) of the people*'

(Cas Mudde and Cristóbal Rovira Kaltwasser, *Populism: A Very Short Introduction*, New York: Oxford University Press, 2017, p. 6; italics in original); see also Jan-Werner Müller, *Was ist Populismus? Ein Essay*, Berlin: Suhrkamp, 2016, pp. 42f.

12 See the detailed profile by McKay Coppins, 'Stephen Miller: Trump's Right-Hand Troll' in: *The Atlantic* (28 May 2018), available online at https://www.theatlantic.com/politics/archive/2018/05/stephen-miller-trump-adviser/561317/; regarding Miller's influence on immigration and asylum policy in the USA, see also Maggie Haberman, 'A Familiar Force Nurtures Trump's Instincts on Immigration: Stephen Miller' in: *The New York Times* (4 November 2018), available online at https://www.nytimes.com/2018/11/04/us/politics/trump-stephen-miller-immigration.html.

13 Quoted in Kruse and Zelizer, *Fault Lines*, p. 219.

14 For more on this and the fundamentals of Reaganomics as viewed through the lens of democratic theory, and from a perspective that is not necessarily critical of capitalism, see Monika Prasad, *Starving the Beast: Ronald Reagan and the Tax Cut Revolution*, New York: Russell Sage Foundation, 2018.

15 See Tooze, *Crashed*, p. 140.

16 The last prominent case was against Microsoft in 1998, specifically, the company's attempts to monopolize the internet browser market. To avoid being split up like AT&T, Microsoft changed its practices, which in turn enabled the rise of Google, Facebook and other internet firms.

3. The Price of Unity: Germany's Shock Therapy in International Comparison

1 'The sick man of the euro' in: *The Economist* (3 June 1999), available online at https://www.economist.com/special/1999/06/03/the-sick-man-of-the-euro. The economic data cited in this essay is based on the updated version of my book *Europe since 1989: A History* and the research I conducted for it. Regarding Germany's crisis in the late 1990s, see also Hartmut Berghoff, 'Die

1990er Jahre als Epochenschwelle? Der Umbau der Deutschland AG zwischen Traditionsbruch und Kontinuitätswahrung' in: *Historische Zeitschrift* 308/2 (2019), pp. 364–400, p. 369.

2 Marcus Böick's book was very important to this debate; see Böick, *Die Treuhand: Idee – Praxis – Erfahrung 1990–1994*, Göttingen: Wallstein, 2018. A major research project being conducted by the Leibniz Institute for Contemporary History will lead to new insights in this area.

3 Regarding the calculation of the exchange rate, see Gerlinde Sinn and Hans-Werner Sinn, *Kaltstart: Volkswirtschaftliche Aspekte der deutschen Vereinigung*, 2nd revised edition, Tübingen: Mohr-Siebeck, 1992, pp. 54–64; regarding the suggestion of the GDR's state bank, see the Deutschlandfunk interview of 28 February 2015, with the bank's vice-president at the time, Edgar Most, available online at https://www.deutschlandfunk.de/25-jahre-treuhandanstalt-eine-einzige-schweinerei-100.html. While giving talks on this topic in recent years, I have often been asked whether there were any alternatives to the currency reform. Options discussed at the time included a lower exchange rate with a better revaluation of savings deposits to give former GDR citizens a kind of seed capital. There was also a wage subsidy scheme which was tested in the 'Rust Belt' and actually implemented in 2005.

4 Regarding these figures and the ones that follow, see Böick, *Die Treuhand*.

5 Regarding east-to-west migration, see Bernd Martens, 'Zug nach Westen – Anhaltende Abwanderung' (30 March 2010), available online at https://www.bpb.de/system/files/pdf/1LYN4H.pdf.

6 See Philip Manow, *Die politische Ökonomie des Populismus*, Berlin: Suhrkamp, 2018, p. 94.

7 See Martin Diewald, Anne Goedicke and Karl Ulrich Mayer (eds), *After the Fall of the Wall: Life Courses in the Transformation of East Germany*, Stanford, CA: Stanford University Press, 2006.

8 See '"Zum Kotzen": Helmut Schmidt wettert gegen Jammer-Ossis' in: *Spiegel online* (11 October 2003), available online at

http://www.spiegel.de/politik/deutschland/zum-kotzen-helmut-schmidt-wettert-gegen-jammer-ossis-a-269386.html.

9 Regarding these figures, see Ivan T. Berend, *From the Soviet Bloc to the European Union*, Cambridge: Cambridge University Press, 2009, p. 61.

10 Regarding the crisis of the German social welfare state, see Gerhard A. Ritter, *Der Preis der deutschen Einheit: Die Wiedervereinigung und die Krise des Sozialstaates*, Munich: C.H. Beck, 2006.

11 According to data cited by Hartmut Berghoff, a total of 3.7 million manufacturing jobs were lost between 1991 and 2002, 3.3 million of them in the old Federal Republic of Germany; see Berghoff, 'Die 1990er Jahre als Epochenschwelle?', p. 390.

12 The exact case numbers have been available online on the website of the Berlin police since 2002; see https://www.berlin.de/polizei/verschiedenes/polizeiliche-kriminalstatistik.

13 Regarding these red-green social and economic reforms, see Edgar Wolfrum, *Rot-Grün an der Macht: Deutschland 1998–2005*, Munich: C.H. Beck, 2013. More context is needed to understand the Hartz reforms, however; for a general overview of the neoliberal reforms in post-communist Europe, see Appel and Orenstein, *From Triumph to Crisis*, pp. 90–116. Tony Blair's New Labour was obviously another important point of reference for Schröder and the Social Democrats; in this respect, it is important not to relativize the co-transformation or interpret it too monocausally.

14 The best-known proposal was the tax model suggested by Friedrich Merz, leader of the Christian Democratic Union's parliamentary group in the Bundestag at the time. His model involved three tax rates with a top rate of 36 per cent (Merz had said that people should be able to work out how much tax they owed on the back of a beer mat, so his proposal has gone down in history as the beer mat model). This idea was apparently enough to earn Merz a reputation as a financial expert, which landed him the position of chairman of the supervisory board of

BlackRock Germany after he left politics. BlackRock is a global finance and investment corporation which specializes in splitting up companies and reselling their profitable segments.

15 The data cited here for Scandinavian and East Central European countries can be found online at http://www.gini-research.org/articles/cr. Each country report includes the respective data as well as an explanation of how it was gathered.

16 The figure of 1.6 billion euros is cited by Jürgen Kühl, '25 Jahre deutsche Einheit: Annäherungen und verbliebene Unterschiede zwischen West und Ost' (4 July 2014), available online at http://www.bpb.de/politik/innenpolitik/arbeitsmarktpolitik/55390/25-jahre-deutsche-einheit. The problem with these estimates is that the German federal government stopped gathering precise data on its transfer payments in 1999. The transfer payments also included development aid (some of which could be applied for in western Germany as well) and extra benefits such as special economic promotion programmes. A comprehensive calculation of all the individual types of expenditures and return flows can be found in Ulrich Blum et al., 'Regionalisierung öffentlicher Ausgaben und Einnahmen: Eine Untersuchung am Beispiel der Neuen Länder', *IWH-Sonderheft* 4/2009, available online at https://www.econstor.eu/bitstream/10419/140919/1/SH_09-4.pdf.

17 These figures are based on collated economic data for all five federal states; see also Ther, *Europe since 1989*. The data cited there for the NUTS2 regions is available on the Eurostat website at https://ec.europa.eu/eurostat/tgm/table.do?tab=table&init=1&language=en&pcode=tgs00006&plugin=1. The Eurostat data is updated regularly; for example, the last census in Germany resulted in changes because population numbers were revised downwards, so per-capita GDP had to be revised upwards. There are, of course, more comprehensive economic measurements than GDP, including the Human Development Index (HDI), but only GDP has been regularly measured on a regional and municipal level since 1989.

18 See, e.g., Luis Cornago Bonal and Delia Zollinger, 'Immigration, Welfare Chauvinism and the Support for Radical Right Parties in Europe' (19 March 2018), available online at https://blogs.lse.ac.uk/eurocrisispress/2018/03/19/immigration-welfare-chauvinism-and-the-support-for-radical-right-parties-in-europe/. This article also cites current literature on the topic.
19 Polanyi, *The Great Transformation*, p. 189.

4. *La Crisi*: Italy's Decline as a Portent for Europe

1 Marx wrote these words in what is perhaps his best essay, 'The Eighteenth Brumaire of Louis Bonaparte'; see *Marx and Engels Collected Works*, vol. 11: *Marx and Engels, 1851–53*, London: Lawrence & Wishart, 2010 (1979), pp. 99–197.
2 For an account of Berlusconi's rise, see Guido Crainz, *Storia della Repubblica: L'Italia dalla Liberazione ad oggi*, Rome: Donzelli, 2016, pp. 306–13.
3 However, he is mentioned by Cas Mudde and other political scientists who have been researching right-wing populism for a long time; see, e.g., Cas Mudde and Cristóbal Rovira Kaltwasser, *Populism: A Very Short Introduction*, New York: Oxford University Press, 2017. In Italy itself, of course, there is extensive contemporary literature on the topic; see, e.g., Nicola Tranfaglia, *Populismo autoritario: Autobiografia di una nazione*, Milan: Dalai, 2010 (who points out interesting connections with Latin American populism) or Marco Tarchi, *L'Italia populista: Dal qualunquismo a Beppe Grillo*, Bologna: Il Mulino, 2014 (who covers more background from 1944 onwards).
4 For the details of the scandal, see Paul Ginsborg, *Italy and Its Discontents: Family, Civil Society, State, 1980–2001*, London: Penguin, 2001, pp. 267ff.
5 All the figures cited here relating to Italy's budget deficits and overall debt are based on a detailed research report from the European House – Ambrosetti think tank (www.ambrosetti.eu). The long version is available upon request through the website. Appendix (*appendice*) 6 covers the development of Italy's debt

broken down by year and government. A short version of the report was published in the newspaper *Corriere della Sera*; see Federico Fubini, 'Cernobbio, il livello record del debito: l'Italia come ai tempi di guerra' in: *Corriere della Sera* (5 April 2019), available online at https://roma.corriere.it/notizie/cronaca/19_aprile_05/livello-record-debito-come-tempi-guerra-df2f9b6a-57da-11e9-9553-f00a7f633280.shtml.

6 For a discussion of this 'managerialism' in 1994 (including quotes from the 1994 election campaign), see Giovanni Orsina, *Berlusconism and Italy: A Historical Interpretation*, translated by Emily and Hugo Bowles, New York: Palgrave Macmillan, 2014, pp. 71–2 and the entire third chapter.

7 See the data in appendix 6 of the report cited in note 5.

8 The precise point at which Italy overtook the UK was fiercely debated at the time; see Paul Ginsborg, *A History of Contemporary Italy: Society and Politics, 1943–1988*, New York: Palgrave Macmillan, 2003, p. 408.

9 For the history of Olivetti, see Giovanni De Witt, *Le fabbriche ed il mondo: L'Olivetti industriale nella competizione globale, 1950–90*, Milan: FrancoAngeli, 2005.

10 Regarding the success of Fiat in the 1980s, see Ginsborg, *A History of Contemporary Italy*, p. 407; regarding Fiat's expansion in Eastern Europe, see Valentina Fava, 'Between Business Interests and Ideological Marketing: The USSR and the Cold War in Fiat Corporate Strategy, 1957–1972' in: *Journal of Cold War Studies* 20/4 (2018), pp. 26–64.

11 An entire economic and social history of Italy could be written based only on Olivetti, Fiat and companies that grew in the context of the public holding company IRI. In light of Italy's decline since the mid-1990s, such an analysis is urgently necessary, not least to determine how the trend can be reversed.

12 See note 2 to this chapter.

13 The new electoral law was nicknamed the 'Porcellum' (after its own author referred to it as a *porcata*, or piece of junk), and it remained in place until the Constitutional Court ruled against it in 2013.

14 From 2010, the regional funds for southern Italy were redirected to fight the crisis and to be used for other tasks; see Francesco Barbagallo, *La questione italiana: Il Nord e il Sud dal 1860 a oggi*, Rome: Laterza, 2013, pp. 207f.

15 Regarding the radicalness of the Lega and its various illegal and sometimes violent activities, see Crainz, *Storia della Repubblica*, p. 326.

16 See 'Fallimenti record per colpa dei debiti Pa' in: *La Repubblica* (3 February 2014), available online at http://www.repubblica.it/economia/2014/02/03/news/fallimenti_record_per_colpa_dei_debiti_pa_cgia_alle_imprese_mancano_ancora_100_mld-7759 2615/.

17 Regarding this comparison between Southern and Eastern Europe, which was inspired by economic history studies from the late nineteenth century on 'Galician misery', see my book *Europe Since 1989*, pp. 235–46.

18 When Berlusconi became prime minister in 1994, Italy's currency was still the lira. This calculation of the country's debt in euros (and according to 2018 prices) is based on the research report from The European House – Ambrosetti (see note 5).

19 Regarding the development of the spread in 2011, see Michela Scacchioli, 'Da Berlusconi a Monti: La drammatica estate 2011 tra spread e rischi di bancarotta' in: *La Repubblica* (10 February 2014), available online at http://www.repubblica.it/politica/2014/02/10/news/estate_2011_spread_berlusconi_bce_monti_governo_napolitano-78215026/.

20 My main points of reference are Ginsborg's history of post-war Italy (*A History of Contemporary Italy: Society and Politics, 1943–1988*, London: Penguin, 1990) and the follow-up volume (*Italy and Its Discontents: Family, Civil Society, State, 1980–2001*, London: Penguin, 2003).

21 See Ginsborg, *Italy and Its Discontents*, p. 108; regarding the expansion of Berlusconi's media empire from the mid-1980s, see Crainz, *Storia della Repubblica*, p. 245.

22 All of these statistics, with various international comparisons,

can be found on the OECD website at https://data.oecd.org/edu att/population-with-tertiary-education.htm; https://data.oecd .org/eduatt/adult-education-level.htm and https://data.oecd.org /eduresource/education-spending.htm; regarding the deficits in the education system, see also Crainz, *Storia della Repubblica*, pp. 330f. Crainz rightly points out that, in light of the rising proportion of children with a migration background, Italy needs to invest far more in its schools.

23 See the data from FLC CGIL, the trade union for educators, regarding the 'Legge di stabilità' from 2010, available online at http://www.flcgil.it/attualita/sindacato/legge-di-stabilita.-confer mati-i-tagli.-pochi-interventi-a-favore-della-conoscenza.

24 Regarding internet connections and the provision of broadband for households, see Heide Seybert, 'Internet Use in Households and by Individuals in 2012' in: Eurostat, *Statistics in Focus* 50/2012, available online at https://ec.europa.eu/eurostat/docu ments/3433488/5585460/KS-SF-12-050-EN.PDF/39000dab-e2 b7-49b2-bc4b-6aad0bf01279. See also Ther, *Europe since 1989*, pp. 243f., which looks at other indicators in addition to internet access.

25 The *reddito di cittadinanza* corresponds to an older Southern European model of the welfare state based primarily on monetary payments instead of solid public institutions and services; regarding this tradition, which is also part of the problem, see Claude Martin, 'Southern Welfare States: Configuration of the Welfare Balance between State and the Family' in: Martin Baumeister and Roberto Sala (eds), *Southern Europe? Italy, Spain, Portugal, and Greece from the 1950s until the Present Day*, Frankfurt: Campus, 2015, pp. 77–102.

26 See Ginsborg, *Italy and Its Discontents*, pp. 68ff.; regarding the increased dependency on family networks (other authors call this 'familialism by default'), see also Martin, 'Southern Welfare States', pp. 88–90.

27 Regarding the data from 1992 and 1993, see Ginsborg, *Italy and Its Discontents*; regarding the statistics from 2018, see 'Italiani mammoni: tra i 18 e i 34 anni il 66% vive coi genitori' in: *Il Fatto*

Quotidiano (17 December 2018), available online at https://www.ilfattoquotidiano.it/2018/12/17/italiani-mammoni-tra-i-18-e-i-34-anni-il-66-vive-coi-genitori-peggio-di-noi-solo-grecia-croazia-e-malta/4843022/ (72.7 per cent of young men lived with their parents, compared to 60 per cent of women in the same age group).

28 See Ther, *Europe since 1989*, p. 252; regarding the low earnings of workers under the age of 35, see also Alberto Magnani, 'Redditi e pensioni, la bomba a orologeria dei giovani in Italia' in: *Il Sole 24 ore* (17 October 2017), available online at https://www.ilsole24ore.com/art/impresa-e-territori/2017-10-16/redditi-e-pensioni-bomba-orologeria-giovani-italia-160402.shtml?uuid=AEv4L1oC.

29 See Ther, *Europe since 1989*, p. 245.

30 Regarding the regional dimensions of the crisis, see Raffaele Ricciardi, 'Il Pil del Sud è il 42% meno del Nord: Così la crisi ha segnato il Mezzogiorno' in: *La Repubblica* (27 November 2013), available online at www.repubblica.it/economia/2013/11/27/news/conti_economici_regionali_istat_nord_sud-72073979/.

31 Regarding clientelism in companies, see Bruno Pellegrino and Luigi Zingales, 'Diagnosing the Italian Disease', National Bureau of Economic Research, Working Paper 23964, October 2017, available online at https://www.nber.org/papers/w23964.

32 The emigration data gathered by Eurostat is available online at http://appsso.eurostat.ec.europa.eu/nui/show.do?dataset=migr_emi2&lang=en. The Italian community in London grew by 150 per cent from 2006 to 2012; see Russell King, 'Migration and Southern Europe: A Center-Periphery Dynamic?' in: Baumeister and Sala (eds), *Southern Europe?*, pp. 139–69, p. 161.

33 See the research report from The European House – Ambrosetti, which lists both the primary surpluses of 1990–2007 and the budget deficit after interest payments (pp. 12 and 16).

34 This is not so apparent, however, because social inequality is measured internationally primarily on the basis of income inequality (the Gini coefficient) and not asset inequality.

35 Regarding the EU investment plan of 2014, see Gustav Theile, 'Juncker feiert seinen Investitionsplan – trotz Kritik' in: *Frankfurter Allgemeine Zeitung* (18 July 2018), available online at https://www.faz.net/aktuell/wirtschaft/konjunktur/juncker-feiert-seinen-investitionsplan-trotz-kritik-15696986.html.

36 See Fabio Tonacci, 'Salvini, il ministro latitante: nel 2019 al ministero solo 17 giornate piene' in: *La Repubblica* (14 May 2019), available online at https://www.repubblica.it/cronaca/2019/05/14/news/il_ministro_latitante-226209342/?ref=RHPPLF-BH-I226216739-C8-P2-S1.8-T1&refresh_ce.

37 Regarding the additional costs for refinancing the bonds, see the research report from The European House – Ambrosetti (note 5).

38 The data on GDP and debt in 2017–20 can be found in a report from ISTAT, the Italian National Institute of Statistics, available online at https://www.istat.it/it/files//2021/03/PIL-E-INDEBITAMENTO-AP_1mar2021.pdf. The report was published in March 2021, and it was not possible to take into account any later data for this book.

39 The IMF floated this suggestion in 2013; see International Monetary Fund, *Fiscal Monitor: Taxing Times* (October 2013), available online at https://www.imf.org/en/Publications/FM/Issues/2016/12/31/Taxing-Times, particularly p. 49.

5. The West, Turkey and Russia: A History of Estrangement

1 Regarding the military coups and Turkey's democratization, see Stefan Plaggenborg, 'Kemalismus und Bolschewismus: Ungleiche Brüder und ihr historisches Erbe' in: *Osteuropa* 68/10–12 (2018), pp. 51–80, pp. 65–9.

2 Plaggenborg estimates that a total of 6,000 people fell victim to the far-left and far-right violence in Turkey in the 1970s (ibid., p. 69).

3 See Tim Szatkowski, *Die Bundesrepublik Deutschland und die Türkei 1978 bis 1983*, Berlin: De Gruyter, 2016, p. 34; Karin

Hunn, 'Nächstes Jahr kehren wir zurück ...': Die Geschichte der türkischen 'Gastarbeiter' in der Bundesrepublik, Göttingen: Wallstein, 2005, pp. 458, 552.

4 Regarding the latter, see, e.g., Jannis Panagiotidis, 'Postsowjetische Migranten in Deutschland: Perspektiven auf eine heterogene Diaspora' in: *Aus Politik und Zeitgeschichte* 67/11–12 (2017), pp. 23–30.

5 See the results of the survey conducted in 2017 by the Körber Foundation, in which 56 per cent of the respondents agreed with this statement; only 41 per cent disagreed. The study is available online at https://www.koerber-stiftung.de/themen/russland-in-europa/beitraege-2017/umfrage-russland-in-europa-2017.

6 One welcome exception is Ruhr University Bochum, where the Department of History has a Chair for the History of the Ottoman Empire and Modern Turkey.

7 For examples of this tendency, see Konrad Clewing, 'Staatensystem und innerstaatliches Agieren im multiethnischen Raum: Südosteuropa im langen 19. Jahrhundert' in: Konrad Clewing and Oliver Schmitt (eds), *Geschichte Südosteuropas: Vom frühen Mittelalter bis zur Gegenwart*, Regensburg: Pustet, 2011, pp. 432–553, pp. 438, 529; for a counter-example of how Ottoman history can be integrated, see Marie-Janine Calic, *Südosteuropa: Weltgeschichte einer Region*, Munich: C.H. Beck, 2016.

8 Quoted in Patrick Bredebach, *Das* richtige *Europa schaffen: Europa als Konkurrenzthema zwischen Sozial- und Christdemokraten – Deutschland und Italien von 1945 bis 1963 im Vergleich*, Göttingen: V&R Unipress, 2013, p. 204.

9 The history of this spatial concept is analysed by, e.g., Maria Todorova in *Imagining the Balkans*, Oxford: Oxford University Press, 1997.

10 Quoted in Szatkowski, *Die Bundesrepublik Deutschland und die Türkei*, p. 35.

11 See Sabine Fischer and Günter Seufert, 'Transformation misslungen: Die EU, Russland und die Türkei' in: *Osteuropa* 68/10–12 (2018), pp. 271–90, p. 278.

12 Regarding these integration problems, see the last chapter in the German edition of my book about refugees, which goes into more detail about German integration fears and labour migrants; Philipp Ther, *Die Außenseiter: Flucht, Flüchtlinge und Integration im modernen Europa*, Berlin: Suhrkamp, 2017, pp. 318–50.

13 Hans-Ulrich Wehler, 'Das Türkenproblem' in: *Die Zeit* (12 September 2002). Wehler's article, which primarily argued against Turkey's accession to the EU, is available online at https://www.zeit.de/2002/38/200238_tuerkei.contra.xml/komplettansicht.

14 These figures come from my book *Die Außenseiter*, pp. 318–44, which includes long series of data with various sociological indicators for the social integration of German Turks (these are not found in the English version – *The Outsiders: Refugees in Europe since 1492* – because the final section of that book has a different focus).

15 Putin repeated this statement in 2017, though he went into more detail on what he meant; see Oliver Stone, *The Putin Interviews: Oliver Stone Interviews Vladimir Putin*, New York: Hot Books, 2017.

16 See Anders Åslund, *Building Capitalism: The Transformation of the Former Soviet Bloc*, Cambridge: Cambridge University Press, 2002, p. 118.

17 See Jan Zofka, *Postsowjetischer Separatismus: Die pro-russländischen Bewegungen im moldauischen Dnjestr-Tal und auf der Krim 1989–1995*, Göttingen: Wallstein, 2015, pp. 290–4. Moscow did support the separatists in Abkhazia, but it is beyond the scope of this book to examine this conflict in detail.

18 Mearsheimer most recently voiced his theories in *The Economist*; see 'Why the West is principally responsible for the Ukrainian crisis', *The Economist*, 19 March 2022 (unlinked because the article is behind a paywall).

19 See M.E. Sarotte, *Not One Inch: America, Russia, and the Making of Post-Cold War Stalemate*, New Haven, CT: Yale University Press, 2021.

20 I discussed the plots of these operas in an earlier book; see Philipp Ther, *Center Stage: Operatic Culture and Nation Building in Nineteenth-Century Central Europe*, translated by Charlotte Hughes-Kreutzmüller, West Lafayette, IN: Purdue University Press, 2008, pp. 213–14. When I wrote the original version of this book in 2008, I had no idea how dangerous Putin's politics of history would become. The year 2004 was the starting point.

21 See Commission of the European Communities: 'Wider Europe – Neighbourhood: A New Framework for Relations with our Eastern and Southern Neighbours' (11 March 2003), available online at http://eeas.europa.eu/archives/docs/enp/pdf/pdf/com 03_104_en.pdf.

22 See, e.g., Mykola Riabchuk, *Dvi Ukrainy: Realni mezhi, virtualni igry*, Kyiv: Krytyka, 2003. Polish and German translations of this work were published later, and several essays on the topic have also appeared in English.

23 See the detailed investigative article by Anastasia Kirilenko, 'Volle Kraft voraus in den Untergang' in: *Frankfurter Rundschau*, 6 December 2016, p. 12, available online at https://www.aca demia.edu/32105753/Volle_Kraft_voraus_in_den_Untergang _Der_Bankrott_der_ostdeutschen_Wadan-Werft_warmutmaßl ich_von_Anfang_an_geplant_Russische_Mafiosi_und_Politiker _unter_Verdacht.

24 This debate is already under way to some extent in journals such as *Foreign Affairs* in the USA and *Osteuropa* in Germany.

6. Eastern Europe as a Pioneer: Polanyi's Pendulum Swings to the Right

1 Regarding Thatcherism, see Harold James, *Europe Reborn: A History, 1914–2000*, London: Routledge, 2003, pp. 352–60; Dominik Geppert, *Thatchers konservative Revolution: Der Richtungswandel der britischen Tories 1975–1979*, Munich: Oldenbourg, 2002.

2 See Madeleine Albright, *Fascism: A Warning*, New York: HarperCollins, 2018; Timothy Snyder, *On Tyranny: Twenty*

Lessons from the Twentieth Century, New York: Tim Duggan Books, 2017.

3 The literature on this topic is vast, so I will limit myself to citing one book which brings together its author's lifelong study of fascism: Martin Blinkhorn, *Fascism and the Right in Europe, 1919–1945*, Harlow: Longman, 2000.

4 See János Mátyás Kovács and Balázs Trencsényi (eds), *Brave New Hungary: Mapping the 'System of National Cooperation'*, Lanham, MD: Lexington Books, 2019.

5 Bálint Magyar, *Post-Communist Mafia State: The Case of Hungary*, Budapest: CEU Press, 2016; regarding corruption, see pp. 73–105 in particular; see also Kovács and Trencsényi, *Brave New Hungary*.

6 Regarding the precursors to this labour market law, see János Köllő, 'Towards a "Work-Based Society"?', in Kovács and Trencsényi (eds), *Brave New Hungary*, pp. 139–58.

7 In the wake of the crisis, Orbán's government claimed it was consolidating the budget and introduced special taxes for banks, energy companies, telecommunications firms and international supermarket chains; international banks had to convert loans issued in foreign currencies using a prescribed exchange rate; and the government also passed laws against foreign service companies. For details on this, see Ther, *Europe since 1989*, pp. 221ff., pp. 233ff.

8 Details of the award ceremony, complete with photos, are available online at https://gobertadvisors.com/en/esemenyek/.

9 The short film is available on YouTube at https://youtu.be/0wEiXUanPfg.

10 In this book I use the Ukrainian names for cities in Ukraine rather than the Russian-derived names more common in the West – hence Kyiv rather than Kiev, and Dnipro instead of Dnieper for the largest river in Ukraine.

11 One of the best books about this is Philip Manow, *Die politische Ökonomie des Populismus*, which also points out regional differences in Germany and elsewhere.

12 See the memoir competition about the transformation organized by the KARTA Center mentioned in the first essay.
13 From 2010 to 2019, Slovakia achieved average annual growth of 3 per cent, while Hungary achieved 2.8 per cent. See the economic statistics from the Austrian Economic Chamber, available online at http://wko.at/statistik/eu/europa-wirtschaftswachstum.pdf.
14 See James Krapfl, *Revolution with a Human Face: Politics, Culture, and Community in Czechoslovakia, 1989–1992*, Ithaca, NY: Cornell University Press, 2013.
15 See Peter Baker, Trump says "I'd take it" if Russia Again Offered Dirt on Opponent in: *The New York Times* (12 June 2019), available online at https://www.nytimes.com/2019/06/12/us/politics/trump-russia-fbi.html.
16 In the end, Berlusconi was only convicted for tax fraud, but the trial for hosting prostitutes at parties in his own home (a scandal referred to as 'Rubygate') also compromised him.
17 These insults became more frequent in 2009, as the investigations into him and his company Mediaset picked up speed, and in 2013, when he was convicted in two trials. For an example of his comments, see the interview with Catholic newspaper *Avvenire*: 'Intervento: La vera anomalia sono i giudici comunisti' in *Avvenire* (28 October 2009), available online at https://www.avvenire.it/attualita/pagine/berlusconi-ballaro-giudici_200910281013049970000.

7. Systemic Competition during the Covid-19 Pandemic

1 See Václav Havel, 'The Council of Europe, Strasbourg, May 10, 1990' in: *The Art of the Impossible: Politics as Morality in Practice, Speeches and Writings, 1990–1996*, translated by Paul Wilson et al., New York: Fromm International, 1998, p. 33. The sociologist Hartmut Rosa used this observation as the basis for developing a theory of late-modern capitalism; see Hartmut Rosa, *Alienation & Acceleration: Towards a Critical Theory of Late-Modern Temporality*, Malmö: NSU Press, 2010.
2 Regarding this term, see Stefan Link, 'How Might 21st-Century

De-Globalization Unfold? Some Historical Reflections' in: *New Global Studies* 12/3 (2018), pp. 343–65 (here pp. 353–6).
3 This data is updated continually on the WHO Coronavirus Dashboard at https://covid19.who.int/.
4 *The Lancet* estimated that there were at least 18 million direct and indirect victims of the pandemic, with uncertainty intervals to cover a range of potentially higher and lower figures. See 'Estimating Excess Mortality due to the COVID-19 Pandemic: A Systematic Analysis of COVID-19-related Mortality, 2020–21' in: *The Lancet* 399/10334 (2022), pp. 1513–36 (here p. 1519). Available online at https://www.thelancet.com/action/showPdf?pii=S0140-6736%2821%2902796-3. Throughout the rest of this book, I use data from *The Lancet*.
5 Ibid. Only Peru recorded an even higher rate of excess deaths in proportion to its population.
6 See 'Estimating Excess Mortality due to the COVID-19 Pandemic', p. 1519.
7 See Tooze, *Shutdown*, pp. 66f.
8 Only about 20 per cent of the Chinese community in Italy works in the industrial sector, however; far more are employed in the service industry. See Ministero del Lavoro e delle Politiche Sociali, *La comunità Cinese in Italia*, 2018, available online at https://www.lavoro.gov.it/documenti-e-norme/studi-e-statistiche/Documents/Rapporti annuali sulle comunità migranti in Italia - anno 2018/Cina-rapporto-2018.pdf.
9 See Manuel Castells, *The Rise of the Network Society – The Information Age: Economy, Society and Culture*, vol. 1, Malden, MA: Blackwell, 1996. The other volumes, *The Power of Identity* and *End of Millennium*, were published in 1997 and 1998.
10 Adam Tooze recounts this in chapter 3 of his book; see 'Wasted Time' in Tooze, *Shutdown*, pp. 65–78. See also the subsection on 'Organized Irresponsibility' (pp. 27–48). Even after the WHO issued its warning, Boris Johnson argued 'for freedom of exchange' and advised the public not to panic about the virus (see ibid., p. 69 – Tooze's book includes many more quotes along these lines).

11 In the winter of 2020–21, the University of Chicago and University of Vienna organized a series of online meetings (in lieu of a traditional conference) with the title 'Deglobalization and Anti-Globalism in Central Europe'. Co-organizer Tara Zahra will soon publish a book on this topic.
12 Adam Tooze's book is also full of quotes that were already embarrassing during the pandemic and seem even more so in hindsight. See, for example, Trump's boast on 24 February 2020, 'We're going to be pretty soon at only five people' (meaning the number of Covid cases), which he embellished with self-praise for the government: 'That's a pretty good job we have done'; see Tooze, *Shutdown*, p. 76.
13 Regarding the mortality rate for Black Americans and other groups, see the study by Elisabeth Gawthrop, 'The Color of Coronavirus: COVID-19 Deaths by Race and Ethnicity in the U.S.', available online at https://www.apmresearchlab.org/covid/deaths-by-race.
14 See Tooze, *Shutdown*, p. 96.
15 George Packer writing in *The Atlantic* came to the dramatic conclusion that the USA was a 'failed state'; see George Packer, 'We Are Living in a Failed State' in: *The Atlantic*, June 2020, available online at https://www.theatlantic.com/magazine/archive/2020/06/underlying-conditions/610261/.
16 Details of the resolution and the subsidies for individual companies can be found in a US Congressional report from March 2021; see 'Operation Warp Speed Contracts for COVID-19 Vaccines and Ancillary Vaccination Materials', available online at https://crsreports.congress.gov/product/pdf/IN/IN11560. Regarding Operation Warp Speed, see also Tooze, *Shutdown*, pp. 239–42.
17 See 'Kanzler Kurz: Das Virus kommt mit dem Auto', available online at https://www.kleinezeitung.at/politik/5853568/Coronavirus_Kanzler-Kurz_Das-Virus-kommt-mit-dem-Auto.
18 Kurz also claimed that migrants from these countries living in Austria were responsible for a third of all infections. This figure

was quickly debunked, but the stigmatization of foreign migrants living in Austria did not abate. See 'Stammt tatsächlich ein Drittel der Fälle vom "Westbalkan"?', available online at https://www.derstandard.at/story/2000122230366/stammt-tatsaechlich-ein-drittel-der-faelle-aus-dem-westbalkan.

19 Pfizer received nearly 2 billion dollars as an advance for developing vaccines, while the German government gave BioNTech the equivalent of 443 million dollars. Regarding these figures, see Tooze, *Shutdown*, p. 240.

20 See 'Putin Hails New Sputnik Moment as Russia is First to Approve a COVID-19 Vaccine', available online at https://www.reuters.com/article/us-health-coronavirus-russia-vaccine-put-idUSKCN25712U.

21 This data is based on the article 'Estimating Excess Mortality due to the COVID-19 Pandemic: A Systematic Analysis of COVID-19-related Mortality, 2020–21', in *The Lancet* 399/10334 (2022), pp. 1513–36, available online at https://www.thelancet.com/action/showPdf?pii=S0140-6736%2821%2902796-3.

22 Current and past data on vaccination rates can be found at https://ourworldindata.org/covid-vaccinations.

23 The problem this time, however, was not so much the stock markets as it was government bonds. Regarding these important details of the crisis, see Tooze, *Shutdown*, p. 112.

24 Tooze characterizes the role of the Federal Reserve as 'a central bank to the world'; see Tooze, *Shutdown*, p. 122.

25 China's gross national product declined by 6.8 per cent in the first quarter of 2020 (see Dana Heide, 'Chinas Wirtschaft bricht ein – Coronavirus beendet jahrzehntelanges Wachstum' in: *Handelsblatt*, 17 April 2020, available online at https://www.handelsblatt.com/politik/konjunktur/nachrichten/konjunktur-chinas-wirtschaft-bricht-ein-coronavirus-beendet-jahrzehntelanges-wachstum/25748974.html). Despite this, the country achieved growth overall in 2020.

26 See Federico Fabbrini, *Next Generation EU: Il futuro di Europa e Italia dopo la pandemia*, Milan: Mulino, 2022, p. 81. The

author is also representative of how the well-educated Italians of his generation have fared; he teaches at an Irish university, but he first wrote this book in Italian. Another important book on the EU response to the pandemic is Luuk van Middelaar, *Pandemonium: Saving Europe*, Newcastle: Agenda Publishing, 2021, pp. 80–91 and 105–112. I like Middelaar's optimistic outlook, but it remains to be seen whether the EU will grow stronger with every crisis, including this particular one.

27 See Fabbrini, *Next Generation EU*, p. 87.
28 See Kiran Klaus Patel, 'COVID-19 und die Europäische Union' in: *Geschichte und Gesellschaft* 46/3 (2020), pp. 522–35.
29 See Fabbrini, *Next Generation EU*, pp. 108–28.
30 This comparison of risk-taking and risk-averse coronavirus policies is based on the book by Peter Baldwin, *Fighting the First Wave: Why the Coronavirus Was Tackled So Differently Across the Globe*, Cambridge: Cambridge University Press, 2021.
31 See Tooze, *Shutdown*, p. 132.
32 The proportion of overweight and obese children amounted to 26.7 per cent; see Gerald Jarnig et al., 'Acceleration in BMI Gain Following COVID-19 Restrictions: A Longitudinal Study with 7- to 10-year-old Primary School Children' in: *Pediatric Obesity* 17/6 (2022), e12890. Regarding psychological disturbances (amongst parents as well), see Ulrike Ravens-Sieberer et al., 'The Mental Health and Health-related Behavior of Children and Parents during the COVID-19 Pandemic: Findings of the Longitudinal COPSY Study' in: *Deutsches Ärzteblatt International* 119/25 (2022), pp. 436–7. It should be noted that both studies were regional, and each looked at only at a single federal state, namely, Carinithia (Austria) and Hamburg (Germany). Some studies determined that symptoms improved from the autumn of 2020, which can be attributed to habituation to the pandemic's restrictions. The following study was based on surveys in several large cities and revealed a less dramatic increase in psychological complaints: M. Döpfner et al., 'Die psychische Belastung von Kindern, Jugendlichen und ihren Familien während der COVID-

19-Pandemie und der Zusammenhang mit emotionalen und Verhaltensauffälligkeiten' in: *Bundesgesundheitsblatt* 64 (2021), pp. 1522–32.
33 This calculation is available online at https://www.worldbank.org/en/news/press-release/2021/12/06/learning-losses-from-covid-19-could-cost-this-generation-of-students-close-to-17-trillion-in-lifetime-earnings.
34 See Tooze, *Shutdown*, p. 101. This neologism appears even earlier in a few articles, and the concept can be viewed as a productive side effect of the pandemic. It was already common knowledge that women bear the brunt of recessions, but this was never before discussed in such direct terms.
35 Detailed figures can be found in an OECD report; see OECD, *The State of Global Education: 18 Months into the Pandemic*, Paris: OECD, September 2021, pp. 40 and 41. Overviews are provided on pages 12 and 17. The report is available online at https://www.oecd-ilibrary.org/education/the-state-of-global-education_1a23bb23-en.
36 Ibid. (all of these figures are taken from the OECD report).
37 This calculation is based on the estimated total expenditure for old-age pensions amounting to more than 300 billion euros. Regarding the pension increase, see 'Deutliche Rentenerhöhung beschlossen', available online at https://www.bmas.de/DE/Service/Presse/Pressemitteilungen/2022/deutliche-rentenerhoehung-beschlossen.html. Pensions in eastern Germany rose even more, by 6.12 per cent. The basis of this increase is a complicated calculation influenced largely by a rise in earned income. Furthermore, the increase that failed to materialize in 2021 was balanced out in 2022. State payments for old-age pensions currently swallow up about one third of Germany's federal budget and account for 23 per cent of the income of pension insurance schemes. Regarding these figures, see the issue of the journal *Aus Politik und Zeitgeschichte* entitled 'Rente' (Pension), no. 20/2022, available online at https://www.bpb.de/system/files/dokument_pdf/APuZ_2022-20_online.pdf. The figure of 300 billion

is taken from the editorial, while the other figures can be found on pages 31 and 37 (there is no space here to cite every single article). In France and especially Italy, the ratio between what is spent on the older population and on school education is even worse than in Germany.

38 Regarding this resolution, see 'Pandemiebedingte Lernrückstände aufholen', available online at https://www.kmk.org/fileadmin/Dateien/pdf/KMK/SWK/2021/2021_06_11-Pandemiebedingte-Lernruckstaende-aufholen.pdf. The programme is based on a resolution of the German federal government for the federal states, which are responsible for education and thus schools in Germany.

39 The documentary, which deals mostly with the outbreak of the pandemic at the start of 2020, can be rented and viewed online. Links to streaming versions are available at https://www.aiweiwei.com/coronation. A discussion with the director about his assessment of the situation in China can also be viewed online; see the interview with the Foreign Correspondents' Club of Japan at https://www.youtube.com/watch?v=-XHYZMDZwYI.

Afterword: A Bad End: The War against Ukraine

1 I tried to draw attention in Germany to the plight of the 1.5 million Ukrainian internally displaced people (IDP) by pledging part of the non-fiction book prize at the Leipzig Book Fair in 2015 to them. But since the Ukrainian IDPs stayed in their home country, unlike the Middle Eastern refugees who arrived in the EU in 2015–16, little heed was paid to them.

Index

Abdülaziz (sultan), 132
Abdülhamid (sultan), 133
Abdülmecid (sultan), 132
Afghanistan, 56
Africa, 149, 184
agriculture, xiii, 25, 173, 189
AKP, 132, 137
Albania, 143
Albright, Madeleine, 164
Alevi, 137–8
Alexander II (tsar), 145
Alternative für Deutschland (AfD), 27, 31, 69, 76–7, 163–4, 175
Amato, Giuliano, 97
Amazon, 46, 61–3
Amsterdam, 96
Ankara, 156
annus horribilis, x, xiv, 27, 90, 164, 182
antiliberalism, xv–vi, 28–35, 51, 170, 178, 180
antisemitism, 33, 158
Argentina, 95
Armenia, 156–7
Asia, xi, 39, 78, 82, 95–6, 128, 184, 194–5
see also crisis
Atatürk (Mustafa Kemal Pascha), 123, 131–2, 134, 137
atheism, 137
austerity, 11, 14, 20, 28–9, 55, 76–7, 101, 112, 119, 192

Australia, 191
Austria, 18, 31, 49–50, 86, 105, 151, 162–3, 177, 227–8
  Covid policy, 189, 191–3, 198–200, 211–17
Austrian Freedom Party (FPÖ), 49, 135, 163, 177
Austrian People's Party (ÖVP), 135, 163, 177
authoritarianism, 12, 27, 109, 125, 150, 154, 156, 165–6, 171, 181
Azerbaijan, 156–7

Babiš, Andrej, 93, 174, 193, 200
Balcerowicz, Leszek, 12–4
Balkans, 130–1, 133, 199, 204
Baltic States, 19–20, 76, 143, 226
banks, 17, 19–20, 29, 56, 59, 73, 96, 102, 111–12, 155, 207
  central, 66, 72, 102, 156, 206–7
  see also European Central Bank
Belarus, 16, 149, 226, 232
Berlin, 68, 71–2, 76, 82, 108, 208
Berlusconi, Silvio, xiii, 60, 88–94, 97–104, 106, 109, 111, 115–9, 163, 179
Bezos, Jeff, 202
Biden, Joe, 39, 56, 171
Black Americans, *see* people of colour
Blair, Tony, 24, 54, 56, 63, 92, 96, 161
Bokros, Lajos, 14

Index

Bolsonaro, Jair, xxv
borders, 72, 79, 127, 145–6, 150, 210, 227, 231
  see also Covid-19 pandemic
Borodianka, 154
Bosnia and Herzegovina, 141–2, 154, 186, 204, 231
Bossi, Umberto, 100–1, 163
Brazil, xxv, 217
Bretton Woods system, 8–9
Brexit, xiv, 20–1, 31, 88, 127, 136, 162
Brown, Gordon, 57
Bucha, 154
Buchanan, Pat, 49, 163
budget, 14, 44, 55, 57–9, 81, 100–1, 166
  deficit, 48, 55, 58, 93, 97, 111–13, 116, 172, 207
Bulgaria, 31, 76, 107, 124, 128–9, 135143
Bush, George H.W., 40–1, 55, 159
Bush, George W., 56–61, 148

California, 48, 51–2, 62
Canada, 228
capitalism, xii–iii, 2–7, 108, 140–1, 156, 189, 202, 204
  embedded, 2, 8, 158, 161
  financial/rentier, 5, 11, 95, 96, 102
  laissez-faire, 2, 6, 9, 11, 16, 22, 66, 158, 164
  see also crises of
Capitol (storming of the), 32, 36–8, 151, 164–5, 182
Čaputová, Zuzana, 174
Catholicism, *see* Christianity
Caucasus, 133, 140, 149, 231
censorship, 155, 200, 220, 231
Chechnya, 140
Chicago School, 3, 9–11, 23, 63, 70, 84, 94
children, 17, 21, 66, 136–7, 170, 181, 183, 194, 214–8
Chile, 4, 10, 13, 160
China, 4, 53, 59, 78–9, 125, 128, 227, 232
  Covid policy, 185–91, 194–7, 202, 204, 206, 220–1
Chinese Communist Party, 202, 221
Christian Democratic Union (CDU), 72, 90, 162–3, 224
Christian Democrats, 10, 92–3, 118, 162–3
  see also Christian Democratic Union

Christian social teaching, 10, 12, 70, 92
Christianity, 38, 130–1, 166, 171, 178, 195–6
citizenship, 50, 139
Civic Platform party, 178
civil society, 46, 63, 138, 180
civilians, 142, 154, 225, 227, 230
class, 3, 10, 23, 65–6, 80, 216
  lower, 28, 46, 183
  middle, 4, 48, 54, 58–9, 77, 90, 111, 137, 155, 162, 170
  working 31, 46, 57–8
climate change, 178, 181, 229, 234
Clinton, Bill, 24, 39–41, 43–5, 51–7, 59, 63–4, 161, 148, 161, 192
Clinton, Hillary, 49, 51, 162
Cold War, 35, 70, 90, 93, 127–8, 143, 148, 155, 203, 228
colonialism, 31, 131, 146, 231
communism, xii, 22, 26, 39, 47, 141, 162, 166
Communist parties, 5, 8
  see also Chinese and Italian Communist Party
'competitive signaling', 15
Confucianism, 194
Congress of Vienna, 130
Conservative Party (UK), 20, 31, 159
conservatives, 30, 37, 60, 135, 163–5, 177, 198
conspiracy theories, 29–30, 78, 169, 191, 202
constitution, 32, 71, 110–11, 135, 165, 167, 170, 178, 180–1, 223
consumer society, 4, 19, 54, 59, 61, 68–70, 74, 199, 217, 230
Conte, Giuseppe, 117
convergence theory, 17, 70
corporations, 7, 23, 31, 56, 60–3, 93, 98, 112, 152–3, 168–9, 202, 230
corruption, 12, 32, 73, 93, 151–3, 156, 167, 172, 174–5, 177–8, 223–4
coup, 36–7, 69, 123–4, 140, 153, 155 // incl. putsch
Covid-19 pandemic, 60–2, 88, 93, 118, 137, 156, 172, 177, 182–221
  border closures, 188–91, 194, 199, 211, 219
  health care systems, 192–4, 196–7, 215, 219
  lockdown, 183, 188, 191–4, 198, 200, 205, 211–13, 217, 220–1

Covid-19 pandemic (*cont.*)
  masks, 185, 190, 193, 195, 197, 199–200, 213
  mortality, 184–7, 190–4, 196–7, 200–1, 204–5, 220
  vaccines, 61, 137, 185–7, 190, 197, 202–5, 211–4, 218–20
crime, 30, 47–8, 82, 141, 175
Crimea, 13, 141, 147, 149–53, 223–7
crises (of capitalism), x–xi, 3, 161, 206, 218
  Asia (1998), 10, 155, 160–1
  Covid-19 (2020), 184, 206–8
  Czech banking, 73
  dot-com (2001), 82, 161
  euro (2011), 14, 20, 28, 102, 111–13, 192, 207–8
  global financial (2008–9), 20, 28–9, 54, 59–60, 76–7, 101–2, 119, 159, 184
  oil (1974), 9, 228–9
  rouble, 155, 160–1
  Savings and Loan (1985), 159
Croatia, 143, 231
currency, 9, 20, 59, 71–3, 119–20, 232
Curzon, George, 131
Cyprus, 124
Czech Republic, 3, 18, 73–4, 77, 85, 142, 172, 174
  Covid policy 193–4, 200, 216, 218
Czechoslovakia, 12, 40, 72–3, 79, 81, 101

D'Alema, Massimo, 97
Dagestan, 231
de Maizière, Lothar, 71
debt,
  -to-GDP ratio, 14, 93–4, 97, 100, 111–12, 119–20
  government, 11, 20, 58–9, 70, 81, 88, 101–2, 207–8, 232
  private, 4, 54, 59, 159
deindustrialization, viii, 4, 6, 18, 21, 52–3, 65–6, 68–9, 160
democracy, 7, 26, 40, 63, 113, 151, 163, 190, 193–5, 226–7
  crisis of, 27, 42, 57, 88, 99, 155, 170
  liberal, 34–7, 100, 150, 162, 165, 177, 180–2, 209
  people's, 23, 160, 171, 206
  pluralistic, 167, 174, 222
Democratic Left Alliance (SLD), 27
democratization, vii, 4, 11, 39–40, 123, 125, 175, 188, 190

Democrats (US), 31, 43–4, 46–8, 51–2, 54, 56, 57–60, 62, 162, 176–7, 180
deregulation, 10–12, 17, 56, 59, 83, 159
Detroit, 53
dictatorship, 10, 115, 134–5, 150, 203, 221, 232
digitalization, 60–1, 104, 195, 208, 210
discrimination, 45–7, 136, 138
Dole, Bob, 51
Donbas, 147, 149–52, 154, 223–6
Donetsk, 150–1
double movement/pendulum (Polanyi), 7–8, 11, 77, 96, 109–10, 120, 140, 161–2
Draghi, Mario, 112, 118–9, 211
drugs, 26, 55–6, 140
Duda, Andrzej, 171

East European bubble, 19–20, 76, 175, 222
Eastern Bloc, 8, 14, 17, 19–20, 73, 95, 140, 162
education, xxiii, 17, 21, 26, 97–8, 103–4, 106, 136, 190
Egypt, 149
Eichel, Hans, 58
election fraud, 32, 36, 201, 222
Emilia-Romagna, 107
energy
  crisis, 228
  prices, 184, 207, 223, 228–9
  renewable, 113, 210, 229
entrepreneurship, 79, 81, 94, 108, 185, 193
environment, xi, 66, 71, 210
Erdoğan, Recep Tayyip, xix, 121, 123–6, 132–3, 135, 138, 156–7, 178
ethnic cleansing, 142, 231
Eurasian movement, 127
European Central Bank (ECB), 29, 101, 112, 115, 119
European Commission, 29, 78, 112, 180, 210–12
European Community (EC), 8, 74, 88, 124, 134, 205, 228
European People's Party (EPP), 163, 199
European Union (EU), 115, 120, 124–6, 148–9, 169, 172–3, 181–2, 196, 223, 229
  Covid policy, 204–5, 207–12, 218
  enlargement, 25, 74, 76, 124–7, 134–6, 143, 148–9

Index

transfer payments, 15, 118, 167, 172, 180–1, 209
eurozone, 88, 97–8, 102, 111, 117–20, 207
exchange rates, 8–9, 20, 70–3, 75, 125
exports, 30, 73, 82, 187, 189, 206, 211, 229

family, *see* gender roles
famine, 144, 184
fascism, 6–8, 34, 90, 96, 153–4, 164–6, 223–4
fear, 37, 83, 86–7, 121, 124, 137, 149, 157, 168, 183
Fico, Robert, 173–4
Fidesz, 18, 32, 151, 163, 166–9, 173–4, 194, 199, 210
financial sector, 12, 17, 20, 29, 102, 112, 159, 206–8
Finland, 147
First World War, 6, 122, 130–2, 139, 196, 224, 233
fiscal policy, 55, 57–60, 88, 96, 100–2, 111–3, 118
Five Star Movement (M5S), 104, 109, 114, 116–9, 175–6
Florida, 57
Foča, 154
food, 21, 25, 55, 91, 184, 189, 215, 219
see also famine
foreign direct investments (FDI), 11, 13, 15–16, 19–20, 168, 173, 226
Forza Italia, 90, 93
Foxley, Alejandro, 10
France, 8, 18, 29, 36, 49, 57, 116, 130–1, 134–5, 177
Covid policy, 197, 216
Frankfurt an der Oder, 76
free trade, 5, 7, 11–12, 30, 53, 74, 113, 156, 223
freedom, 158, 171, 213, 219
economic, 16
of the press, xvi, 171–2
of speech, 201
Friedman, Milton, 3, 9–10, 13, 54, 63–4, 89
Fukuyama, Francis, vi–ii, xii, xviii, 44

Gaddafi, Muammar, 90, 115
Gallipoli, Battle of, 122
GDP, 13, 43, 74, 118, 220, 232
per capita, 17–18, 85, 94, 107, 124

Geithner, Timothy, 59
gender roles, 30, 103, 105, 107, 216
genocide, 131–2, 144, 154
Gentiloni, Paolo, 115
Georgia, 144, 146–7
German empire, 17, 122, 132
Germany, 8–9, 26–7, 57–8, 111–5, 120, 126, 136–8, 151–3, 208–9, 224
Covid policy, 189, 192–4, 200, 202–3, 205, 212, 216
(co-)transformation, 21, 25, 40, 68–87
Gingrich, Newt, 48
Giuliani, Rudolph ('Rudy'), 48
Global South, 4, 186, 197, 204–5
globalization, viii, 4–6, 28, 43, 96, 125, 184, 186, 189–90, 213
Gorbachev, Mikhail, 69, 127, 140
Gore, Al, 44–5, 57
government bonds, 102, 111–12, 116–17
Great Depression, 2, 6–7
Greece, 14, 29, 101, 116, 119, 122–3, 128–9, 131, 134, 176
Green parties, 23, 83, 177
Greifswald, 153
Grillo, Beppe, 109
growth, 10, 68, 112, 118, 159, 184, 207
in post-communist countries, 13, 16, 18–20, 173–4
see also GDP
Guadalajara, 4
Gusenbauer, Alfred, 151

Habsburg empire, xviii, 74, 109, 128–30
Haider, Jörg, 163
Hartz, Peter, 23
Havel, Václav, x, 183
Hayek, Friedrich, xiii, 9
health care, 17, 21, 43–4, 47, 55, 81, 83, 98, 186, 192
see also Covid-19 pandemic
Hitler, Adolf, 158, 165
Hollande, François, 29, 162
Holodomor, 144
housing, xxi, 29, 59, 62–6, 71, 105–6, 159, 207
human rights, 142
Hungary, 3, 14, 18, 128–31, 142, 165–9, 174–5, 180–1, 209–10, 227
Covid policy, 187, 193–4, 199–200
HZDS party (Movement for a Democratic Slovakia), 175

identity politics, 44–6
imperialism, 31, 33, 130, 139, 143–4, 146, 149, 155–6, 186, 223
India, 128, 154, 227
indices, 16, 185
industrial relocation, 4, 15, 53–4, 73–4, 82, 96, 136, 189, 228
industrialization, 4–5, 17, 22, 52, 61
industry
 aerospace, 52, 78
 automotive, 52–3, 73, 95–6, 168, 230
 electronics & computer, 4, 52, 78, 94–5, 188, 207
 heavy, 53, 78, 85, 228
 oil, gas & chemical, 52, 96, 140, 160, 172, 207, 224, 227–9, 232
 pharmaceutical, 186
 service, 4, 46, 53, 69, 162, 176, 213
 telecommunication, 12, 60–2, 95
 shipbuilding, 77–8
inequality
 regional, 3–4, 18, 21–2, 52–3, 84–5, 106–7, 170, 173, 192
 social, 18–19, 46, 52, 65–6, 83, 112, 170, 173, 184, 213, 216
inflation, 9, 11, 64, 98, 119–20, 125, 172, 184, 207, 213
Intellectuals, 34, 123, 127, 131, 150, 160, 225
interest rates, 64, 102, 111–12, 116–20, 207
International Monetary Fund (IMF), 11, 13, 16, 20, 29, 76, 119–20, 160, 227, 232
interventionism, 6, 203, 213
Iran, 148
Iraq, *see* war
Ireland, 52, 76
Islam/Muslims, 122, 130–4, 137–8
 anti-Muslim sentiment, 30, 34, 50, 85, 137, 169, 177
Israel, 149
Istanbul, 122–3, 127, 131, 134–5, 138
Italia Viva, 117
Italian Communist Party (PCI), 8, 90, 92–3, 97
Italy, xiii, 8, 18, 49–50, 60, 88–120, 131
 Covid policy 188–9, 194, 196–7, 211–2, 214

Jinping, Xi, 191, 202, 204, 220
Johnson, Boris, 31, 164, 190, 198, 212

Judaism, Jews, 5, 158, 160, 169
judicial system, 151, 178–80
Juncker, Jean-Claude, 112, 163

Kaczyński, Jarosław, 169, 171–2, 174, 178, 193, 209
Kaliningrad, 145, 226
Kern, Christian, 151
Keynesian policy, 8–10, 159, 206
Kharkiv, 225–6
Kherson, 226
kindergartens, 104, 106–7, 216
Klaus, Václav, 12, 73
Kohl, Helmut, 71–2, 81, 161
Kołodko, Grzegorz, 13
Kosovo, 142–3, 231
Kurds, 123, 137–8
Kurz, Sebastian, 177, 193, 198–200
Kyiv, 172, 225

labour market, xx, 12, 15, 30, 52, 76, 82–4, 105, 110, 167–8
 see also migration
Labour Party, 8, 21, 24, 83, 159–60
Latin America, xi, 11, 39, 95, 184, 217
Latvia, 20, 76, 119, 143
Law and Justice party (PiS), xv, 18, 27, 78, 169–73, 175, 178, 210
Lázár, János, 169
Le Pen, Jean-Marie, 163
League of Nations, 131
Lega/Lega Nord, 60, 100–1, 116–8, 163, 176
Leipzig, 71–2, 84
LGBT, 30, 44–6, 48, 176
(the) Left, xii, 28, 62, 66, 77, 97–100, 105, 153, 161–2, 170, 176–7
liberalization, 10–13, 16, 74, 79, 83, 110, 125, 140, 159, 221
Libya, 90, 115
life expectancy, 12, 26, 55, 110, 140, 204, 215
Lipton, David, vii
Lithuania, 20, 76, 143–4, 266
Lombardy, 107, 196
London, 20, 108, 141, 190
Los Angeles, 62
Luhansk, 151

Macron, Emmanuel, 116
Manafort, Paul, 151
Marchionne, Sergio, 95

Index

Mariupol, 154, 225
market(s), 2, 6–7, 10, 15–16, 22–3, 48, 53, 66, 74, 79, 219
  black, 71, 73
  emerging, 10, 16, 24, 183, 218
  see also labour and stock market
market economy, 2, 4, 9, 39, 61, 70, 124–5, 160, 206, 213
Marshall Plan, 134
Marx, Karl, 90, 92
Marxism, 5–7, 22, 33, 47, 146
Mattarella, Sergio, 118
Mečiar, Vladimír, 175
media, 89, 98–99, 103, 114, 133, 166–7, 171–2, 180, 200–2, 224
  social, 28, 32, 114, 176–7, 190, 193, 201–2, 214, 232
Medvedev, Dmitry, 223
Meloni, Giorgia, 90, 115, 119
men, 25, 90, 105, 164, 201
Merkel, Angela, 26, 111, 114, 115, 147, 162–3, 181, 198, 205, 224
Mészáros, Lőrinc, 168
Mexico, 4, 50, 53, 216
Mezzogiorno, 84, 106–7
Middle East, 85, 137, 148–9, 184, 228
migration, 20, 31–4, 49–50, 90, 115, 124, 176–7, 194, 199–200
  forced, 131–2
  labour, 20, 25, 30, 76, 86, 107–8, 122, 136–8, 176, 189
  illegal, 30
  inner-German, 25, 70, 72–3, 75–7, 81
  see also refugees
Milan, 93, 190
military, 44–5, 55, 121–4, 132, 140, 142, 165, 203, 208, 227, 231–3
Miller, Stephen, 50–1
Milošević, Slobodan, 33, 142, 231
mining, 85, 160
minorities, 33, 49, 131–4, 137–9, 142–4, 174, 176–7, 226
mobilization
  for the labour market, xx, 21, 23–5, 83–4
  (para)military, 154, 164
  political, xx, 27–8, 30, 33, 57, 176, 201, 221, 228
modernization, 4, 15, 26, 125, 133, 208–9, 229
Modrow, Hans, 71
Moldova, 149

Mondale, Walter, 159
monopolies, 2, 62–3, 98, 108, 247
Montenegro, 143
Monti, Mario, 109–10, 112–3, 118–9
Morawiecki, Mateusz, 172, 209
Motyzhyn, 154
Munich, 108, 125
music, 98, 121, 130, 140
Musk, Elon, 201
Muslims, *see* Islam
Mussolini, Benito, 164–5
Mykolaiv, 225

Napoleon I, 144
Napoleon III, 92
nation, 12, 31, 50, 63, 92, 131, 139
nationalism, 27, 31–5, 49–51, 77, 87, 120, 125, 163, 171–7, 186–7, 231
nation-state, 8, 113, 130–3, 139, 143
NATO, 124, 127, 134, 143, 154, 175, 226–7, 231
  enlargement, 141–4, 146–9, 152, 222–3, 233
neoclassical synthesis, 10–11
neoliberalism, 2–5, 9–17, 24, 31, 96, 102, 184, 194, 208, 213
  in Central Europe, PL, 173
  in the US and UK, 48, 53–4, 59, 63, 160, 192
neoconservatives, xii, 6, 16, 22, 34, 48–51
Netherlands, 18, 96, 107, 135, 151, 195
neutrality, 122–3, 147, 226, 233
New Deal, 8, 66–7
New York, 28, 46, 48
New Zealand, 191
NGOs, *see* civil society
Nicholas II (tsar), 133, 139
Nord Stream 2, 152, 224, 227
North Macedonia, 143
nostalgia, 38–9, 74
nuclear power, 148, 188, 231, 233

Obama, Barack, 29, 43, 51, 58–9, 161–2, 192
obesity, 26, 214–15
Ocasio-Cortez, Alexandria, 46, 62
older people, 55, 77, 106, 110, 195, 201, 203–4, 212, 214, 217
oligarchs, 12, 140–1, 161, 202, 222
Orbán, Viktor, 14, 30–3, 99, 163, 166–9, 172, 174–5, 180–1, 199–201, 209–10
Orientalism, 128, 132–3

Ottoman empire, 121–2, 128–33, 156
outsourcing, see industrial relocation
Owen, Robert, 7, 160

paradigm of inevitability, xxiii–iv, 26–7, 75–9
Paris Peace Conference, 130–1
Partito Democratico (PD), 92, 109–10, 114–17, 119
Party of Democratic Socialism/Die Linke (PDS), 77, 79, 175
party system, 38, 123, 164
PASOK party (Greece), 29
peace, x, 148, 150, 225–7, 233–4
pendulum (Polanyi), see double movement
pensions, 14, 17, 55, 75, 81, 83, 110, 217
people of colour, 45, 47–8, 64–6, 99, 165, 192
Piasecki, Bolesław, 166
Piedmont, 94, 104, 107
Pinochet, Augusto, 4, 10–11
planned economy, xi, 22
Podemos, 176
Poland, 12–14, 17–19, 27, 76–8, 95, 142, 144, 152, 165–6, 169–73, 178
  Covid policy, 193–4, 201, 211, 216, 218
Polanyi, Karl, 2–8, 22–3, 33, 66, 86, 111, 158, 160
police, 20, 37, 80, 133, 179, 221, 223
Polish-Lithuanian Commonwealth, 129, 144
political coordinate system, 51, 161–3
political polarization, xiv, xxi–ii, 34, 99, 165
population replacement theory, 49, 108
populism, 50, 58, 88, 116–7
  left-wing, 27–8, 104–5, 109, 116–8, 154, 175–8
  right-wing, 27, 30–5, 48–50, 77, 86–93, 99, 162–4, 168–80, 187, 228
Post-communists, 14–15, 161
  see also Democratic Left Alliance, Party of Democratic Socialism
poverty, 14, 17, 22–6, 47, 61, 65, 107, 160, 184, 192, 218
Powell, Colin, 44–5
Prijedor, 154
privatization, 10–17, 73–5, 77–8, 83, 95–6, 98–9, 140–1, 159, 167, 192
Prodi, Romano, 97, 99–100

propaganda, 8, 31–2, 140–1, 169, 171, 194, 198, 203–4, 224–6, 231–2
prosperity, 17, 43, 47, 70, 75, 86, 122, 175, 184
protest, 18, 21, 28–9, 62, 121, 165, 174–5, 213, 221–3, 231
  parties/votes, 30, 77, 168, 170, 175
Protestantism, see Christianity
public infrastructure, 54, 56, 62, 85, 97, 104, 111, 208, 232
purchasing power, 10, 59, 98
Putin, Vladimir, 12–13, 125–7, 139, 142–57, 161, 164, 181–2, 201, 203, 207, 222–33

racism, 31–4, 49, 51, 58, 65
Reagan, Ronald, 9, 19, 38, 40, 48–9, 54–5, 60, 63, 148, 158–60, 192
real estate bubble, 17, 19–20, 59–60, 76, 159
recession
  in post-communist countries, 12–13, 80
  in the West, 20, 29, 40, 74, 82, 94, 101–2, 125, 160–1, 195, 206
redistribution, 21–2, 26, 54, 102, 213
refugee(s), 50, 123–4, 133, 137, 142, 267
  crisis (2015/16), 31–2, 85–6, 115, 124, 163, 173, 194
regional divide, see inequality
religion, 32, 130, 133, 137–8, 194–6
  see also Christianity, Islam, Judaism
Renzi, Matteo, 92, 99, 109–13, 115, 117, 162
Republican People's Party (CHP), 123
Republicans (US), 36, 48–9, 51, 55, 57–61, 94, 99, 165, 196, 201
revolution, 6, 39–40, 72, 133–4, 144, 146–7, 150–1, 153, 175, 222–3
Roma, 142
Romania, 16, 19–20, 65, 76, 107, 124, 128, 148
Rubin, Robert, 56–7
rule of law, 78, 136, 167–8, 173, 178–9, 181, 209
Russia, 3, 12–13, 33, 124–9, 139–57, 160–1, 181, 222–34
  Covid policy, 185–6, 197, 203–4, 219
Russian empire, 127, 130, 133, 139–40, 144
Rust Belt, 6, 53, 57–8
Rutte, Mark, 135

Index

Sachs, Jeffrey, vii, 13–4
Şahin, Uğur, 137
Salvini, Matteo, 90, 101, 113–7, 119, 176, 209
Samoobrona, 175, 178
Samuelson, Paul, 10
San Francisco, 63
sanctions, 152, 181, 224, 227–31
Sarkozy, Nicola 135
Sarrazin, Thilo, 136–7
Scandinavia, 18, 83, 192, 195, 216
Schäuble, Wolfgang, 55, 70, 114
Schengen area, 199, 211
Schmidt, Helmut, 80, 134
Schmidt, Mária, 169
schools, 46, 62, 64–5, 98, 104, 107, 213–18
Schröder, Gerhard, 26, 54, 56, 63, 81, 92, 151–3, 161
Schumpeter, Joseph, 7, 108
Schüssel, Wolfgang, 151
Seattle, 63
Second World War, 2, 120, 122, 139, 148, 158, 196
self-employment, 79–81, 213
self-radicalization, 32, 34, 49, 92, 153, 169
separation of powers, 166–7, 209
Serbia, 95, 128, 141–2, 154, 191, 197, 204, 231
Shanghai, 220
Sheffield, 53
Shenzhen, 4
shock therapy, 10, 12–13, 15, 39, 75, 80
Singapore, 191
Slovakia, 16, 18, 25, 173–5, 200, 230
Smer, 18, 173–5 //originally social democratic, then pivoted
social democracy, xii, 39, 176–8, 205
Social Democratic Party (SPD), 23, 26, 57, 81, 83 152, 224
Social Democrats, xxiv, 10, 27, 57–8, 92, 161–2, 176–8, 195
  see also Labour Party, Partito Democratico, Republican People's Party, Social Democratic Party
social diversity, see inequality
social mobility, 57, 80, 83
social recognition (Polanyi), 23, 80
socialism, 162
  state, xxiii, 3, 14, 22, 25, 38–9, 74
  democratic, xiii, 7–8, 108, 160
Socialist Unity Party (SED), 71, 80
Socialists (France), 29, 57
Socialists (Italy), 90, 93, 97
society, 6, 22
  see also civil and consumer society
solidarity, 106, 113, 172, 205–6
Solidarność, 12
Soros, George, 162, 169, 194
South East Europe, 18, 95, 128–32, 134, 143, 199, 204
South Korea, 195
South Ossetia, 147
Southern Europe, 20–1, 95, 107, 111–12, 123, 192, 207
sovereignty, xxvi, 31, 117–18, 143, 147
Soviet Union, 54, 95, 127–9, 133–4, 139–40, 144, 169, 188, 203, 228
Spain, 28, 95, 176, 194, 197, 207, 216
sphere(s) of influence, 141, 143, 146, 149, 196
Srebrenica, 154
Stalin, Joseph, 34, 140, 144–5, 155, 160
standard of living, 24, 26, 85, 107, 184, 218
state, 9, 16–7, 21–3, 48, 53, 78, 93–4, 203, 206, 208, 213, 219
  state-controlled/owned companies, 16, 77–8, 96, 151, 159
Stiglitz, Joseph, 3
stock market, 28–9, 31, 44, 56, 61, 207
  crash, 2, 17, 60, 159, 161
strike, 62, 77, 160
Summers, Larry, 59
surveillance, 22, 188
Sweden, 76, 147, 149, 177, 193, 195, 216
Switzerland, xxvi, 141, 216
Syriza party, 29
systemic competition, 8, 151, 185–7, 191, 197, 202, 204–6, 220
Szálasi, Ferenc, 166
Szczecin, Gdynia, 77

taxes, 9, 14, 62–3, 81, 132, 159, 181, 201, 208
  breaks, 55, 59–62, 116
  evasion/fraud, 94, 179
  flat, 17, 26, 83, 173
  low-tax ideology, 16, 31, 54
terrorism, 30, 37, 137, 161, 187
Thatcher, Margaret, xxiv, 9–10, 12, 21, 26, 94, 96, 159–60
'third way' economies, 11, 160
trade deficit, 59

trade unions, 6, 10, 40, 58, 81–2, 97, 110, 159–62, 176
transformation, vii–xi, 3–5, 27, 187
  late-capitalist, 34, 43, 53, 66
  losers, viii, 18, 21, 23, 81
  post-socialist, 13, 19, 21, 39, 72–5, 81–7, 140, 149–50, 171
transition, vii, 43
Tremonti, Giulio, 101, 104
Trump, Donald, 30–3, 36–8, 49–51, 58–61, 164–5, 178–9, 190–2, 197, 200–2, 232
trust, 118–19, 146–8, 195, 203, 213, 220, 233
Tsipras, Alexis, 29
Türeci, Özlem, 137
Turkey, 33, 95, 115, 121–8, 131–57, 178, 182, 199, 227
Tuscany, 107
Tusk, Donald, 178

UK Independence Party (UKIP), xxi
Ukraine, 15–16, 18–20, 139, 144–57, 181, 186, 222–34
uncertainty, 19, 38, 72, 77, 84–6, 147, 171, 193, 225
unemployment, 13, 19–21, 23–5, 27, 29, 53, 68, 73, 79–85, 213
  youth, 97, 104–6, 110
United Kingdom, 8, 20–22, 24, 31, 57, 94, 127–8, 159–60, 164
  Covid policy, 193, 197
United Nations, 185
universal basic income (UBI), 105–6, 116–17
universities, 98, 104, 128, 162–3, 167, 183, 210, 218
urban centres, 18, 84, 176, 223, 230
Uruguay, 95
USA, 8–9, 25–6, 29–31, 36–67, 141–3, 148, 152, 158–9, 164–5, 228
  Covid policy, 185, 188, 191–3, 197, 201–3
Uzbekistan, 16

Veneto, 196
Vienna, 7, 65, 108, 129, 141, 169, 213, 228
Vietnam, 79, 188

violence, 132–4, 142, 146, 155, 164–6
visa regulations, 124, 134, 141, 145–6
Visegrád group, 81, 210–11
Višegrad, 154
voter turnout, xx, xxii, 27, 40, 57, 170
voting
  rights, 99, 134, 138, 165, 176, 180, 217
  system, xxi, 99, 123, 164–6, 201
Vox party, 176
Vučić, Aleksandar, xxvi, 204

wages, 4, 15, 25–6, 72–3, 75, 78, 82, 84–5, 95–6, 168
Waigel, Theo, 70
war, 56, 129–30, 133, 147, 156–7, 159
  Iraq, 32, 56, 143, 148, 154
  in Ukraine, 126, 145, 147, 150–2, 154–6, 172, 184, 207, 223–34
  in former Yugoslavia, 141–3, 150, 154, 231
  see also Cold War, First World War, Second World War
war crimes, 142, 154, 233
Washington Consensus, 11–12, 74
Washington, D.C., 41, 46–7
  see also Capitol
Wehler, Hans-Ulrich, 137–8
Weiwei, Ai, 220
welfare system, 8–9, 17, 20–6, 28, 52–5, 86, 107, 170, 192, 213
'the West', 13, 35, 42, 70, 124–6, 140–8, 151–5, 162, 185, 229
women, 25, 44–5, 47–8, 108, 134, 136, 216
World Bank, 11
World Health Organization (WHO), 184–5, 188, 202
Wuhan, 188, 191

Yanukovych, Viktor, 150–1, 222–3
Yeltsin, Boris, 140–1, 155, 161
youth, 19, 21–2, 25, 28, 64, 104–6, 164, 167–8, 183, 214, 217–18
  see also unemployment
Yugoslavia, 11, 80, 95, 150, 160, 231

Zegan, Tommy, 164
Zelensky, Volodymyr, 181, 225–6
Ziobro, Zbigniew, 173, 178